SOUTHWEST
GARDENER'S HANDBOOK

Quarto is the authority on a wide range of topics.

Quarto educates, entertains and enriches the lives of our readers—enthusiasts and lovers of hands-on living.

www.quartoknows.com

First published in 2016 by Cool Springs Press, an imprint of Quarto Publishing Group USA Inc., 400 First Avenue North, Suite 400, Minneapolis, MN 55401 USA.
Telephone: (612) 344-8100 Fax: (612) 344-8692

quartoknows.com
Visit our blogs at quartoknows.com

Cool Springs Press titles are also available at discounts in bulk quantity for industrial or sales-promotional use. For details contact the Special Sales Manager at Quarto Publishing Group USA Inc., 400 First Avenue North, Suite 400, Minneapolis, MN 55401 USA.

10 9 8 7 6 5 4 3 2 1

ISBN: 978-1-59186-647-3

Library of Congress Cataloging-in-Publication Data

Names: Maranhao, Diana, author.
Title: Southwest gardener's handbook / Diana Maranhao.
Description: Minneapolis, MN : Cool Springs Press, 2016. | Includes index.
Identifiers: LCCN 2015039051 | ISBN 9781591866473 (pb)
Subjects: LCSH: Gardening--Southwestern States.
Classification: LCC SB453.2.A165 M37 2016 | DDC 635.0979--dc23
LC record available at http://lccn.loc.gov/2015039051

Acquiring Editor: Billie Brownell
Project Manager: Alyssa Bluhm
Art Director: Cindy Samargia Laun
Layout: Kim Winscher

Printed in China

SOUTHWEST
GARDENER'S HANDBOOK

YOUR COMPLETE GUIDE:
SELECT • PLAN • PLANT • MAINTAIN • PROBLEM-SOLVE

TEXAS, ARIZONA, NEW MEXICO,
OKLAHOMA, SOUTHERN NEVADA, UTAH

DIANA MARANHAO

COOL SPRINGS PRESS
Home and Garden Experts™
MINNEAPOLIS, MINNESOTA

DEDICATION

This book is dedicated to my husband, Steve, in gratitude for sharing your expertise in all matters of horticulture, arboriculture, plant science, soils, and irrigation. Thank you for your encouragement and support while I was glued to the computer; for Friday flowers; rolled tacos; tending the dog, cat, chickens, and bees; and countless other things you do that allow me to garden with abandon.

ACKNOWLEDGMENTS

I need to acknowledge the unending support and love of my son, Steve, who always tells me, "You can do it, Ma!" and daughter, Destiny, who led me down this career path and encouraged me to write about my passion.

I owe a debt of gratitude to my editor, Billie Brownell, who is the essence of time management and organization. You help me make sense of my words so I can get them out of my head and to the reader.

The gardening expertise in the book is through the combined efforts of a group of incredible Cool Springs Press garden authors. Thank you for sharing and for your continued contributions to gardeners and professionals in the landscape industry: Mary Irish, Judith Phillips, Linn Mills (in loving memory), Dick Post, Steve Dobbs, Dale Groom, John Cretti, Jacqueline A. Soule, Greg Grant, Nan Sterman, and Joe Lamp'l. I also want to acknowledge Jeri Deneen and Jon Powell/DPA Inc. for their beautiful illustration on page 18.

CONTENTS

FEATURED PLANTS

USDA COLD-HARDINESS ZONES FOR THE SOUTHWEST

Most of the plants listed in this book will thrive in all USDA Zones in the Southwest and Oklahoma. Exceptions are addressed in the individual plant profiles.

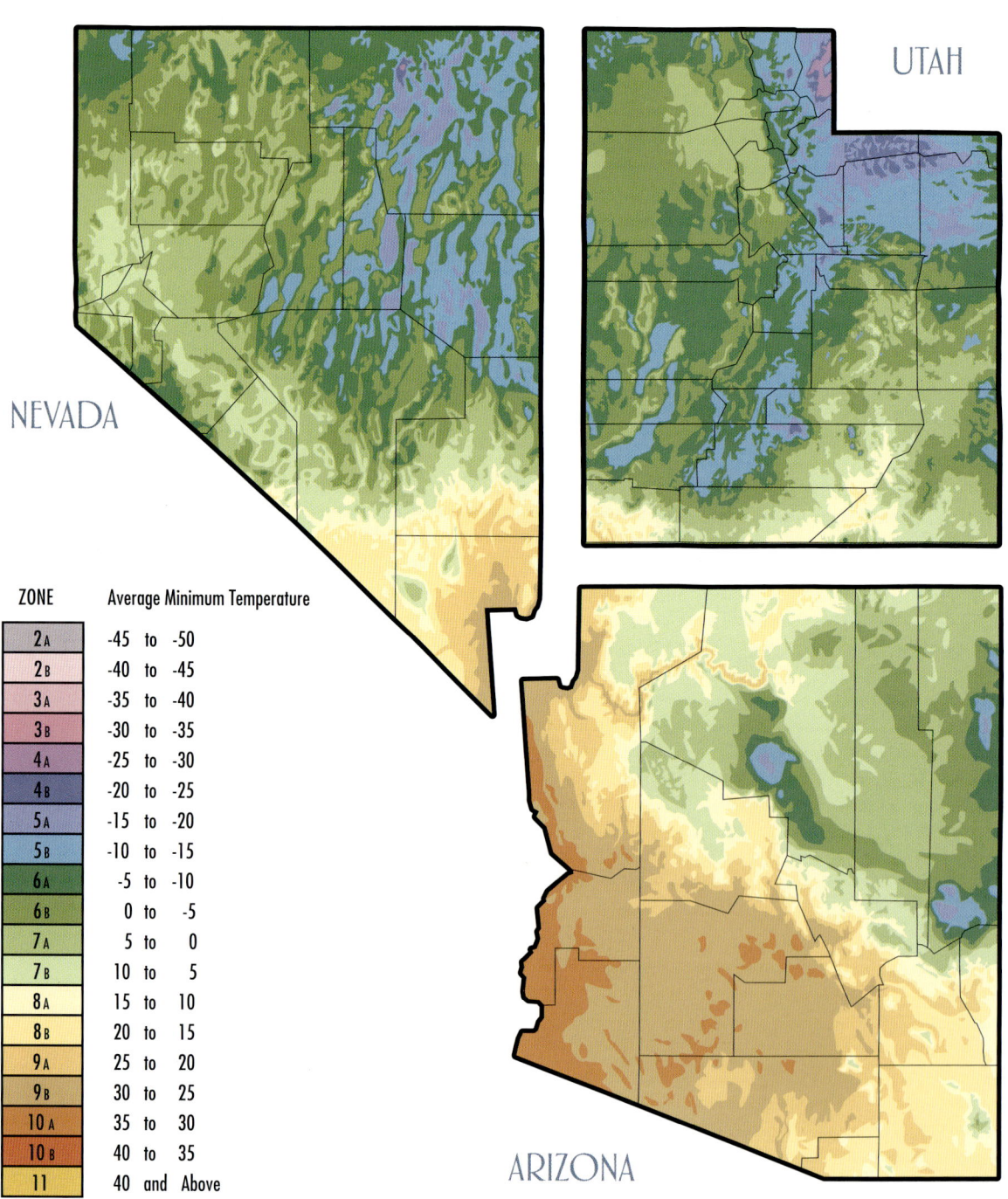

ZONE	Average Minimum Temperature		
2 A	-45	to	-50
2 B	-40	to	-45
3 A	-35	to	-40
3 B	-30	to	-35
4 A	-25	to	-30
4 B	-20	to	-25
5 A	-15	to	-20
5 B	-10	to	-15
6 A	-5	to	-10
6 B	0	to	-5
7 A	5	to	0
7 B	10	to	5
8 A	15	to	10
8 B	20	to	15
9 A	25	to	20
9 B	30	to	25
10 A	35	to	30
10 B	40	to	35
11	40	and	Above

NEVADA

UTAH

ARIZONA

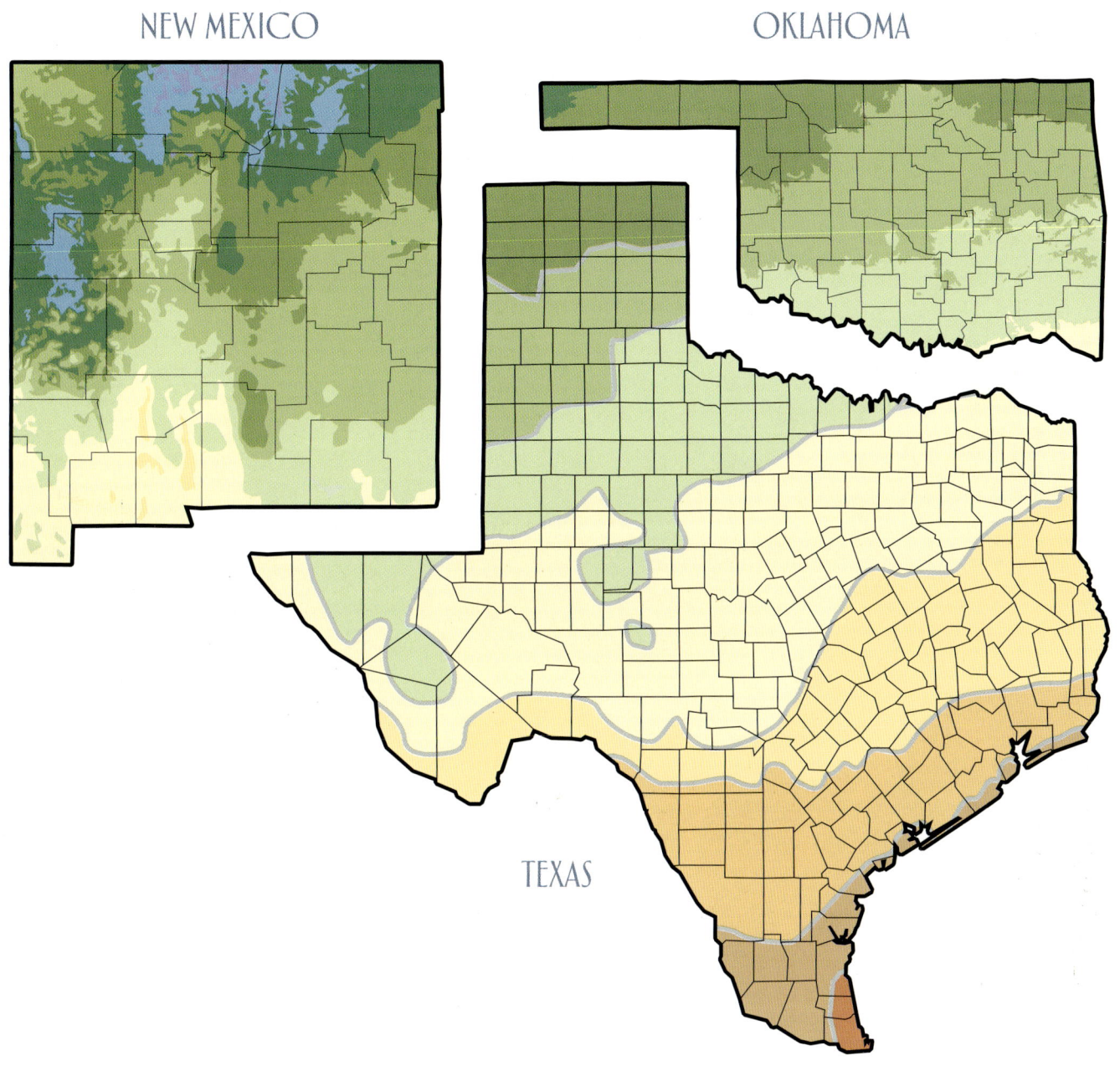

NEW MEXICO

OKLAHOMA

TEXAS

USDA Plant Hardiness Zone Map 2012. Agricultural Research Service, U.S. Department of Agriculture. Accessed from planthardiness.ars.usda.gov.

GARDENING
in the Diverse Southwest

There is something that keeps us gardening in the Southwest— though there are plenty of challenges. In April, a freezing cold wind comes first, the skies darken at midday, hail bounces off the deck, the air warms just a bit for it to turn to snow, and it blankets the flowering fruit trees, putting an end to the promise of harvest. Or a beautiful succulent garden, designed and planted to fill a sunny bed, becomes scorched and shriveled in the intense heat of the summer sun. Early morning hours find us on bended knees, new design sketch in hand, digging up the succulents and transporting them to their new home under the dappled shade of a tree. They are planted, watered, and mulched before the sun rises, their struggles already forgotten. Hot, scorching winds send us running to the vegetable garden, shade cloth and string in hand, to shelter the pepper plants, bending sideways in the wind, their leaves curling in protest. The weather report sends out frost warnings and we grab the wheelbarrow, fill it with mulch, tree boughs, and burlap to cover the shrubs that we knew are marginal in our zone, but we've planted them anyway.

As gardeners, we take our cue from Mother Nature and watch plants for their signals to tell us when we need to take action. When we don't readily see a solution to a problem, we turn to our references and seek advice from professionals. Much of our gardening tasks are based upon years of gardening experience, the successes and failures that taught us how to diagnose and treat ailing plants, when to supply nutrients, how and when to water, and a multitude of other experience-based skills. Gardening in the Southwest is full of challenges that change from day to day, season to season. It takes all of our resources, our experiences, and the continued quest to learn more to build our gardens. It is the challenge, the adversity, the continual learning, the successes, and the rewards that keep us gardening.

GARDENING IN THE DIVERSE SOUTHWEST

The Southwestern areas included in this book (Texas, Arizona, New Mexico, Oklahoma, southern Nevada, and Utah) are diverse. This diversity ranges from the arid Mojave Desert, where average rainfalls total just 4 inches a year, to the humid southeastern corner of Oklahoma, which receives an excess of 50 inches of rain a year. The rest of us are at the low end of rainfall averages, between 9 to 20 inches per year. Most of our rain occurs in the cooler winter months, when plants slow their growth. Summer monsoons can sometimes bring welcome relief and a bit of extra water when we need it the most.

Low-desert elevations from sea level to 600 feet are shared in Texas, southern Nevada, and Arizona, where temperatures commonly exceed 100 degrees Fahrenheit in summer. The high deserts in New Mexico and Utah have the summer heat as well as winter snow and freezes. Mountain regions, from 4,500 to 15,000 feet, have a dramatic impact on the weather. With every 1,000-foot increase in elevation, the last frost dates change safe planting times by as much as a month. Our seasonal lengths may vary, but not having enough water, long and short droughts, widely fluctuating temperature extremes, and high winds are common threads that bind Arizona, southern Nevada, Utah, Texas, New Mexico, and Oklahoma gardeners together.

LIVING ON THE ZONAL EDGE

The United States Department of Agriculture (USDA) Cold Hardiness Zones give us guidelines for plant selection. Most of the plants listed in this book will thrive in all USDA Zones in the Southwest and Oklahoma. Exceptions are addressed in the individual plant profiles.

In the coldest zone of the Southwest, USDA Zone 5, winter temperatures can plummet to minus 20 degrees Fahrenheit, but in reality, the coldest temperatures may be in the single digits in winter, and cold winds and snow are common. I have learned that anything can happen here, so it's best to plan for the extremes. A good majority of the Southwest falls between Zones 6 to 9, with those gardening in USDA Zone 9 experiencing occasional frosts during winter. That is the best time of the year to garden there, due to over-the-top summer heat. Whatever zone you garden in, Southwestern gardeners push their zone limits frequently when selecting the plants that we want to grow. Whether it's to beat the heat by siting a favorite plant in a semi-shady spot, giving it more water and mulch, or to protect it from cold beyond its tolerance with a thick cover of branches, when our efforts pay off, we gloat. When it doesn't, we go to the nursery and buy something else to replace it. Our losses teach us lessons.

GARDENING WITH THE SEASONS

First and last killing frost dates are a reliable guideline for determining when to safely plant in the garden. I learned this lesson the hard way the first season I gardened in southern Utah. Lulled into a sense of security by warm, springlike days during the first week of April and by the colorful, lush displays of plants available to buy at the nearest nursery, I moved my nurtured vegetable and flower seedlings into the newly prepared garden bed. My home is 1,000 feet higher in elevation than the local nursery in town, a fact I did not consider. Around the third week of April, the daytime temperatures plummeted by 20 degrees. As soon as the sun set behind the mountain at 4 p.m., the temperature fell to 30 degrees Fahrenheit, and it just got worse. By the end of the week there were 4 inches of snow on the ground. Our last frost date is around the end of April, so I now don't plant anything out in the

garden until after Mother's Day. Your local Cooperative Extension keeps the last killing frost dates current; consult them for this and other gardening information.

Summer is the longest of the seasons for gardeners in the Southwest. The heat and sun can cause plants to fail and wreak more havoc on them than the occasional single digit winter night. Summer temperatures dictate the type of plants we grow; where we grow them; and when we plant, fertilize, and water. Arid climates experience hot, dry, fierce winds that speed up evaporation, causing leaf and tip burn, desiccated leaves and stems, and defoliation. Already humid areas that receive summer rains face stifling heat with no air movement, threatening plants' foliage and roots with mold, mildew, and fungus. In those areas, even short periods of drought can be the demise of plants that are accustomed to regular moisture. Careful plant selection, well-draining soil, planting within your gardening season constraints, deep watering, adding mulch, and providing nutrients, if and when the plants need them, are practices that create beautiful, thriving Southwest gardens able to survive the dog days of summer.

BEST PLANTS FOR SOUTHWEST GARDENS

The best plants that we grow in Southwestern gardens have deep roots; strong scaffolds with open canopies; finely divided leaves; and coated, waxy, shiny, or fuzzy foliage—all characteristics that help them survive the heat, sun, and wind. Deep roots anchor a plant to the ground and grow into the soil profile, giving plants the ability to draw upon water resources that remain long after the soil surface has dried. A vast web of roots, extending far beyond the drip line of a plant, absorbs water and nutrients from the soil. Open and airy scaffolds allow wind to pass freely without causing damage, and the airflow limits the establishment of molds and mildew. Finely divided leaves with their feathery foliage have less surface area, so there's less evaporation. Leaves that have waxy, shiny, fuzzy, or rough surfaces are protected from the sun and wind.

Plants native to our region have these characteristics. When selecting and growing native plants, success depends upon mimicking their natural habitat as closely as possible. If they grow naturally alongside streambeds and waterways, then they require regular watering and may tolerate a slow-draining soil. If they are found growing in sandy low deserts in full sun, then they need a sunny spot in the garden and a well-draining, lean soil. Most native plants never need fertilizing; some will even show toxicity to fertilizers, failing in heavily amended, fertile garden soils. Native plants are slower growing—their longer development time contributes to their strength. Give them regular, deep watering and it'll speed their growth and establishment in your garden. After that, they will survive on their own.

Native plants are difficult to propagate and cultivate in a production setting, so they are not easily found in quantities at garden centers and home-improvement stores. Growers specialize in native plants offer selections of adaptable natives for sale, along with valuable siting, growing, and watering advice. Native plant growers can also recommend combinations for interplanting, which closely mimics the symbiotic relationships plants have in their native habitat. Seek out local native plant societies to lead you to growers and nurseries that specialize in native plants for your area as well as for valuable cultivation information.

Some native plants are available as seed, so you can try your hand at germination. A great many native grasses are available as seed, commonly in

GERMINATING SEED INDOORS

Often, the "best" plants are the ones you grow yourself from seed. The choice of variety is far greater from seed than transplants. To germinate seed indoors:

Use new containers. Wash repurposed pots, packs, flats, benches, and the heat mat. Soak containers for an hour in bleach solution (1 part bleach: 10 parts water), lay everything out on the heat mat and propagation bench and drench all, using a watering can with the bleach solution (also sterilizing the watering can). Dry completely before filling with soil.

Seeds require a light, well-draining soil mix. When you purchase the formulated seedling mix, buy an additional bag of perlite and mix 3 parts seedling mix, 1 part perlite blend. An ultralight, airy mix is essential for seeds to push growth out of the soil and for their tiny roots to form.

Thoroughly water the soil in the container, set the temperature on the heat mat, and leave the filled containers on the mat for a day to bring the soil temperature to desired level.

Sow the seed according to spacing directions on the package. Be careful not to bury the seed deeply, covering lightly with perlite or vermiculite to keep the seed from drying out.

Provide light by direct sunlight or with grow lights, 8 to 10 inches above the soil surface.

Set the heat mat thermostat to between 70 to 75 degrees Fahrenheit, taking into account that lights emit heat as well. Double-check the soil temp with a soil thermometer.

Label everything, even if you think you will remember. Time passes and seedlings look similar among species. It's easy to confuse tomato or pepper types.

Mist two to three times a day, using a spray bottle or a seedling mist nozzle to eliminate dispersing or flooding the seed. Cover the seed at night with bubble-wrap or a plastic lid to hold in moisture and heat.

Keep seedlings on the heat mat until they have at least two sets of leaves, then elevate them slightly above the heat mat (an inverted flat works well) for a week before moving to another bench to harden off.

After seedlings are 3 to 4 inches tall, fertilize using a water-soluble fertilizer at half-rate. Fertilize when soil is damp, not dry.

Transplant when seedlings have 6 to 8 sets of leaves, then apply water-soluble fertilizer weekly until planting outdoors in the garden.

Southwestern soils vary in physical and chemical structure from region to region and from one area of the landscape to another.

bulk packages from a quarter-pound or more. Direct-sowing the seed into the garden often gives better germination rates, although the results may not be seen for a couple of seasons. Natives may be slow to start, but once they gain foothold, they'll be in your garden forever.

Some native plants have invasive tendencies when they are taken out of their natural challenging environments and moved into the easy life in our gardens. Look for cultivars that are less invasive and deadhead spent flowers to control reseeding. Never dig plants out of the wild to transplant them.

Native plants are comfortable sharing space with non-native plants that have similar needs, especially drought-tolerant plants that also thrive in well-draining soils. Blending the two types makes a textural, interesting, colorful, lush, and hardy landscape. Plant researchers are constantly performing trials on species from around the world to determine if they will grow under cultivation.

Plant breeders develop these introductions and create improved hybrids and cultivars to expand the selections. Their work gives us various size ranges and forms with prolific blooms in more colors; variegated or patterned foliage; cold, heat, or drought tolerance; and disease resistance.

The plant choices are seemingly endless, so narrow the search to plants that grow within or close to your USDA Hardiness Zone and that match your water resources and soil type. Local nurseries are in the business of selling plants to repeat customers, so you can usually rely on the selections they offer as being good choices for your area. If a plant is on the zonal edge, the label will give you that information. Reputable mail order and Internet plant growers offer gardeners the opportunity to try even more new and different plants. And, of course, gardeners always love to share. A large portion of my garden has come by way of cuttings, seeds, and divisions shared by other gardeners throughout the Southwest.

IT'S IN THE SOIL

"Dirt is what you get out of the vacuum cleaner. Soil is what gardeners dig in." These were the first words my soil science instructor used to open a memorable course. Chemistry was never one of my strong points, but by digging in the soil all these years, I have learned much and continue to learn every time I put a shovel in the earth. Gardening experiences, regular soil tests, text teachings, and new soil information I pick up along the way make sense of soil chemistry and emphasize the importance of building healthy, well-draining soils, which are vital to growing thriving plants.

Southwestern soils vary in physical and chemical structure from region to region and from one area of the landscape to another. The physical structure is comprised of three main soil particles that form together to form aggregates; it's their arrangement that creates soil texture. In our arid Southwest, soils have large percentages of sand, the largest soil particle. Clay is sometimes dominant in our soil. It is the smallest soil particle and carries a negative charge, which allows it to attract and hold water and nutrients, an asset in small amounts. The problem arises when there is a high percentage of clay, creating a slow draining, heavily charged soil

that holds onto water and nutrients so tightly that they are unavailable to the plants.

A well-draining soil has airspaces that allow water to percolate into the soil profile, carrying nutrients present in the soil to plant roots, where it is absorbed, then transported up through a plant's vascular system to its growing tips. As the water moves beyond the root zone, it carries excess salts with it. In a well-draining soil, tiny root hairs penetrate easily into the soil airspaces, where they grow into strong, deep-reaching roots. Strong, deep root systems anchor a plant and have access to moisture residing deeply in the soil long after the surface has dried.

Poorly draining soils affect plant vigor and root health. Plants may be stunted, exhibit nutrient deficiency symptoms, show yellowing leaves, and defoliate, finally leading to stem collapse and root rot. A slow or poorly draining soil commonly occurs in soils with high clay content or from compaction. To correct poorly draining soils:

- Thoroughly incorporate topsoil, organic amendments, compost, humus, aged manure, or peat. Rototill or dig the amendments in as deeply as you can. It takes at least three seasons working the soil before you'll begin to notice an improvement. In plant years, that's a short period of time, considering they will have good health for years to come.
- Loosen compacted soil. Thoroughly and deeply water the area, allow it to dry a few days, then turn and work the soil. Rototilling can be done initially to loosen the soil and get it to the point where you can work it but should only be done on alternate years until the soil has recovered.
- Import soil and incorporate with native soil to build raised beds, hills, berm, or mounds that direct the water away from the root zone.

The chemical analysis of soil is pH. Most urban soils range between 5.0, acidic, to 8.0, alkaline. Our soils tend to be alkaline in the Southwest, typical in areas that lack rainfall. Acidic soils are prevalent in areas that have consistently moist soils.

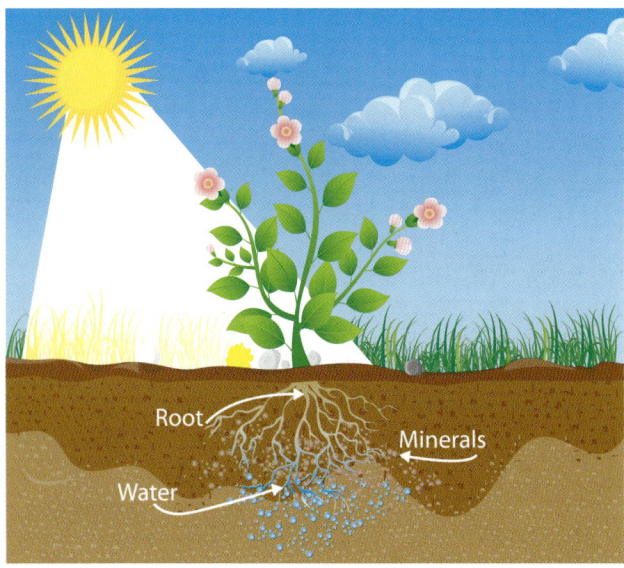

A well-draining soil allows water to percolate past its root zone, encouraging deeper, stronger root growth.

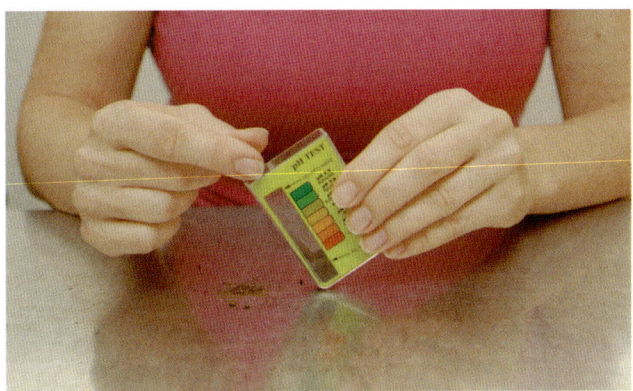 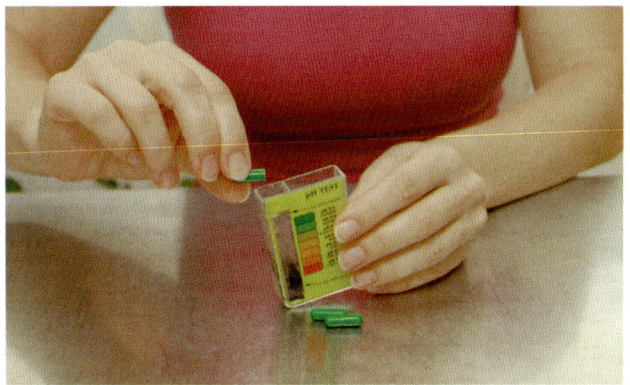

A soil test will reveal the pH of your soil, or you can check it yourself with an easy-to-use testing kit. The best practice is to choose plants that can grow in your soil pH range rather than trying to change the soil chemistry.

pH cannot be changed; it can only be altered for a short time. When peat is added to the backfill in an alkaline soil, a plant gets off to a good start, but eventually the plant roots extend far beyond the acid-enhanced planting hole. A more sensible approach is to select plants that thrive in your alkaline or acidic soil. If you have a favorite acid-loving plant (and live where soils are alkaline), then try container growing with a peat-based, rich, potting soil.

TO FERTILIZE OR NOT TO FERTILIZE?

Some plants need no supplemental nutrients, others receive all they need from fertilizer given at planting to get them growing. A few require timed-release fertilizer applied each season until they establish. The more fertilizer that's applied, the more new growth—and the more water a plant requires. In the past, fertilizer was applied on a schedule, rather than by a plant's need. Today, Southwestern gardens are built on the premise that if we create a healthy soil and give the plant the water it needs to develop strong, healthy roots, then it will get all its nutrients from the soil. Healthy plants can withstand onslaughts of pests and are rarely bothered by disease.

If you suspect your plants are lacking nutrients in their diet, are not growing as vigorously as you want, or are spindly and weak, then there might be nutrient deficiencies at play. Do some research before bringing out a fertilizer. Chlorosis occurs commonly in alkaline or slow-draining soils, exhibited by yellowing between the leaf veins, and is attributed to a lack of iron. An application of chelated iron will quickly remedy the problem. Yellowing or dropping leaves; purple-tinted new foliage; and weak, brittle trunks or stems can signal nutrient deficiencies but also are signs of overwatering and heat, cold, root, or stem rot. Stressed plants are subject to insects and disease, so you may be seeing after-effects of cultural issues. If you are not sure if the problem is a deficiency, take a discolored leaf and a healthy leaf (for comparison) to the local Cooperative Extension or nursery professional for diagnosis and treatment.

Have a soil test done (check with your local Cooperative Extension) before planting new garden spaces and every few years for established landscapes. Submit individual samples and list what you intend to grow for each landscape situation—turf, vegetables, trees or shrubs, and so forth. Soil tests list the low and high levels of nutrients, comparing it to the desired levels for the plant types. Request recommendations for supplemental nutrients, chemical or organic formulations, whatever your preference, along with application rates. Soil tests confirm the soil pH and give application rates for treating extreme acidic or alkaline soils as well as recommendations for supplemental nutrients in chemical or organic formulations. Salinity levels are checked as well.

A small berm directs the water into the adjoining shallow impression or basin in this meadowlike planting. The captured water is used to support the plants.

Soils high in salinity are common for regions that have low rainfall and use drip irrigation. Soluble salts, present in fertilizer, water, and soil, build up and affect a plant's ability to absorb water and nutrients, but that's easily corrected by leaching through a seasonal deep soaking.

IT'S ALL ABOUT WATER

Lack of rain and snow, overtaxed waterways, depleted water resources, and short- and long-term droughts are situations Southwest gardeners are accustomed to. Nurturing our gardens on limited water budgets is challenging, but if we make the most out of the water we have, protect it as best we can from evaporation, select drought-tolerant plants, and direct and capture the water's flow, we can have our gardens while conserving too.

Drip irrigation systems take the work out of moving a trickling hose from plant to plant to prevent sprinkler evaporation, overwatering with sprinklers, and water loss from overspray. The water is applied slowly, dripping water or spraying large droplets through emitters, whose output is measured in gallons of water per hour (from 2 gph to 6 gph). Drip irrigation system components are readily available and are easy for homeowners to install. Most major manufactures offer design services at a minimal cost, saving you the task of deciding which emitters/tubing and system layout to use. Spray irrigation heads deliver water measured in gallons per minute (from ½ gpm to 5 gpm). Spray systems, which require professional or manufacturer design services, are the most efficient method for watering lawns, meadows, and for germinating seedbeds.

Capturing rainfall, directing the flow of water, and minimizing erosion and runoff make use of water that falls from the sky. Rainbarrels are readily available and only take minutes to install. A 50-gallon rainbarrel can supplement the water needed by a small lawn or supply water for container gardens. Directing the flow of water from the rain gutter to a nearby tree berm and basin can eliminate watering for a month's time. Digging a series of berms along the contour of a slope can slow the water, cutting back on rainwater runoff and soil erosion. Terraces, built from natural materials on hand, stabilize a slope, while slowing and capturing the water for use in the excavated beds.

WATER NOW, SAVE WATER LATER

If you can supply the water plants need through their first summer (succulents, turf, and ornamental grasses), a few growing seasons (perennials, shrubs, groundcovers, roses), or even five to six years (trees) until they are established, they will require less supplemental watering at maturity. After a few seasons of weaning them by spacing out the time between waterings, they will survive on natural rainfall. Even in a long-term drought, a monthly deep watering will keep them happy. Using more water to get them established gives years and years of beauty and enjoyment. That's a very good return on your water investment.

JUST ADD MULCH

Whether you water by hand or have an irrigation system, a thick layer of mulch protects your water investment. After planting, add a thick, 3- to 4-inch layer of mulch. Mulch cools the soil and the roots; protects the plant from accelerated evaporation from heat, sun, or wind; and the thick layer creates darkness, discouraging weed seed

germination. Organic mulches need to be replenished yearly as they decompose. Inorganic mulches (like rock or rubber) need a layer of weed-barrier fabric between the mulch and the soil to allow water to percolate into the soil while creating a barrier that limits weed germination and keeps the mulch from working into the soil. Mulches can be used in all planted areas, on slopes, in pathways, for seating areas, and in spaces where there is no landscaping at all.

RIGHT PLANT, RIGHT PLACE

"Right Plant, Right Place" is a slogan that's about more than matching a plant to soil, cold hardiness zone, moisture, sun, or shade. The practice also means paying attention to the plant's maximum height and width at maturity, then locating it in a spot where it can grow naturally to its tall and broad size. A healthy plant requires less maintenance, less fertilizer, and, with drought-tolerant plants, less water as it establishes in the landscape.

When I see a gardener on hands and knees in the heat of the day, shears in hand, carefully trimming a groundcover into neat, straight lines so it doesn't invade the sidewalk, I want to help them up from their knees, give them a cool drink, and say, "Just leave it be. It's fine." Their labors could have been eliminated if the right plant had been chosen to fit the space, and the plants would be healthier if allowed to grow into their natural shape and mature size.

Pruning shrubs into squares and circles is commonly seen both in commercial and residential sites because it's easier and faster to shear a plant than to selectively prune, which requires technical skill and an understanding of how plants grow. The results are not attractive, nor does the practice lead to optimum plant health. Pruning plants into defined shapes is sometimes a design style choice (as with formal design style) and some plants are more tolerant than others to this type of pruning. If this is your style, then be aware that hard pruning such as this stresses a plant as it strives to heal the wounds. More water and additional fertilizing are often required in order to maintain vigorous, healthy growth.

Whenever I see a tree that is topped because it is getting in the way of a power line, I can't help but make my dismay be known to the perpetrator. We all know the dangers of that practice, but sadly, it still occurs. Selecting trees that are smaller in size when mature would be the better choice, as they would require minimum pruning. Trees are the longest-living and largest plants in the garden, so research into selecting the right tree to serve the purpose will assure its success.

Careful plant selection in the design phase can all but eliminate constant pruning, saving you labor and creating a healthier landscape. Space shrubs to accommodate their width at maturity, allowing the natural growth to form a hedge, make a screen, or provide background to other plantings. Select groundcovers that are tidy growers for small spots, mounding types to grow in drifts, or sprawling forms to cover a slope. Choose a tree to provide a broad shade canopy, to grow tall to block the wind, or to bring color and structure as a focal point in a small garden—using its natural form and attributes. Then you can put the pruners, the shears, or the clippers away.

Remember to enjoy your garden. Sit in the shade; have a cool drink; and admire the healthy, bushy, sprawling, climbing, clumping, stately, beautiful, and carefree landscape you have made. That's what gardening in the Southwest is all about.

Papaver rhoeas

ANNUALS
for the Southwest

Annuals are underrated. I often hear them referred to in conversation, "Oh, that plant? It's just an annual." Annuals are often an afterthought, a filler plant, a plant to add to a container combination, a spot of color to bring to the garden after a long winter. Typically they are marketed in full bloom to ensure immediate sales. Once in their new home, they proceed quickly through their flowering cycle and, being "just an annual," they decline in a few weeks, their short lives forgotten and their contributions unheralded.

But annuals are stars in my landscape. There are the repeat performers that self-sow in early spring as the ground warms, requiring no effort on my part. There are annuals that are the first to flower in spring, annuals that continue to bloom through triple-digit heat in summer, and annuals that prefer cooler temps and bring color and texture to the bed when all others are slowing and fading into dormancy. Annuals are profuse and long-period bloomers, making a statement in the landscape throughout their short lives. The best selection is from what you can grow yourself.

STARTING FROM SEED

For the best variety and for the longest-blooming plants (see Germinating Seed Indoors, page 14), grow your annuals from seed. It's a little time consuming, but the results are well worth the effort. Check the seed packets to determine the optimum time to sow outdoors. Based on that, sow the seed indoors four to six weeks before planting time plus an additional two weeks to harden them off before planting outdoors. During that two weeks, bring seedlings outdoors to a shady location during warm days, but move them indoors at night before the sun sets and night cold sweeps in. In the second week, let seedlings bask in the full sun, but in late afternoon, move them to part shade so their roots don't overheat. Leave them outside under the shelter of a roof overhang at night if no frost threatens. At week three, if soil temps are warmed, plant them outdoors.

PROPAGATING FROM CUTTINGS

Some annuals can be grown from cuttings taken from active new growth (before the first frost). Cut stems 6 to 8 inches long to start, place in a jar of water and keep them cool until planting. Use a well-draining, lightweight potting soil not heavy in organics, as the cuttings rot easily. Moisten and pack the soil into the container. You want a damp soil, but not one that's wringing wet. Make holes for cuttings using a dibble or

Pick off any leaves on the stem that will be buried in the soil. Use a lightweight, well-draining potting soil. Rooting hormone is optional. Keep the soil warm and damp until the cuttings root.

a pencil. Prepare the cuttings by clipping each to just below a node (where the leaf meets the stem); that is where roots form. Finished cuttings should be at least 4 inches long and contain four or more nodes. Strip any leaves off the stem that would be buried in soil or touching the soil surface and remove flowers. If any remaining leaves are larger than 2 inches across, use scissors to cut each leaf in half. This keeps some green for photosynthesis and shading, but decreases the leaf surface that needs water. Stick the cutting in the soil; it should stand up on its own and include two nodes that are buried in the soil. Pack the soil around the cutting, and give the cuttings a thorough overhead watering. You can stick up to 50 cuttings of various types in a flat, spaced 1 inch apart, or stick six to eight cuttings into a 6- or 8-inch pot. Allow the surface of the soil to dry before you overhead water again. Keep the container in a shaded location (at least out of direct sunlight). After a few weeks, give a (very) gentle tug to see if there is resistance. When cuttings are fully rooted, they will start sending out new foliage. After four or more new leaves form, transplant.

SELF-SOWING ANNUALS

You can allow annuals to reseed in the garden, or you can actively collect seed to sow the following season. Calendula, cosmos, amaranth, marigold, poppy, sunflower, alyssum, and zinnia are all reliable self-sowers. After four to six weeks of flowering, stop deadheading spent flowers to allow the plants to set seed. When the plants have started to dry, softly bend them down to ground. This minimizes the seed being spread by the wind or birds. They will lie there quietly until spring when Mother Nature takes over. Or, collect the seed by cutting the entire plant off at the base, with flowers intact. Hang upside down inside a large, labeled paper bag in a dry, cool spot. After the stems and flowers are completely dry, cut off the entire flower head, collect any seeds from the bag, and store in a cool, dark, dry space. In the spring separate the seeds and plant indoors or out. Note that poppies need to be dried in summer for fall sowing.

By growing annuals, you can cover a slope or create a border and do it all in living color for just a few dollars. Plant a few, sow a lot, and trial many. You will never run out of choices or spaces for annuals.

OVERWINTERING ANNUALS

Some annuals are perennials in warmer climates. Those plants can be overwintered in pots in the house or greenhouse. Geranium, sweet potato vine, coleus, copper plant, impatiens, and begonia can be dug up, potted, and brought into the house or greenhouse for winter. Pull the mulch away from the base of the plant, use a round point shovel and dig around the entire rootball, forming a circle. Lift the rootball out of the bed. Clean up the roots, clipping the torn ends. Transplant into a pot larger than the rootmass. Clip the plant crown back by half, cutting each stem back to the node (save the cuttings for rooting new plants). Use a lightweight bagged potting soil and plant at the same level the plant was while in the ground. Tamp the soil around the roots as you backfill, building the soil up to final level, and leaving enough space for water. Water slowly and deeply, filling the pot to the brim with water then let it drain thoroughly. Bring the pot into a window with bright, indirect sunlight or set it on a greenhouse bench out of direct sunlight. Move it to its preferred exposure until when it sends out new foliage.

AFRICAN DAISY
Arctotis hybrids

Why It's Special—African daisy is a reliable, drought-tolerant annual that basks in the sun and heat. Masses of daisylike ray flowers are held above deep green serrated foliage, providing color and texture. Tuck single plants into rock garden crevices or into container gardens. Plant them *en masse* as a groundcover, in drifts as foreground fillers, in color beds, and in the home meadow.

How to Plant & Grow—In mild-winter areas, sow seed in January for early spring bloom. Otherwise sow or plant starts in early spring for summer flowers. Water regularly while they're germinating and establishing; then water deeply once a week. Provide well-draining soil. There's no need to fertilize at planting or during its growing cycle.

Care & Problems—African daisy has no pests or diseases. These freely reseeding plants can become invasive. If you're concerned, pull plants as soon as flowers fade.

Water Needs—Upon establishment, water once a week. Avoid overwatering.

Bloom Color—Shades of yellow, orange, white

Peak Season—Early spring in warm-winter areas; summer in colder climates

Mature Size (H x W)—6 to 15 inches x 12 inches

AGERATUM
Ageratum houstonianum

Why It's Special—Ageratums are long-blooming annuals with heart-shaped leaves that become hidden under the quantities of fluffy buttonlike blooms covering the plant. Plant compact forms in container gardens and as edging in color borders. Plant drifts of taller types in cottage gardens and perennial beds.

How to Plant & Grow—Sow seed in flats or packs eight weeks before garden planting. Provide bottom heat for 70-degree Fahrenheit soil temperature. Plant seedlings after all danger of frost is past in a well-drained soil.

Care & Problems—Ageratum flowers continuously through warm weather with occasional deadheading. If plants stretch or become lanky, pinch back lightly to encourage bushy new growth. It's prone to powdery mildew and root rot; give ageratum adequate spacing for air movement. There's no need to fertilize. Avoid overhead watering.

Water Needs—Water slowly and deeply when soil is dry down to an inch. Do not overwater; allow the soil to dry out a bit between waterings.

Bloom Color—White, purple, lavender, pink

Peak Season—Spring through frost

Mature Size (H x W)—6 to 15 inches x 12 inches

BIDENS
Bidens ferulifolia

Why It's Special—Bidens is a long-season, lightly scented bloomer, thriving in summer heat. It is a standalone plant in a hanging basket, window box, or container. In the landscape, it can be planted *en masse* to cover mounds and slopes quickly. Use it as a foreground plant in color beds, as a bright edging along a walkway, or interplant with other trailing annuals and perennials for contrasting colors and textures.

How to Plant & Grow—Plant in a well-drained garden soil in early spring when soil and air temps are on the rise. Bidens break easily, so location is important to minimize trodding or handling. Mulch just after planting.

Care & Problems—There are no pests or diseases. No deadheading is needed. To encourage bushiness, cut back by half at midseason and apply a water-soluble fertilizer at half-rate. Fertilize container plants once each month.

Water Needs—Water garden plants twice weekly; water containers daily during summer.

Bloom Color—Yellow, some white selections

Peak Season—Spring until first frost

Mature Size (H x W)—1 to 2 feet x 1 to 2 feet

CALENDULA
Calendula officinalis

Why It's Special—Calendula flowers when other plants are not yet blooming in early spring and in fall when heat-lovers are finished. Large, tight, disk-like flowers make them excellent fillers in the perennial bed, a mass of color in the fall border, and a great change-out plant in a fading container garden. Calendula make the best impact planted in groups in the landscape, but their branching habit fills a pot quickly if planted singly. Check out new cultivars that offer more colors and types.

How to Plant & Grow—Sow seed seven weeks before planting in late summer for fall blooms. In mild-winter areas, plant in fall for spring flowers. Pots and packs transplant easily in any well-drained soil. Calendula self-sow in fertile garden soils.

Care & Problems—They are fairly drought tolerant, pest and disease resistant, and require no fertilizing. Deadhead to prolong flowering.

Water Needs—Water to a depth of 6 inches, twice weekly.

Bloom Color—Orange, yellow, cream, apricot

Peak Season—Fall through spring in mild-winter areas; fall elsewhere

Mature Size (H x W)—36 inches x 18 inches

COCKSCOMB
Celosia argentea var. cristata

Why It's Special—The bold colors of cockscomb are not for the faint of heart! Plant plume types for bright linear accents in containers, for midground drama in the cottage cutting garden, and in drifts lining a path. Crested types form tight mounds of color in the border, enhance a focal point, or provide contrast interplanted with grasses and reed-like plants in containers.

How to Plant & Grow—Sow seeds in flats or packs eight weeks before the last frost date. Plant hardened off seedlings in early spring. If soil is well draining and moderately fertile, no additional fertilizer is needed. Cutting plume types for bouquets and deadheading crested cockscomb prolongs flowering.

Care & Problems—Watch for root rot in wet weather. A well-draining soil minimizes this problem.

Water Needs—Cockscomb is drought tolerant once established so avoid overwatering. Water the soil, not the foliage, whenever it's dry to 2 inches below the surface.

Bloom Color—Red, orange, pink, yellow

Peak Season—Summer though fall

Mature Size (H x W)—6 to 30 inches x 6 to 18 inches

COLEUS
Solenostemon scutellarioides

Why It's Special—The many sizes, foliage color combinations, patterns, and exposure tolerances move coleus out of the interior plant environment and into the landscape (although it is still an excellent houseplant!). Coleus is a multitasking plant that brightens a dark shady entrance, overflows a hanging basket, drifts along to define a pathway edge, or creates a tropical groundcover beneath a focal point tree or shrub.

How to Plant & Grow—Coleus is available at garden centers in early spring and can be planted in the garden after the last frost. It needs a well-draining fertile soil. Apply a topdressing of a timed-release fertilizer at planting, followed by one or two applications of a water-soluble fertilizer every eight weeks. Mulch to cool the soil and conserve moisture.

Care & Problems—Remove flowers to encourage new growth. Search out and destroy slugs and snails. Pinching stems encourages bushiness.

Water Needs—Maintain regular, deep watering.

Bloom Color—Foliage in combinations of red, purple, chartreuse, yellow, cream, salmon, brown, purple

Peak Season—Season-long foliage

Mature Size (H x W)—6 to 24 inches x 12 inches

COPPER PLANT
Acalypha wilkesiana

Why It's Special—Copper plant tolerates aridity, humidity, and high summer temperatures. Use its bright foliage as background in the color bed, planted in sweeps under the light shade of open branching trees, along a drive where it doesn't mind the reflective heat, in containers as a focal point, or even as a houseplant. Interplant with white-flowering plants or variegated green-and-white foliage plants for contrast.

How to Plant & Grow—Plant in early spring after last frost when temperatures are consistently above 65 degrees Fahrenheit. Work organic amendments into the soil before planting for well-draining soil, use organic mulch, keep moist until established. Apply timed-release fertilizer midseason. Shear (do not pinch) to encourage bushiness.

Care & Problems—In shade that is too dense, foliage color fades. Variegated yellow/cream types need more afternoon shade. Occasionally, mealybugs attack; squish bugs, spray off, or apply controls according to package directions.

Water Needs—Provide regular, deep watering throughout the season

Bloom Color—Red with variegated burgundy, pink, yellow-cream foliage

Peak Season—Spring through fall foliage

Mature Size (H x W)—2 to 4 feet x 2 to 4 feet

COSMOS
Cosmos spp.

Why It's Special—Cosmos is a heat-loving annual with a long-season bloom, reseeding yearly. Plant cosmos in drifts in the cutting garden using monochromatic seed packs for individual blocks of color. Plant dwarf types in annual borders or containers, taller forms as a background summer floral screen, broadcast in the home meadow, and companion-plant with vegetables to attract pollinators.

How to Plant & Grow—Sow or plant in fall in frost-free areas; otherwise, after last frost. Cosmos like a well-draining soil, but not too organically rich. Cover direct sown seed lightly, keep moist until germination and plants are 4 inches tall. Incorporate timed-release fertilizer before planting into sandy, quick-draining soils. Otherwise, no fertilizer is needed.

Care & Problems—There are no pests or diseases to bother cosmos. There will be fewer flowers and more foliage in organic-rich soils or excess nitrogen.

Water Needs—Wait until soil dries before watering deeply, once a week in summer. Water twice monthly in cooler months.

Bloom Color—Pink, white, rose, red, red-orange, burgundy, lavender

Peak Season—Summer through fall

Mature Size (H x W)—1 to 6 feet x 1 to 2 feet

GAZANIA
Gazania rigens

Why It's Special—Gazania are summer garden workhorses, a short-lived perennial in frost-free zones. Clumping types come in bright colors and combinations, their ray-type petals meeting at a yellow center ringed in black or brown. Use trailing types, which have fuzzy foliage in green with white undersides and yellow blooms, for slopes and groundcovers. Plant clumping forms in drifts, sweeps, or groupings in borders and as filler in container gardens.

How to Plant & Grow—Plant into warm soils, early spring to summer and fall in low-desert regions. Incorporate slow-release fertilizer at planting in containers or if planted in fast-draining garden soils; otherwise no soil amendments are needed. Water deeply once a week to establish.

Care & Problems—Trim back to encourage groundcover spread. No fertilizer required. Gazania is subject to root rot if overwatered, but no pests bother it.

Water Needs—Allow soil to dry between waterings, twice monthly.

Bloom Color—White, orange, red, mahogany, apricot, red, pink, yellow

Peak Season—Late spring through summer

Mature Size (H x W)—6 to 12 inches x 12 to 24 inches

GERANIUM
Pelargonium × hortorum

Why It's Special—Geranium gives lasting blooms on plump plants that become lush filler plants when not in bloom, with ruffled, hairy, and variegated leaves. Scented geranium has the added bonus of spicy, herbal aromatic leaves. Plant in containers and overwinter indoors, plant a drift for a bright focal points in the color border, in monochromatic sweeps as foreground plantings, and *en masse* in the dappled shade of a tree's understory for a part-shade groundcover. Use scented types along a path where their perfume activates when brushed against.

How to Plant & Grow—Plant in spring. Incorporate organic amendments or timed-release fertilizer at planting. Water twice a week to establish.

Care & Problems—Geraniums have no pests or diseases. Locate in full sun in milder summers, otherwise, in part shade. Deadhead to prolong blooms. Avoid waterlogged conditions.

Water Needs—Water deeply, regularly once a week.

Bloom Color—White, red, orange, lavender, pink, salmon, maroon

Peak Season—Spring, summer, fall

Mature Size (H x W)—12 to 24 inches x 8 to 18 inches

GLOBE AMARANTH
Gomphrena globosa

Why It's Special—Globe amaranth is heat, wind, rain, and drought tough, making it summer hardy for easy growing in the arid desert or hot humid climes. There are more compact types good for containers and in sweeps in the annual border. Plant groupings of taller, branched forms as midground to background plantings in the perennial border or cut flower garden. Its cloverlike blooms hang on through the heat, drying on the plant, while maintaining their color.

How to Plant & Grow—Sow seed directly in packs (eliminating transplanting from flats later), cover with soil for darkness, keep soil warm (70 degrees Fahrenheit) and moist until germination. Plant hardened-off seedlings in the garden in spring. Incorporate a timed-release fertilizer at planting. Water twice weekly to establish.

Care & Problems—Aphids may appear on juvenile foliage; spray off until a plant establishes. Deadhead to prolong bloom. No fertilizer is needed.

Water Needs—Water deeply, once a week during blooming.

Bloom Color—Purple, white, pink, lavender, red

Peak Season—Summer

Mature Size (H x W)—6 to 36 inches x 12 to 24 inches

IMPATIENS
Impatiens balsamina

Why It's Special—Impatiens flourish and flower in partial to full shade, yet defy summer heat. It's good for hanging baskets and containers, in sweeps curling in and out of tree understories, and in drifts in color borders. Use impatiens to their full measure in shady alcoves, entranceways, under arbors, tucked into the base of shrubs, and anywhere you need a spot of color to brighten an otherwise-dark space.

How to Plant & Grow—Plant in spring after last frost. Incorporate 3 inches of compost or timed-release fertilizer at planting. Use drip irrigation, covering tubing with 3 inches of organic mulch. Pinch back midsummer to promote bushiness, blooming, and minimize heat stress.

Care & Problems—Occasionally it suffers from aphids, mealybugs, slugs, and snails. Use bait for slugs and snails. Keep plants healthy to combat insect pests.

Water Needs—Maintain a moist (but not soggy) soil throughout the season.

Bloom Color—White, pink, red, purple, lavender, orange, salmon

Peak Season—Summer to first frost

Mature Size (H x W)—6 to 18 inches x 6 to 18 inches

MARIGOLD
Tagetes spp.

Why It's Special—Marigold takes summer heat, is not particular about where it lives, critters and pests leave it alone, it flowers all season, and it self-sows for the next season. There are tall branching America marigolds with round mum-sized blooms for the cut flower garden; willowy, diminutive marigolds for the edible garden; and dwarf types for color borders, sweeps along driveways, and containers.

How to Plant & Grow—Grow marigolds from seed to take advantage of the many forms and flower colors. Start seed in light, starter soil mix six weeks before the last frost. Harden off seedlings before planting them in a well-worked soil; add timed-release fertilizer in lean soils. Plant deeply, apply an inch of organic mulch, and water deeply, infrequently, for two weeks until established.

Care & Problems—No pests or diseases bother marigold. No additional fertilizer past planting is needed. Deadhead to promote bloom.

Water Needs—Water deeply, twice weekly; dry between waterings. Do not overwater.

Bloom Color—Orange, yellow, burgundy, red, creamy white

Peak Season—Summer

Mature Size (H x W)—6 to 36 inches x 10 to 36 inches

MEXICAN SUNFLOWER
Tithonia rotundifolia

Why It's Special—Mexican sunflower is drought and heat tolerant, flowering until first frost, making blooms available to pollinators long into fall. Bushy, strong, and tall plants form a garden border or green floral screen. Plant *Tithonia* in drifts in the cut flower garden and in sweeps along drives or anywhere you need long-lasting background plantings that make a statement with knock-your-eyes-out blooms.

How to Plant & Grow—Sow seed in mid-spring when the soil has warmed. Plant 1 inch deep, firming the soil, and cover with bird netting until germination if necessary to keep birds and critters at bay. Mexican sunflower doesn't like a rich soil, so don't amend or use pre-plant fertilizers. Drip irrigation keeps soil evenly moist for germination. Mulch when plants are 6 inches tall.

Care & Problems—It has no pests after plants are established but well-drained soil is essential. Cut blooms for bouquets to encourage more flowers.

Water Needs—Allow soil to dry before deep watering.

Bloom Color—Orange, gold, yellow

Peak Season—Summer

Mature Size (H x W)—2 to 6 feet x 2 to 4 feet

MILLION BELLS
Calibrachoa cultivars

Why It's Special—Million bells is a floriferous, heat-loving workhorse that's perennial in frost-free areas. Use trailing types for groundcover, making a lush, quick cover; in drifts along a sunny drive, and *en masse* on slopes. Long favored for hanging baskets or spilling over a container's edge, there are mounding types for the color borders and foreground fillers in perennial or shrub beds.

How to Plant & Grow—Plant in early spring after last frost into a well-draining soil. Use well-draining potting soil in containers. Incorporate timed-release fertilizer into soil before planting. Keep transplants deeply watered three times a week until they're over any transplant shock and sending out new growth.

Care & Problems—Whiteflies can be a nuisance but they don't harm plants. Root rot occurs in poorly draining soils.

Water Needs—Water deeply, twice a week with drip irrigation during summer; water containers daily.

Bloom Color—Pink, rose, white, blue, violet, lavender, yellow, apricot

Peak Season—Summer

Mature Size (H x W)—4 to 6 inches x 24 to 36 inches

MULLEIN
Verbascum bombyciferum and hybrids

Why It's Special—White in the garden makes all other colors and textures pop! Mullein is a drought- and heat-tolerant, self-maintaining plant that brings white to the midground and whose towering bright yellow blooms make their statement in the background, fulfilling two design features at once. Use singly as a focal point, plant in groups in perennial beds, in drifts as a colorful border, and *en masse* to fill hot, dry spots.

How to Plant & Grow—Plant seedlings after the last frost. Sow seeds outdoors in mid-spring when the soil has warmed. Barely cover seed, then press into the soil and keep moist until germination. Thin to 12 inches apart. Do not amend soil or fertilize. Water deeply, twice a week for just two weeks until plants recover from transplant shock.

Care & Problems—No pests or disease bother mulleins. Cut off blooms to avoid reseeding.

Water Needs—Water deeply, irregularly, when soil completely dries out, no more than once a week in summer.

Bloom Color—Yellow

Peak Season—Summer

Mature Size (H x W)—3 to 6 feet x 1 foot

NASTURTIUM
Tropaeolum majus

Why It's Special—Nasturtium provides a spring/summer vine on a fence or a trailing groundcover with lush, deep green foliage (there are some variegated cultivars). Then it produces lightly scented, tropical-looking blooms (which you can eat, as well as the foliage). Slower to climb, quicker to ramble, train tall forms up a trellis or arbor or plant on a slope or open area as a groundcover. Interplant bushy types in color borders or vegetable gardens to discourage squash bugs.

How to Plant & Grow—In the low desert, sow seed in fall for winter and early spring bloom. In other areas, sow seed in spring for summer to fall blooms. Nasturtium needs a well-draining soil. Incorporate 1 inch of compost or timed-release fertilizer into soil before planting. Keep seedbeds moist until germination. Mulch and begin training to supports when plants are 4 inches tall.

Care & Problems—No pests or diseases bother nasturtium. No supplemental fertilizer is needed.

Water Needs—Water deeply once a week.

Bloom Color—Orange, red, yellow, cream, white, maroon

Peak Season—Spring to fall

Mature Size (H x W)—2 to 10 feet x 2 to 10 feet

PANSY
Viola × wittrockiana

Why It's Special—Pansies can be grown throughout the Southwest as a cool-season bloomer. In hot summer regions, plant in sweeps, drifts, and clusters for fall to early spring blooms. In cooler climes, they make a good foil for bulb beds, planted in a monochromatic mass. They begin their long flowering cycle in early spring and continue into to early summer when the temperatures begin to rise.

How to Plant & Grow—*Viola tricolor* (Johnny Jump Ups) can be broadcast-sown in fall for spring to early summer blooms; they self-sow. Plant other types from packs in fall for hot-summer areas, otherwise plant in spring. Plant in compost-amended soil or incorporate a timed-release fertilizer. Mulch and keep moist.

Care & Problems—No pests or diseases affect pansies. Pinch hard halfway through their cycle, top-dress with timed-release fertilizer, and you may get another bloom cycle before summer heat.

Water Needs—Keep soil moist; water twice monthly in winter. Otherwise deeply water once a week.

Bloom Color—Purple, lavender, pink, yellow, white, maroon, combinations

Peak Season—Fall, winter, spring

Mature Size (H x W)—6 to 12 inches x 12 inches

PHLOX
Phlox drummondii

Why It's Special—Phlox is a long-season, prolific bloomer available in tall cultivars that create a floral green screen in the color border, as mid-sized bushy plants that drift throughout the color bed, and as dwarf mounding types that fill a space with a blanket of color. Use them wherever you want a continuous show of color from fall to summer or spring until first frost, depending upon your summer heat pattern.

How to Plant & Grow—In the low desert, plant packs in fall; otherwise plant in early spring right after the last frost. Buy plants that haven't yet sent out blooms or are bud-tight. Provide a compost-enriched soil or incorporate timed-release fertilizer at planting. Mulch and keep moist, watering deeply twice a week until established.

Care & Problems—Deadhead to prolong blooms. Spray off spider mites with water.

Water Needs—Keep soil moist, watering deeply twice or three times a week in hot summers.

Bloom Color—White, pink, red, peach, yellow, lavender bicolored

Peak Season—Spring to fall

Mature Size (H x W)—6 to 20 inches x 10 to 15 inches

POPPY
Papaver **spp.**

Why It's Special—Poppies come in bright and pastel colors, with double or single petals, providing foil for bulb beds, mass plantings at meadow edges, and sweeps of color in cutting gardens. Poppies make bold statements interplanted in the perennial garden and blanketing a slope with color through summer. Drought tolerant and heat and wind resistant, poppies will self-sow for a few years if you leave the seedpods (which make great dried arrangements) for the wind and birds to carry the seed.

How to Plant & Grow—Broadcast fine seed mixed with sand in fall for spring/summer bloom or in early spring as soon as ground can be worked for summer to autumn bloom. Sow in raked, unamended soil, cover lightly, and keep seedbeds moist until germination.

Care & Problems—No diseases or pests bother poppies. Do not fertilize.

Water Needs—Water shallowly, simulating a summer rain, only in periods of extended drought.

Bloom Color—Red, pink, white, salmon, blue, purple, yellow, orange

Peak Season—Spring through summer

Mature Size (H x W)—2 to 10 feet x 2 to 4 feet

SALVIA
Salvia splendens

Why It's Special—Annual salvia is a heat- and sun-loving plant, at its best when other plants fade and falter. Lush foliage makes a good contrast to its brilliant blooms that grow in tall, fluffy spikes. Planted *en masse*, salvia make a bold statement along driveways, in sweeps in the color or perennial borders, as a foil to bulbs, in groupings in containers, and in drifts under the dappled shade of open-canopy trees.

How to Plant & Grow—Grow from seed in early spring after last frost. Keep compost-amended seedbed moist until germination. When plants are 4 inches tall, top-dress with granular fertilizer and mulch. Plant packs into amended soil, mulch after planting. Water deeply twice a week until established.

Care & Problems—Sometimes spider mites occur in hot, dry summers; hose off foliage occasionally. Apply a timed-release fertilize to transplants halfway through summer and deadhead to prolong bloom.

Water Needs—Water deeply once a week; water twice weekly if extreme summer temperatures persist.

Bloom Color—Red, purple, white

Peak Season—Summer to fall

Mature Size (H x W)—6 to 36 inches x 12 inches

SCAEVOLA
Scaevola aemula

Why It's Special—Scaveola is a heat- and sun-loving, long-blooming, drought-tolerant, low-growing, and wide-spreading annual that does double and triple duty in the landscape. It's perennial in frost-free climates. Scaevola makes a season-long hanging basket or container plant, while upright types add color and texture in sweeps of color or cottage gardens. More compact forms planted *en masse* look great to line a sunny pathway, and sprawling forms make a quick-blooming groundcover.

How to Plant & Grow—Plant in spring into a well-draining soil once the soil is warmed. Mulch with shredded or chipped tree trimmings. Water deeply, letting soil dry a bit between waterings to establish. No fertilizer is needed.

Care & Problems—Overwatering and waterlogged soils are a threat. Treat chlorotic leaves by applying water-soluble fertilizer to damp (not waterlogged) soil.

Water Needs—Water deeply, but infrequently, only when soil has dried to an inch below the surface.

Bloom Color—Blue, white, pink, purple

Peak Season—Summer

Mature Size (H x W)—4 to 6 inches x 12 to 36 inches

SUMMER SNAPDRAGON
Angelonia angustifolia

Why It's Special—Summer snapdragon sets the mood for the tropics by its showy, orchidlike blooms appearing on tall spikes, while having the characteristics needed to stand up to tropical warmth and humidity. Long after other, not-so-stalwart annuals are melting in the heat and humidity, summer snapdragon grows and flowers on. Its bushy habit makes it a focal point and it's perennial in frost-free climes. Plant in drifts through meadows and *en masse* in color or cutting gardens. Grow summer snapdragon massed in a large pot.

How to Plant & Grow—Plant transplants in early spring after the last frost into compost-amended, well-drained soil or incorporate timed-release fertilizer. Mulch and water deeply; keep soil moist until plants are established.

Care & Problems—No pests or diseases bother *Angelonia*. There's no need to deadhead, stake, or fertilize.

Water Needs—Water deeply, infrequently (but more often in drought).

Bloom Color—Purple, white, pink

Peak Season—Summer

Mature Size (H x W)—18 to 24 inches x 10 to 15 inches

SUNFLOWER
Helianthus annuus

Why It's Special—Sunflower still has a place for those who love its blooms but don't want towering giants. Dwarf branching types tuck into cut flower gardens, into containers, and in color borders. If the classic, bright yellow sunflower doesn't work in your pastel palette, select from new offerings in pale and muted colors. Dinner-plate blooms attract pollinators and produce seed. Sunflowers create a garden fence or floral screen in sweeps, form a grove or line a pathway in groupings, or edge the meadow when planted *en masse*.

How to Plant & Grow—Sow seed early spring through fall, as long as daytime temperatures remain above 70 degrees Fahrenheit, into well-draining soil. Maintain moist seedbeds until germination. Mulch when plants are 4 inches tall.

Care & Problems—Protect the seedheads from birds. There are no pests or diseases.

Water Needs—Water deeply, avoiding overhead watering, allowing soil to dry to 2 inches deep before repeating.

Bloom Color—Yellow, orange, brown, red, pink, cream, bronze

Peak Season—Spring through fall

Mature Size (H x W)—2 to 10 feet x 2 to 4 feet

SWEET ALYSSUM
Lobularia maritima

Why It's Special—Sweet alyssum's scented blooms (some love it, some do not!) bring bees and butterflies by the droves. The soft foliage is all but hidden when sweet alyssum blooms, its pastel flowers blanketing the ground. Use alyssum in the veggie garden to attract pollinators, plant in drifts along pathways, under the dappled shade of fruit trees, in the color border in sweeps, in containers as filler, and broadcast-seed throughout the meadow.

How to Plant & Grow—Sow seed directly or plant cell-packs in early spring when soil is warming. Cool soils cause sporadic, weak germination. Incorporate timed-release fertilizer; keep soil moist until established.

Care & Problems—No pests or diseases bother sweet alyssum. Pinch back lanky plants in midsummer to encourage repeat bloom or leave for self-sowing the following season.

Water Needs—It's fairly drought tolerant if deeply watered to a depth of 10 to 12 inches once a week.

Bloom Color—White, purple, lavender, pink, rose

Peak Season—Spring through fall

Mature Size (H x W)—4 to 6 inches x 10 to 12 inches

SWEET POTATO VINE
Ipomoea batatas

Why It's Special—Sweet potato vine has lush, tropical-looking foliage on a drought-tolerant plant that grows best in lean, well-draining soils. Give it room to perform. Use it to cover the ground quickly and thickly, drifting throughout the shrub bed, surrounding a focal point tree, meandering in and out of tall perennials, and tumbling out of pots. In frost-free areas, it is perennial.

How to Plant & Grow—Plant pots in spring when air and soil temperatures are warm. Plant in well-draining and well-worked soil, but no amendments or fertilizer are needed. Water deeply and infrequently to establish. Add mulch.

Care & Problems—Control growth and encourage side growth by pinching the tips. Spider mites occur in extended dry periods; occasionally wash off foliage. Aphids may feed on new growth; spray them off or wait them out. No fertilizing is needed.

Water Needs—Water deeply, infrequently, allowing soil to dry between waterings.

Bloom Color—Chartreuse, purple, gray or pink variegated foliage

Peak Season—Spring through fall foliage

Mature Size (H x W)—12 to 18 inches x 4 to 6 feet

TIDYTIPS
Layia platyglossa

Why It's Special—Tidytips is indeed a tidy, clumping, low-mounding annual, having perfectly symmetrical, bright yellow blooms tipped in white that just barely rise above its foliage on strong narrow stems. A neatly growing, drought-tolerant, and carefree plant, use tidytips in containers, planted *en masse* along driveways or at the meadow's edge, in sweeps lining color borders, and in clumps in the foreground of the perennial garden.

How to Plant & Grow—Sow seed mixed with sand in fall for spring bloom in hot-summer regions. Lightly cover fine seed and sprinkle every three days until germination. In milder-summer sites, sow seed or plant seedlings in early spring. Plant in a well-draining soil, which can be rocky, sandy, lean, or clayey. Water deeply and infrequently until plants establish.

Care & Problems—There are no pests or diseases to bother tidy tips. No fertilizer or deadheading is required.

Water Needs—Water deeply once a week if there's no rain.

Bloom Color—Yellow

Peak Season—Spring

Mature Size (H x W)—4 to 10 inches x 5 to 10 inches

WALLFLOWER 'BOWLES' MAUVE'
Erysimum linifolium 'Bowles' Mauve'

Why It's Special—The wallflower 'Bowles' Mauve' is a compact, long-blooming, drought-tolerant, durable, carefree annual that often persists and flowers into a second season before it finally gives up its floral show. Use it freely in perennial gardens, in annual borders, singly in pots or in combinations, planted in blocks in formal gardens, and in sweeps along a path.

How to Plant & Grow—Plant in spring after danger of all frost is past into a well-drained soil amended with a few inches of compost and incorporated with timed-release fertilizer. Mulch and water deeply to a depth of 18 inches to establish.

Care & Problems—No pests or diseases bother wallflowers. Trim off spent blooms midseason to encourage more blooms and keep the plants compact.

Water Needs—Water once a week, deeply to 24 inches in summer when temperatures exceed 85 degrees Fahrenheit; then, twice monthly as temperatures cool; once a month in cooler weather.

Bloom Color—Pink-purple

Peak Season—Spring through fall, all season in mild winters

Mature Size (H x W)—18 to 24 inches x 18 to 24 inches

WAX LEAF BEGONIA
Begonia semperflorens

Why It's Special—The most carefree, long-blooming, adaptable begonia among this genus, wax leaf begonias bring color to densly shaded beds and stand up to the heat in full sun exposures too. Growing and flowering through winter in desert regions, they perform in cooler zones from spring to fall. Use in color borders, in the dappled shade of a broad canopied tree, in pots, in shady alcoves or entrances, or drifting along the edge of a stream.

How to Plant & Grow—Plant cell packs in spring, two weeks after last frost, into well-draining, compost-amended soil. Plant in fall in frost-free areas. Mulch. Water deeply, and avoid wetting foliage; keep soil moist until established.

Care & Problems—Snails are the wax leaf begonia's only pests. Use snail bait following package directions. If plants begin to fade midseason, apply a timed-release or water-soluble fertilizer. Deadhead and clean up faded foliage.

Water Needs—Keep deeply watered, allowing the soil's surface to dry before watering.

Bloom Color—White, red, pink

Peak Season—Spring, summer, fall

Mature Size (H x W)—6 to 12 inches x 8 to 12 inches

ZINNIA
Zinnia angustifolia

Why It's Special—Zinnia is a heat- and drought-tough annual. Taller zinnia works in the midground of perennial beds or at the background of patio gardens, *en masse* in cut flower gardens, in drifts at a meadow's edge, and as foil to bulb beds lining a drive. Fill a pot or a bed with zinnia's rainbow colors or individual colors melting from one to another.

How to Plant & Grow—Sow seed or plant starts in fall in low-desert regions; otherwise, plant two weeks after the last frost. Incorporate compost or timed-release fertilizer at planting. Cover lightly with soil, keeping seedbeds moist until germination. Mulch when plants are 4 inches tall or immediately after planting. Deeply water three times a week until established.

Care & Problems—Zinna's biggest problem is powdery mildew. Provide good air circulation and avoid watering foliage. Cut blooms for bouquets or deadhead.

Water Needs—Water deeply twice a week.

Bloom Color—Red, orange, cream, yellow, chartreuse, lavender, purple, pink

Peak Season—Spring to fall

Mature Size (H x W)—6 to 48 inches x 6 to 18 inches

ANNUALS MONTH-BY-MONTH

JANUARY

- As soon as annual wildflowers pop up along roadways and in open areas, that is your signal to sow cold-season annual seeds in the garden. Direct-sow poppies, Johnny Jump Ups, and Mexican hat for early spring bloom.

- In colder climates, order annual seeds for February sowing in the greenhouse. Select new annual types in different colors, varieties, and mixes. Go for the unusual. Try *Cosmidium burridgeanu*, common name Phillipine, whose blooms have an aroma like chocolate with yellow-tipped petals and maroon centers.

- Prepare the soil for planting cool-season seedlings that are available in the garden centers and home-improvement stores. Work in organic amendments if the annual requires a nutrient-rich soil or if the native soil is slow draining. Otherwise, dig and turn the native soil manually, rather than risk overtilling. You will increase airspace needed for drainage and minimize disruption of the soil microbes occurring naturally in the soil.

FEBRUARY

- Prepare a list of annuals to plant outdoors after the threat of frost. Plan when to sow (count weeks back from planting out time, noted on packet) and schedule two additional weeks for hardening off before setting starts out in the garden.

- Sow warm-season annual seeds in a light potting soil mix according to package directions. They need a warm soil, so use a grower's heat mat or a heating pad (wrap the heating pad in a towel to avoid overheating the soil). Place under grow lights or in a sunny window. Cover seed flats with bubble wrap or plastic wrap at night to maintain moisture.

- Maintaining seedling flats requires due diligence. Once seedlings have a couple sets of leaves, the soil should be moist, but not saturated. Mist using a fine nozzle whenever the soil surface feels dry. Keep them on the heat mat until transplanting and for an additional week to recover from transplant shock.

MARCH

- Part-shade, cool-season annuals such as pansies can be kept flowering into the summer if planted in a spot with afternoon shade, mulched, pinched back by one-third, and then fertilized. They will rebloom before succumbing to the heat.

- Direct sow warm-season annuals into the landscape. Place markers in the center of the bed or at the end of the rows to help you remember where you have sown so you can keep the seedbed moist until germination. Cover the seed lightly to protect it from drying out and from the birds, which will be hungry for new seed after a long winter.

- Cool-season annuals are finishing now, so pull them out and replace with starts of warm-season annuals. For the hungrier, warm-season annuals, incorporate compost or timed-release fertilizer at planting. This minimizes additional fertilizer applications in the heat of the summer that can cause leaf burn.

APRIL

- Poppies are most likely done blooming, with seedpods remaining on tall stems. If pods are holding color, leave them in the landscape. If seedpods are brown, tromp the stems to the ground for self-sowing next year. To save seeds and pods, place upside down in a paper bag to capture the seeds before using the pods for dried arrangements. If you still hear tiny seeds rattling around when you give them a shake, insert a pin into the tip, and shake remaining seed into the bag. Store in a cool, dark dry location for fall sowing.

- Pull expired cool-season annuals from container gardens to replace with warm-season lovers. Fluff up container soil, adding fresh if it's depleted. If you are concerned about soil pathogens in used soil, spread the soil out in flats and place in the sun for a few days; the sun will cook anything lurking.

- Drip irrigation is the most efficient way to water in the Southwest. Some systems are available with hose end connections, others are installation-user friendly. Select from leading manufacturers and purchase extra fittings and emitters at the time of purchase for later repairs. Drip irrigation systems are not standardized. Some tubing is metric and others are not, so parts are not interchangeable.

MAY

- Harden off annual starts, homegrown or purchased from local garden centers, which may have shipped directly from a greenhouse to the garden shelves. Take at least a week to acclimate plants. Place them in the shade for a few days and keep them watered; move to morning sun, part shade in the afternoon for a few days; then set them in their final home still in the pots for a day or so before planting. Afternoon sun beating down on little cell packs and black pots can cook the roots. If the starts heat up, move them to the shade to cool them down, and water. Once they are in the ground, the soil will insulate their young roots.

- Direct-sow seeds of warm-season annuals in the garden or in pots. The seedbeds will dry out quickly outdoors from wind and sun, so mist once or twice a day until germination.

- Rather than plant annuals in straight soldier-like rows (unless that is your style), experiment with sowing or planting in drifts or sweeps. Even the classic marigold takes on a new look when it's planted as if it flowed into the scene.

JUNE

- Temperatures are heating up, but some annuals like it hot; sow Mexican sunflower, moss rose, marigold, sunflower, and zinnias that will bloom until first frost.

- Don't fertilize this month. Fertilizing in hot weather can cause leaf burn. Water is key. Deeply water the soil and roots, not the foliage. If the mulch has degraded, top it off with fresh mulch. Maintain a minimum of 3 inches of mulch.

- Wilting can be the plant's defense mechanism against the heat; leaves will unfurl as evening temps cool. Wilting may also be signs of root rot as the leaves collapse because the vascular system is compromised. Stop watering, allow the soil to dry out completely, then water deeply and slowly, allowing soil to dry out again. Repeat this process and the plants may generate new roots if the plants aren't too far gone.

JULY

- Refresh annual container gardens. Move them into partly shaded locations or areas that get a bit of shade in late afternoon when the sun is the hottest. Deadhead, cut trailing plants back by one-third, fill the container with water, and allow it to drain freely out the bottom to leach out salts. Top with shredded or chipped bark mulch.

- You can still plant lantana in the garden and it is usually available at nursery garden centers through the season. Lantana already planted may start to set berries. It will slow its growth then, but pick up speed in August, finishing up with its usual floral show before frost.

- Watch for powdery mildew this month. Intense heat, summer monsoons, too much shade, lack of breezes, and crowding encourages mildew, although sometimes it is just the nature of the plant. Mildew doesn't affect the blooms as much as the foliage. Water the roots, not the leaves; mulch to prevent backsplash; thin overgrown plants; and trim and dispose infected leaves.

AUGUST

- If you have decided to have a wildflower garden or a home meadow, then get out the seed catalogs to order now. There are mixes tailored to our area that include natives and other drought- and heat-tolerant types perfected for the Southwest.

- Prepare new seedbeds by thoroughly deep soaking the area to a depth of 12 to 18 inches, extending the soaker hose to deeply water at least a foot out from the perimeter of the bed. This broad soaking will eliminate the chance of the drier soil wicking away water from the seedbed.

- Sunflowers are long-lasting cut flowers. You may notice ants parading up and down the stems, common visitors in the heat. Cut the stems and plunge the flower heads directly into a bucket of water, allowing them to soak a few minutes. The ants will fall off. Give the bloom a few shakes before fresh cutting and inserting into a vase.

SEPTEMBER

- As warm-season annuals begin to set seed, take note of ones that worked and that you want to invite back to the garden. Stop deadheading and allow the plant to fade. Marigolds, nasturtiums, and sunflowers often reseed in the same place. To collect seed, cut the plants off at ground level, place upside down in a paper bag until completely dry, then separate seed from plant, bag, and store in a cool, dry location until spring.

- Sow seeds for cool-season annuals as soon as temperatures level out below 100 degrees Fahrenheit. Top with seed-starter mix so they don't dry out while germinating. Poppies and pansies can be sown now. Pansies are a bit of challenge to germinate in the ground, but Johnny Jump Ups are quite user friendly and once started will reseed for three or four years before needing a refresher sowing.

- Buy cool-season annuals bud-tight, rather than full in flower, so they last longer in the garden. Otherwise, deadhead before planting to encourage blooming.

OCTOBER

- If you have always wanted a wildflower or meadow, now is the time to start it. Thoroughly wet the seedbed (see September), then using a heavy rake, rake out debris and dead plants. There's no need to till or add amendments. Native soil, rocks, and alkaline lean soils are what these plants are used to in their native habitat. It's best to mimic their surroundings for good germination and strong plants.

- Mix small seed with sand before broadcasting then scatter in sweeps or drifts (just like Mother Nature) onto moistened soil. Scatter seed in front of you while you back out of the seedbed. Sow in early morning or late afternoon to avoid the wind carrying seed out of the area. Once a bed is seeded, scatter a topdressing of soil or sand to protect the seed. Top-dress while walking forward so your footsteps gently press the seed into the soil.

- Sprinkle or mist once a day in the early morning or evening to maintain moisture until seeds germinate. If the heat kicks in or the wind blows, you may need to spritz twice daily.

NOVEMBER

- First frosts in some areas may finish off warm-season annuals. Pull up any expired plants, invest in new mulch or compost, and refresh the beds while you simultaneously nourish the soil.

- Geraniums are perennials in frost-free areas and overwinter well in the home or greenhouse. Ivy and zonal geraniums should be cut back and brought indoors into indirect light and a cool room. They will go semi-dormant, dropping some leaves and slowing in growth. Water only when soil dries through winter. Scented geraniums grow year-round. Cut them back by half, put in a sunny window, away from heat source and water once a week. Don't fertilize until spring.

- Coleus are houseplants in colder climates. If they are growing in the garden, cut them back by half (save the cuttings), pot up in fresh, lightweight potting soil, water in, and place indoors in indirect light, out of the way of vents or heat sources. Root cuttings in the same pot, clean the leaves off, cut at the node, pushing into soil so two nodes are buried. You'll get a bushier plant in no time.

DECEMBER

- In frost-free lower elevations, set out starts of cold-tolerant calendula, pansy, petunia, and sweet alyssum. Water well after planting, mulch, then water deeply once a week in cooler weather. Overwatering at this time can cause rots and mildews.

- If you have a heat mat, take cuttings off the new growth on scented geraniums; the smaller-leaved types root easily. Make cuttings 3 to 4 inches long, pull off foliage on the lower stem, 1 to 1½ inches, stick four to six cuttings per quart pot for a quick finished plant.

- Pick off yellowed leaves and clean out debris in the pots on overwintering plants that are slowed in growth or are dormant. Cooler indoor temperatures will keep pests at bay. Warm greenhouses should be monitored for pests. Limit fertilizing to discourage tender new growth that pests love.

BULBS
for the Southwest

Bulbs were the first plants I grew on the property in Utah where I eventually moved with my husband. I planted a handful of daffodils on both sides of the driveway to have something cheery to greet us when we returned for a visit the following spring. I hand-dug the holes, twice as deep as the plump bulbs, plopped them in, covered them over with the toe of my boot scraping the dry soil into the hole, then dragged a hose out and let water trickle while we loaded the truck for our return trip to California. We returned the following spring, early, just as the snow melted, and there they were, a dozen happy yellow and orange daffodils, swaying in the breeze. Each fall I plant more and they get the same amount of attention as that first handful, yet they continue to grow and thrive. That is the way of most bulbs.

Just to clarify, in this book, I use the term "bulb" to refer to any sort of plant that grows by way of underground storage receptacle, whether it's a rhizome (iris), corm (gladiolus), tuber (caladium), or bulb (daffodil).

WHAT ABOUT THE SOIL?

One thing bulbs have in common is their love of a well-draining soil. They are not particular about a lack of organics, but soggy, cold, wet soils can put an end to their growing before they even sprout. A well-draining soil has ample air spaces that allow the water to move through the soil profile, going deeply to the roots that absorb the water and nutrients.

If you are gardening in soils heavy in clay or in areas that get more rain than the soil can absorb and can drain, then incorporate organic amendments to increase drainage over time. If you are dealing with a soggy bog conditions, consider planting on a berm or slope, building raised beds using imported soil, or growing bulbs in containers.

Some bulbs like more nutrients and organic matter at the start, in which case spreading 3 inches of compost over the entire planting area, then incorporating it thoroughly into the soil fulfills that requirement. Some bulbs prefer situations closely resembling their native habitat, thriving in lean, rocky, or sandy soils on hillsides, or among scrubby outbacks or on slopes. That makes planting prep a bit easier, no amendments needed.

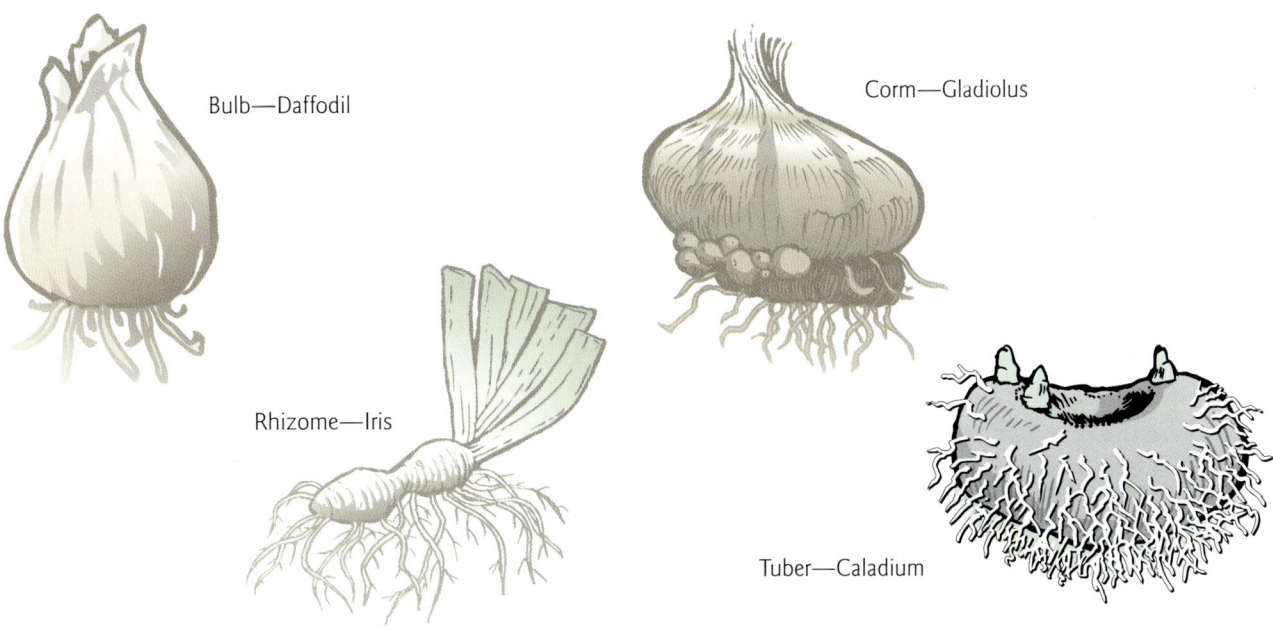

Bulb—Daffodil

Rhizome—Iris

Corm—Gladiolus

Tuber—Caladium

A handheld dibbler makes easy work out of digging perfect-sized bulb holes every time.

HOW MUCH WATER IS ENOUGH?

Bulbs are storage units for water (and nutrients). When bulbs are dormant or slowed in growth, they don't require any water. When you see the first signs of growth in spring, it's time to resume watering. But the soil is still cool and may be holding moisture from recent rain or snow melt, so check the soil first and allow the soil to dry to the touch before watering. Rot in early spring is common, so take care not to overwater.

When they are actively growing and flowering and temperatures are heating up, bulbs need regular, deep watering to keep them hydrated and to nurture developing roots and foliage. Drip tubing with inline emitters works well for bulbs, directing the water to the roots of the plant. If the soil drains slowly, water, allow the water to percolate into the soil, then water again, repeating the process until the water reaches the desired soil depth.

After blooming, maintain infrequent, deep watering (allowing the soil to dry to a few inches) until bulb foliage turns completely yellow or brown. The bulbs are actively storing resources during this time so it is important to maintain soil moisture. If you interplant annuals or perennials into the bulb bed, the water you give those will suffice for bulbs.

MULCH, MULCH, MULCH— DID I SAY MULCH?

Gardening in the Southwest means we have to make the most out of our water resources. All bulbs enjoy a layer of mulch to protect them from our intense air and soil summer temperatures. A thick layer of mulch cools the soil, shades the roots, holds in moisture, adds nutrients to the soil (as organic mulch breaks down), and contributes to good drainage. A thick layer of mulch protects the bulbs in winter, especially in areas where the ground freezes and soil heaving can occur. Using mulch discourages weed seed from germinating and, if the weeds do take hold, they slip out of the soil more easily, eliminating the need to cultivate around the bulbs. Apply mulch just after planting and check the layer in spring and fall for areas that might need a refresh. A good rule of thumb is, if you see soil, add mulch.

TO FERTILIZE OR NOT TO FERTILIZE?

I rarely fertilize my bulbs. Sometimes the tulips get a bit of timed-release scattered on the soil before I replenish the mulch in spring, and I feed the gladiolus as I plant them. The amount of fertilizer necessary depends upon the soil's nutrient levels. If the bulbs sprout forth, put on their foliage, and continue to bloom, don't worry about fertilizing. If their foliage shows telltale

For a natural-looking bulb bed, dig out a swath of soil deep enough to accommodate the bulb planting.

Toss handfuls of bulbs onto the bed, set them upright, then cover them with soil.

signs of deficiencies or chlorosis, the plants appear stunted, or buds are few and far between, then feed them. Container-grown bulbs need fertilizer, as constant watering in soilless mixes leaches out nutrients quickly. Use water-soluble bulb formulations or timed-release fertilizer in containers. Never fertilize a dry soil, either in a pot or in the garden.

NO PAMPERING NEEDED

I have a friend who dutifully divides her iris every three years, painstakingly pulling off dead leaves each spring, trimming the green leaves with scissors into beautiful fans, fertilizing regularly, and deadheading the faded stalks as soon as they decline. What do I do? Maybe I divide every five years and I make fast work of that business. In fall, I deeply water the bed so I can easily sink a shovel, then I dig the entire space at once. It's like this: grab a clump, cut out the older center rhizomes, cut the remaining rhizome into chunks. When all is dug up, I give a few passes with the rake, toss the divisions out, shove them into the soil, top with mulch and I am done. To eliminate dead foliage in spring, I use a heavy landscape rake, plow it into the mass of dead foliage, and rake the bulb bed hard enough to collect most of brown foliage in one or two passes. Some rhizomes pop out of the soil, so I give them a little bonus divide, and then push them back into the soil. I only deadhead when I need some cuts for the house, never fertilize, and you can see that bed of iris blooming from the street. So little attention, so many rewards. That is how gardening with bulbs should be.

45

ALLIUM
Allium spp.

Why It's Special—Allium encompasses a wide range of ornamental and edible onions that munching and digging animals stay away from. Heat, cold, and drought have no effect on their bloom and they naturalize and reseed without any coaxing whatsoever. For impact, plant them *en masse*, in drifts, sweeps, and clumps in the background, midground, or foreground (depending upon the bloom/stem height), in the perennial or cut flower bed, under the canopy of fruit trees, or in the edible landscape.

How to Plant & Grow—Plant allium, spaced bulb to bulb, in fall or early spring into a pre-moistened soil that has been well worked and is well draining. No soil amendments or fertilizers are needed. Water deeply once a week until established.

Care & Problems—There are no pests and allium are not hungry feeders. Cut blooms for fresh or dried arrangements and to deter self-sowing. Chives (*Allium schoenprasum*) can be invasive in small gardens.

Water Needs—After establishment, water deeply every few weeks during summer.

Bloom Color—Purple, white, burgundy, lavender, pink

Peak Season—Summer

Mature Size (H x W)—6 to 36 inches x 6 to 12 inches

BEARDED IRIS
Iris spp.

Why It's Special—Bearded iris retain some foliage in cold winters, making them semi-evergreen. They can take cold, heat, wind, drought, and lean soils. Plant sweeps of monochromatic colors for big impact along a drive or in the midground of garden beds for their linear foliage.

How to Plant & Grow—Plant rhizomes in fall in cold-winter areas; otherwise, plant in spring in well-worked, well-draining, pre-moistened soil. Incorporate a timed-release fertilizer. Plant rhizomes just below the soil surface. Water deeply after planting, once a week until it's rooted.

Care & Problems—Iris need partial shade in the hottest desert regions. Dense shade or overfertilization inhibits blooming. Divide every three to five years in fall, culling out older, central rhizomes. Give the bed a good heavy raking to remove dead foliage in spring.

Water Needs—Deep water once a week through bloom cycles; twice a month until winter; once a month in winter if no rain or snow.

Bloom Color—All colors and combos

Peak Season—Spring to summer

Mature Size (H x W)—8 to 32 inches x 15 to 24 inches

BLAZING STAR
Liatris spicata

Why It's Special—Blazing star is heat and cold tough and not particular about soil, if it's well draining. Its juvenile foliage forms a grassy mound, softening bed edges and intermingling with other ornamental grasses. Tall, linear flower spikes draw the eye to the back of color borders or perennial beds. Plant blazing star in groups, drifts, or in geometric patterns for its full effect.

How to Plant & Grow—Plant rootstalks in spring or containers anytime into well-worked, well-draining soil. Mulch and water deeply, allow soil to dry just a bit before each watering. (You can grow some bulbs from seed. It is a bit more challenging and takes longer for bloom. They form bulbs as they mature.)

Care & Problems—They're not hungry plants, but if chlorosis shows, side-dress with timed-release fertilizer. No pests bother liatris. It may rot in cold, consistently damp soil.

Water Needs—Water deeply once a week in summer, but rarely in winter.

Bloom Color—Purple, pink, white

Peak Season—Summer

Mature Size (H x W)—2 to 4 feet x 1 to 3 feet

CANNA
Canna hybrids

Why It's Special—Canna are at their best in the heat of summer. Plant *en masse* as a long-season, summer focal point in containers, along streambed edges, in flower borders, or perennial beds. Use taller types as a foliage and floral wall or screen, plant drifts along an entrance drive, and install as accents under the dappled shade of a specimen tree.

How to Plant & Grow—Plant bulbs or plants in early spring into well-amended and well-draining soil. Install drip irrigation; apply 3 to 4 inches of mulch. Top-dress with timed-release fertilizer every eight weeks.

Care & Problems—Snails and slugs are common; bait according to directions. Deadhead to prolong bloom. Cut back foliage to the ground in fall to rejuvenate plants and divide every three years.

Water Needs—Deep, regular watering, twice a week in the heat of summer.

Bloom Color—Yellow, orange, pink, red, cream, coral, salmon

Peak Season—Spring through summer

Mature Size (H x W)—2 to 8 feet x 2 to 3 feet

Hardiness—Zones 8 to 11

CALADIUM
Caladium bicolor

Why It's Special—Caladium brings brightly colored foliage to shady gardens where there always seems to be a deficit of plants that can survive the heat, yet lighten up a dark area. Use caladium's colored foliage as a floral carpet in a dark entryway, in drifts in dappled shade, in sweeps in shady perennial gardens, or in containers.

How to Plant & Grow—Plant when tubers are available or from containers when temperatures are consistently above 70 degrees Fahrenheit into well-amended and well-draining soil. Top-dress with a timed-release fertilizer. Add 2 to 3 inches of mulch. Water deeply after planting until established.

Care & Problems—Bait to treat snails and slugs. Apply water-soluble fertilizer once a month.

Water Needs—Provide regular, deep watering two to three times a week; daily for containers.

Bloom Color—Variegated foliage in pink, white, shades of green, red, silver, bronze

Peak Season—Summer to frost

Mature Size (H x W)—1 to 3 feet x 1 to 3 feet

Hardiness—Zones 8 to 10. Overwinter containers indoors or dig tubers in fall, store, and replant in spring if they're not hardy.

CLIVIA
Clivia miniata

Why It's Special—Clivia are long-lived in frost-free climes, naturalizing in dry shady locations and preferring to be clumped together in close quarters. Evergreen, large, straplike leaves lend a tropical, lush feel when planted *en masse* in the shady alcove or entryway. The blooms are large and boisterous, brightening up the darkest corner and the show doesn't end until the berries fade away.

How to Plant & Grow—Plant rhizomes in fall in frost-free areas; otherwise, plant in early spring after last frost into well-amended, well-draining soil. Apply mulch and water deeply, regularly until established. Apply timed-release fertilizer in late winter, before flowering. Fertilize containers with water-soluble fertilizer monthly during flowering.

Care & Problems—Root rot is possible by overwatering in winter. Occasionally mealybugs attack clivia. No dividing required.

Water Needs—Water deeply, allowing soil to dry out between waterings; only minimal watering needed in winter.

Bloom Color—Orange, yellow, cream

Peak Season—Late winter through spring

Mature Size (H x W)—18 inches x 14 inches

Hardiness—Zones 9 to 10. Grow in pots for spring blooms, then bring potted clivia indoors to overwinter.

CRINUM
Crinum spp.

Why It's Special—Crinum live long, don't mind heat or drought (after establishment), and they like being grown closely together. Crinum grow naturally in meadows and on rocky hillsides, making them right at home planted in drifts or groupings along a driveway, at a meadow's edge, and in open areas where they can naturalize freely. Use them in a shady alcove or under an arbor in hot-summer regions.

How to Plant & Grow—Plant in spring through summer in well-worked native soil with good drainage. Incorporate a timed-release fertilizer. Mulch and water deeply once a week, twice a week during hottest summer months for the first season. They may take a few seasons to establish and bloom. They never need dividing.

Care & Problems—Top-dress with timed-release fertilizer in spring. May repeat bloom in late summer so avoid pulling yellowed leaves from plant midsummer.

Water Needs—After establishment, water deeply every few weeks in the heat of summer.

Bloom Color—White, pink, cream, wine

Peak Season—Spring and summer

Mature Size (H x W)—2 to 4 feet x 2 to 4 feet

CROCUS
Crocus spp.

Why It's Special—Crocus are the first bloomers in late winter and some species flower later in autumn, brightening up a spot where summer flowers have ebbed. They are at their showiest planted *en masse* along a path, in drifts along the meadow edge, in swaths through the bulb bed, in the understories of open branching trees, and clustered together in the rock garden.

How to Plant & Grow—Plant spring-blooming crocus in fall; plant autumn-flowering types in August. Crocus are not picky about soil, so there's no need to amend, but work the site well before broadcasting corms. Mulch and water deeply, allowing the soil to dry just a bit before watering again

Care & Problems—There are no pests other than rabbits, which spy a crocus' first leaves as they poke through the snow.

Water Needs—No watering in cold winters where the ground freezes; otherwise, water deeply and infrequently through winter. Resume weekly, deep watering in spring.

Bloom Color—White, yellow, purple, blue

Peak Season—Late winter, early spring, autumn

Mature Size (H x W)—8 inches x 4 inches

DAFFODIL
Narcissus spp.

Why It's Special—Daffodils require no attention once planted, are undemanding in their nutrient or water requirements, naturalize freely, and are a welcome sight heralding spring with their cheerful blooms. Grow them *en masse* on slopes, at the meadow edge, along a driveway or garden path, and in sweeps under deciduous or open canopied trees. Plant diminutive types in rock gardens and along dry streambeds. Site scented daffodils close to gathering spots.

How to Plant & Grow—Plant daffodils in well-worked native soil in fall. Top with a 2 to 3 inches of mulch, and water deeply.

Care & Problems—Deadhead to maintain a tidy look. Don't remove foliage until it is crispy yellow or just leave it to fade away with winter. Bulbs rot if they get too much water. No insects or pests bother daffodils.

Water Needs—Water deeply at first signs of growth in spring, but not during dormancy. In hot summer areas, water deeply once a month.

Bloom Color—Yellow, white, salmon, peach, pink, orange

Peak Season—Spring

Mature Size (H x W)—6 to 24 inches x 4 to 12 inches

DAYLILY
Hemerocallis spp.

Why It's Special—Daylilies are drought tolerant once established, making them the go-to naturalizing bulb for spring-through-fall blooms in water-challenged gardens. Hundreds of cultivars are available, providing a size and bloom color for every garden. Plant in sweeps and drifts to fill open areas, as a groundcover in hot, windy meridian strips, on steep slopes, singly, or with companions in containers.

How to Plant & Grow—Plant bulbs bare root or in containers all year-round, except in winter. Plant into a well-worked soil, incorporating balanced timed-release fertilizer. Mulch and water deeply. Allow the soil to dry a bit before watering again. Fertilize with a timed-release fertilizer in early spring.

Care & Problems—Occasionally aphids, snails, and slugs can be problems. Daylilies are subject to bulb rot if they're overwatered. Divide overgrown clumps every four years.

Water Needs—Deep, regular watering is needed during bloom cycles; otherwise, allow soil to dry between waterings. No water is needed when they're winter dormant.

Bloom Color—Yellow, orange, pink, maroon, red, purple, apricot, lilac, cream

Peak Season—Spring, summer, early fall

Mature Size (H x W)—1 to 3 feet x 1 to 2 feet

FREESIA
Freesia spp.

Why It's Special—Deliciously scented spring blooms, freesia are dormant in summer, needing no water when the rest of the garden is guzzling. Plant bunches among part-shade foliar plants to serve as foil to the fading freesia leaves. Site potted freesia near the front entrance to greet visitors with their scent. Use drifts in the cut flower garden and bring their heavenly fragrance indoors with long-lasting blooms.

How to Plant & Grow—Plant in fall in pre-moistened, well-draining native soil. Water if there's no rain or snow in winter, allowing the soil to dry thoroughly between deep waterings. Divide every few years.

Care & Problems—Dig and store for replanting in fall in rainy summer climes.

Water Needs—Cut back watering after blooming, as soon as leaves begin to turn yellow. Water infrequently, deeply in spring, every two to three weeks thereafter.

Bloom Color—White, purple, red, pink, yellow, orange, blue

Peak Season—Spring

Mature Size (H x W)—12 inches x 6 inches

Hardiness—Zones 9 to 10; Freesia can remain in the ground during winters that stay above 20 degrees Fahrenheit.

GLADIOLUS
Gladiolus spp. and hybrids

Why It's Special—Gladioli are hard to to beat for their long-lasting blooms and linear attributes in the garden. Site in drifts or clumps in the midground of perennial beds or in sweeps along a path. *Gladiolus byzantinus* is cold hardy to Zone 5; it's less apt to need staking or as much water.

How to Plant & Grow—Plant every two weeks in spring as soil is warmed or begin bimonthly plantings in January in desert climes. Plant in pre-moistened, compost-enriched, well-draining soil. Incorporate timed-release fertilizer at planting. Keep soil moist with frequent deep watering.

Care & Problems—Watch for thrips. Plants may require caging supports for tall flower stalks. Cut as soon as top bud shows color.

Water Needs—Deep water once a week in cool spring climates; twice a week in hot summers.

Bloom Color—All colors except blue

Peak Season—Spring, summer

Mature Size (H x W)—2 to 5 feet x 1 foot

Hardiness—Zones 8 to 10. Leave hybrids in the ground if temps remain above freezing; otherwise, dig in fall, store, and replant in spring.

GRAPE HYACINTH
Muscari spp.

Why It's Special—Grape hyacinth are hardy, tidy plants that push their bright flowers even through the snow, blooming through spring. They send out grassy clumps of foliage after blooms fade, making their presence known until fall in rock gardens, in drifts under open tree canopies, at meadow edges, or in the foreground of color borders.

How to Plant & Grow—Plant in fall into well-worked and well-draining soil, incorporating balanced bulb fertilizer. Water well after planting. In low-desert climates, pre-chill bulbs a couple of weeks before planting in January.

Care & Problems—Muscari has no pests except for gophers or moles. Divide every few years if they have reseeded or outgrown their space. There's no need for seasonal fertilizing. Cut back foliage only when it is crispy.

Water Needs—Water in winter only if there is no rain or snow. Provide deep, irregular watering when first leaves first emerge in spring. Allow the soil to dry before watering. It's drought tolerant once established.

Bloom Color—Purple, blue, white

Peak Season—Spring

Mature Size (H x W)—6 to 12 inches x 6 to 12 inches

LILY
Lillium spp.

Why It's Special—Lilies make a statement in the garden with their large tropical blooms sitting atop tall stems lined with deep green foliage. Grouped in perennial gardens, drifting among shrubs in the landscape, sweeping under the dappled shade of trees, naturalizing on slopes—lilies are no longer relegated to a pot at Easter, although they do make excellent container plants.

How to Plant & Grow—Plant in early spring in a well-amended soil with good drainage. Lilies like their "heads in the sun, feet in the shade" so apply a 2- to 3-inch mulch layer. Water well after planting. In lower-desert climates, plant in part sun to part shade.

Care & Problems—Aphids are common. Lilies are slow to colonize; dig and divide in fall after four or more years. Allow foliage to die back naturally, remove them, and apply timed-release fertilizer.

Water Needs—Regular, deep watering in growing seasons, supplemental watering if there's no winter moisture.

Bloom Color—White, salmon, purple, red, yellow, pink

Peak Season—Spring to fall

Mature Size (H x W)—1 to 6 feet x 1 to 3 feet

RAINLILY
Zephyranthes spp.

Why It's Special—Rainlilies are native to prairies, desert scrub, and dry meadows, giving clues to their place in the garden. Plant them *en masse* on slopes, at meadow edges, in sweeps along drives, interplanted with annuals and perennials, and in the understories of open branching trees. They make a summer appearance whenever they get water, fade away, then resurface again if given another drink at the end of the season.

How to Plant & Grow—Plant bulbs in fall into well-worked native soil, incorporated with a balanced bulb fertilizer, then water deeply. Rainlily can be grown from seed; sow after soil reaches 70 degrees Fahrenheit. Keep seedbeds moist until germination. Transplant container-grown plants when the foliage is actively growing.

Care & Problems—Rainlilies are drought tough and disease and pest resistant. Remove withered leaves after they are brown and crumbly. Divide only every five or more years or allow rainlilies to naturalize.

Water Needs—Water blooming plants once a week; no winter watering needed.

Bloom Color—Yellow, white, pink

Peak Season—Summer

Mature Size (H x W)—6 to 12 inches x 6 to 12 inches

SNOWDROPS
Galanthus nivalis

Why It's Special—Snowdrops do indeed grow in the snow. Their crisp, white, diminutive blooms enhance the greening-up of early spring, bringing their pop! to other flowers that are early to rise. Snowdrops naturalize easily and, due to their moisture requirements, are perfect companions for turf and meadow plantings. Plant sweeps under deciduous trees and in drifts throughout the shrub bed. Use their small size to line a streambed and to tuck into rock gardens.

How to Plant & Grow—Plant in fall in amended, well-worked, pre-moistened soil that drains well. Site in part shade in hot summer regions. Space closely together, incorporate a balanced, timed-release fertilizer, mulch, and water deeply. Maintain moist soil for establishment.

Care & Problems—No pests or diseases bothers snowdrop. Maintain a thick layer of mulch. Snowdrops are rarely divided; but if so, divide after blooms fade.

Water Needs—Deeply water to 6 inches, twice weekly in summer, once weekly in spring and winter if there's no rain or snowfall.

Bloom Color—White

Peak Season—Late winter, early spring

Mature Size (H x W)—4 inches x 4 inches

SPIDERLILY
Lycoris spp.

Why It's Special—Spiderlilies require long summer dormancy, making them perfect xeric bulbs for dry climates. They make their presence known in spring (in fall in mild-winter areas) with green, straplike leaves that fade in summer. Large bright blooms appear at summer's end, into fall, just when all else is swooning in the heat. Plant groups, sweeps, or drifts in open areas or in the dappled understory of native trees where they can slumber away in summer, but brighten the landscape late in the season.

How to Plant & Grow—Plant bulbs in late summer in any well-draining soil. Mulch and water deeply and regularly until flower stalks appear.

Care & Problems—If summers are wet and they're sited in poorly draining soils, grow in a container. Slugs or snails are common.

Water Needs—Water growing foliage deeply, but irregularly. Water monthly if there's no rain or snow in winter. Once foliage fades, do not water during summer dormancy; resume watering when flower stalks appear.

Bloom Color—Red, pink, white, yellow

Peak Season—Late summer and fall

Mature Size (H x W)—1 to 2 feet x 1 foot

TULIP
Tulipa spp. and hybrids

Why It's Special—Tulips come in every color imaginable, with literally hundreds of hybrids that need minimal water in summer dormancy and naturalizing drought-tolerant species. Plant sweeps, drifts, and mass plantings to line driveways, border a path, fill the foreground in the perennial bed, blanket a slope, and fill a pot with blooms.

How to Plant & Grow—Pre-chilling is required in low-desert-climates; plant in fall into a pre-moistened, well-draining, compost-amended soil. Top-dress with bulb fertilizer. Use thick layer of mulch, water deeply.

Care & Problems—Aphids in spring; rodents munch bulbs and foliage. Hybrids reappear for a few seasons while *Tulipa* species naturalize. Protect from high winds. Top-dress with bulb food in early spring.

Water Needs—Water monthly during dormancy if there's no winter rain or snow. Water every two weeks as foliage appears, once a week while blooming.

Bloom Color—All colors and combinations except blue

Peak Season—Spring

Mature Size (H x W)—4 to 36 inches x 4 to 12 inches

Hardiness—Zones 3 to 7; in warm-winter climates, dig bulbs after foliage fades, store, and replant in fall.

BULBS MONTH-BY-MONTH

JANUARY

- In low desert, warmer-winter areas, daffodils start to show themselves and bloom. If they are planted at a meadow's edge or in a lawn, take care not to mow their tops down when you mow the grasses. If they are not yet sprouting, you can get in a final mowing over the entire area and not damage the bulbs.

- In these same areas, it is time to plant the tulips and hyacinth that have been pre-chlling in the refrigerator. Before you plant, prepare the soil. Thoroughly water the site, extending the watering to least 1 foot beyond the space. By wetting the area beyond the planting bed, you eliminate the possibility of the drier soil wicking away moisture.

- Crocus is a favorite salad for squirrels, chipmunks, and rabbits. They will nibble as soon as the bulbs show green. Beat them to it and cage the bulbs with chicken fencing, so they can't slip through the wire holes.

FEBRUARY

- When irises awaken and send out new green foliage, you can get them cleaned up for the spring bloom show. Using a heavy rake, clean out the dead foliage. As long as you do it early enough in the season when the new foliage is small, you won't damage the rhizomes and it makes an easy chore out of this seasonal maintenance. Apply a slow-release granulated fertilizer; water in well.

- In low-desert areas, prepare to plant crinum and amaryllis. Where summers are ultra-hot, site these in dappled or full shade. Once bulbs send out green growth, add 3 to 4 inches of mulch to keep them cool and to hold in moisture.

- As soon as pansies, veronica, and yarrow become available, plant them between the bulbs that are beginning to put out new foliage now. Both the bulbs and starts need regular watering and the plants will be in place to serve as foil when the bulb foliage fades.

MARCH

- Narcissus, rain lilies, and grape hyacinth are blooming in high desert and colder winter elevations. Provide deep, regular watering if there is no rain to help continue the bloom and to build up their storage reserves. Cut the blooms just before fading and bring indoors to brighten any room. They make long-lasting cut flowers. Their foliage remains green and is a good accent (for some time) before fading to yellow and dormancy, so get the most out of the plant while they're in the landscape.

- In warmer climates, clean up cannas in the landscape by cutting out the old, browned foliage, cutting back the plant, and fertilizing. Container cannas are available in garden centers and home-improvement stores, so add to your collection or start a new bed, spacing them at 10 to 12 inches to avoid having to divide for some time. Top all canna plantings with 3 to 4 inches of mulch.

- As soon as soil temperatures rise above 65 degrees Fahrenheit, caladium can be planted. The warmer the summer, the more shade caladium require, making them perfect for the dry shade garden. In colder climates, start caladium indoors to set out plants when the soil heats up in April.

APRIL

- Tulips are blooming in colder winter climates. It is not unusual for snow to fly now too. Tulips will ebb and flow with the snow, but the winds can strip their petals off overnight, right when they are fully opened and beautiful. Drive some 2-foot stakes into the ground and cage them in frost-protection cloth until winds subside.

- Iris are in full bloom and need regular, deep waterings to continue flowering. They can grow in part shade, but full shade diminishes flowers. If you can't thin a dense tree canopy, then move the non-flowering iris in fall to a sunnier location. They can be moved now, but will need extra attention to get them established and growing before the heat of summer sets in.

- Grape hyacinths and starflowers are fading, but still have green leaves. If you leave them in the ground through the seasons, top them with a few inches of fresh mulch. They will continue to store nutrients, but will slip into dormancy unnoticed while the fresh mulch tidies up the bed.

MAY

- If the last frost date has passed, summer bulbs can be planted. The bins at the garden centers should be full of gladiolus and cannas. Dig the soil well and incorporate amendments. Pre-moisten the soil deeply, but allow it to dry enough so that when you make a ball of soil, it holds together, but crumbles away from the edge of the ball easily, with no water dripping between your fingers.

- Yarrow is a good foil for tulips and other bulbs. It is usually dormant in colder climes about the time the tulips pop up, and yarrow's lacy foliage is filling in nicely by the time tulips are fading.

- As iris complete their bloom, reduce watering to every 10 days or so. They don't need as much water when they're not blooming, but they'll keep their green foliage so they need some water through summer.

JUNE

- Alliums like the heat! They bask in it, bloom in it, naturalize in it. Some alliums, like chives, can be invasive in a small garden. Plant them in a pot and then plant the pot in the ground. You can pull it out anytime, but it will require less water if the pot is buried so the soil acts as insulator. If it's in a clay pot, clay will wick water from the soil; if it's in a plastic pot, the soil will keep the roots cooler and the pots will require less water.

- Make sure summer bulbs have plenty of mulch. If you are using organic types, then they will decompose quickly with higher temperatures and more water. If you see soil, it's time to add 3 to 4 inches of mulch.

- Cannas grow tall, but their stems can snap in high winds. Use taller plants as a wind block or provide supports.

JULY

- Move bulbs growing in containers to a spot that gets afternoon shade in the heat of summer. Group them closely together to insulate and offer wind protection to one another. Use drip irrigation with spot emitters on spikes to water them deeply, while increasing the surrounding humidity. Add mulch to containers to conserve water and cool the roots. You will need to fertilize more since they are in a light mix and daily watering leaches out nutrients.

- Daylilies can be planted anytime from containers and won't miss a beat in the flowering cycle. They are planted in the hottest spots imaginable in some areas—meridian strips, parking lots, alongside concrete patios, and still they bloom. If you plant now, plant in the morning or evening, into deeply moistened, well-worked, and amended soil. Make sure you cut off any circling roots and make a few vertical slices in the rootball before planting or the roots will continue to circle and will not generate new roots. Water deeply, slowly, a few times to make sure you have deeply watered beyond the root zone. Apply 3 inches of mulch, then maintain regular watering.

AUGUST

- Iris are winding down in some areas. Maintain watering at least every 10 days to keep the soil moist until you divide or until they go dormant or slow growth for winter.

- Dividing iris every three or four years will increase the blooms. As it matures, the center of a rhizome stops blooming and starts to shrivel. In the wild, iris rhizomes naturally divide, with the centers dying and the outside rhizomes spreading to increase the colony. Sometimes they won't bloom while they're regenerating. You may see fewer blooms the following year while a plant rejuvenates, but you will still have beautiful iris foliage to enjoy.

- Stop fertilizing all bulbs except for those in containers.

SEPTEMBER

- Prepare the beds for daffodils. Deeply water to a depth of 12 to 18 inches. Allow the soil to dry until it's damp, but not soggy. Spread 3 to 4 inches of compost over the entire planting area if you have a particularly lean, sandy, or slow-draining soil, then turn it into the native soil. Otherwise, you will only need to deeply turn and work the native soil.

- Pull the soil away from the bed to allow for the proper planting depth (two to three times the size of the bulb), mounding it up on the edges. Scatter the bulbs in the area, set them upright, and then cover with soil. Tamp the soil down, water well, and apply 2 to 3 inches of mulch.

- In areas with mild winters/hot summers, it's time to prechill tulips and hyacinths. Put them in a paper bag or box, but never in plastic. Then place the bulbs in a refrigerator where they can't wick up moisture; an empty crisper drawer is perfect. Check on them every so often to make sure they are not rotting or shriveling. They will need to stay there for six to eight weeks.

OCTOBER

- In areas with cold winters, you can plant tulips, alliums, grape hyacinths, and snowdrops. Mark where you plant them; it's easy to forget exactly where they are over a long winter. In areas where the ground freezes, add an extra-thick layer of mulch to protect them and plant a little bit deeper. In spring, when they send out foliage, you may need to remove a bit of mulch to let the sun in.

- Dig up gladiolus in cooler climates or leave them and plan to replace them in spring. There is a hardier glad now available, hardy to Zone 4 if it's heavily mulched. Reports indicate it blooms in September to October in its first season, lighter its second, then heavily blooms in the third season after planting.

- Dig caladium in cooler climates to overwinter in a cool area, 45 degrees Fahrenheit. A garage or cellar makes a good winter home, as long as it doesn't freeze. In frost-free areas, they can stay in the ground year-round, but space waterings to avoid rot.

NOVEMBER

- Amaryllis, paperwhites (narcissus), and hyacinths are great holiday gifts and a way to bring color and scent to the home in winter. Start them now for the holidays; they're easy to force either in pots with soilless mix or in vases with pebbles and water. Plant them closely together, sides just touching, in any receptacle that is 2 to 3 inches deeper than the bulb; bulbs should be buried so that one-third of the top is exposed. Keep in indirect light, 65 degrees Fahrenheit, until they sprout, then move to brighter light until they bloom, then bring them indoors to enjoy.

- In frost-free areas, plant gladiolus from now through January. Plant freesia, anemone, amaryllis, and bearded iris.

- Cut back on watering in warmer-winter areas and cease watering in colder climates. Fertilize only container plants that are actively growing.

DECEMBER

- For every ½ inch of rain that falls, skip a watering in warmer climates, In cold climates, there should be no need to water. The real concern is freezing soil so make sure at least 4 inches of mulch covers the bulb beds.

- Check bulbs growing in a greenhouse in pots for soil moisture before you water. In a cool house, bulbs may go as long as two weeks before they need water. Rot is common in cool, damp soils. Don't fertilize this month either.

- It's easy to let the record-keeping go during the holidays, but if you haven't sketched your planting plans for the bulb beds by now, do it while it is still fresh in your mind so you can plan to interplant annuals and perennials in spring.

EDIBLES
for the Southwest

No matter where you live in the Southwest, there is an edible you can grow in the landscape, in the garden, in a pot, or on a windowsill. Rising food costs, the availability of organically grown produce, and increasing desire for healthy eating have caused a resurgence in growing our own food. For some gardeners, the dedication to supplying their family with homegrown produce becomes the focus in their garden. Others may be limited on space, but still share the goal of growing their own, so patios become container gardens, filled with all sorts of veggies you never imagined you could grow in a pot. Small containers hold herbs; mid-sized ones are homes to tomatoes, bush beans and peppers; small fruit trees, clusters of corn stalks, and even potatoes fill a barrel or box. Urban gardeners, in their quest to grow their own food, find a bit of space to tuck a tomato plant, a drift of lettuce and spinach, or to espalier a fruit tree.

EDIBLES LOVE GOOD SOIL

Edibles thrive in a designated garden where many seasons of digging amendments into the soil has created a nutrient-rich home. Some types can be replanted in the same space every year (lettuce, garlic, beans, corn), while others should be rotated for pest and disease deterrents (onions, peppers, melons). Most can be intercropped to make the best use of soil and water resources, some benefiting one another by deterring pests or attracting pollinators. Radishes interplanted with cantaloupe deter squash beetles and, allowed to flower, attract bees to the melon flowers. Basil, with its aromatic foliage, can be planted between bell peppers and tomatoes to deter pests. Carrots can share space with the tomatoes, ready to dig after the tomatoes have given up their last fruits.

Edibles grow wonderfully in containers. New cultivars are available in bushier, smaller plants; just about every edible you grow in your garden can be grown in a container. Growing edibles in containers offers benefits to the gardener with less weeding, easy pest monitoring, and ease of harvest.

Growing in pots gives us the ability to move these containers to a more favorable environment if they get too hot or if frost threatens. Edibles can be grown singly in a pot, combined with other vegetables or even ornamentals for colorful combinations. Herbs grown in pots can be overwintered indoors or in a greenhouse, making fresh herbs available year-round.

Edibles can share resources with perennials, shrubs, and trees in the landscape—a practice called *foodscaping*. Use a dwarf fruiting apple tree as a focal point in a small yard. Try various colors of leaf lettuce to make a dense and pretty groundcover. Peppers can border the scented garden, filling the foreground with foliage and red and green fruits. Hardy perennials deserve a permanent place in the landscape. Have oregano trail over a stone terrace wall while garden sage grows in mounds, making a bold and beautiful statement in the landscape.

NEW BEGINNINGS

Growing edibles from seed provides endless opportunities to try new cultivars, to broaden selections, and to germinate seed collected from your favorite edibles from the previous season. For gardeners growing in areas with long winters, it provides strong, well-established plants to set out in spring, giving a head start on the shorter growing season. Greenhouse and indoor growing offers the ability to grow edibles during winter with stocky, early-flowering greenhouse tomatoes and all sorts of cool-season leafy greens and herbs. See page 14 for steps on growing from seed.

PREPARING PLANTS

Whether you grow from seed, buy starter plants in packs or pots, or purchase fruit trees and vines in containers, acclimate the plants to their surroundings before planting in the ground. Starter seedlings have been shipped directly from the grower, loaded into trucks from the greenhouse;

To amend a garden bed, spread 2 to 3 inches of compost or other organic matter on the surface, and then cultivate the amendment into the existing soil.

tree and vine transplants have been potted bare root and pumped with fertilizer to encourage leafy growth; and plants are grown in larger containers in controlled environments to bring early blooms and fruits. All these situations create lush growth but soft plants.

Harden-off plant starts over a period of weeks— one week in the shade, indoors at night; one week in full/partial sun, indoors at night; then outdoors day and night. Trees and vines need a week in the shade or under shelter to prevent full sun from burning the tender foliage and from wind that may snap or bend young stems and branches. Set the plants in their containers in the planting spot for a week to make sure they are happy in their surroundings.

BUILD THE SOIL

Building a nutrient-rich, well-draining soil takes time. Annual edibles use most of the nutrients in the soil each season, so incorporate amendments each spring. Adding 3 to 4 inches of compost or organic topsoil to the area and incorporating it deeply gives

a fairly decent soil in three to five years. Spread any manures on the beds after the final harvest in fall so they decompose and leach out salts during winter. Incorporate into the soil in spring. Plant fruit trees and vines into well-worked, compost-amended soil, then top-dress with organics in spring, manures in fall, or top- or side-dress with organic fertilizers throughout the growing season. Nutrient deficiencies can be avoided if you have a soil test done every few years (check with your local Extension).

WATERING

Drip irrigation delivers water slowly, evenly, and deeply to the roots where the plants need it and minimizes water loss through overspray, drift, or surface evaporation. If you must handwater, avoid wetting foliage, which leads to fungus, leaf tip burn, mold, and mildew. Intertwine a soaker hose throughout the bed or around a tree's drip line for deep and widespread coverage that waters the entire root zones, deeply and slowly. Always apply 3 to 4 inches of mulch to cool the soil and to slow evaporation.

Once you bite into the first tomato of the season, pluck a sprig of basil for a salad, or throw a handful of beans into the soup pot, you join the ranks of gardeners who know that homegrown is always better. From the garden to your table, the thrill of growing your own is renewed every season.

Anchor in-line emitter tubing with wire pins to hold it in place. Plant seedlings next to an emitter to keep young roots near the water source.

APPLE
Malus domestica

Why It's Special—Apples need chill hours but don't mind the heat, and they bloom later so they're not affected by late-season frosts. Apples are long-lived trees, producing fruit the third year after planting. Their fruits last for long periods, as fresh as the day they were picked if kept in dry cool storage or frozen, canned, or dried for good eating years later. Apples make a great shade tree with all-season interest too.

How to Plant & Grow—Plant bare-root or containerized transplants (preferably sourced locally) in late winter or early spring as soon as the soil can be worked. At least two trees are required for pollination; maximum spacing of 25 to 45 feet apart. Amend a well-draining soil with compost, work the soil well, and moisten. Mulch and water deeply after planting. Water weekly, deeply, through the growing season; no winter watering unless extended periods of drought.

Care & Problems—Fertilize with a timed-release fertilizer each spring for an apple's first three years. Prune to train for the desired form immediately upon planting. Prune yearly to maintain good supporting structure.

Harvest & Best Selections—Harvest late summer through fall. Some selections with short chill hours are 'Anna', 'Braeburn', 'Delicious', 'Jonagold', 'Granny Smith', 'Fuji', and 'Gala'. Apple scab-resistant types include 'Akane' (also mildew-resistant); 'Chehalis', very scab-resistant; and 'Spartan', scab, mildew, and fireblight resistant.

APRICOT
Prunus armeniaca

Why It's Special—Apricots need few chill hours and do handle the heat, but they flower early in the season, making them susceptible to fruiting failure due to late-season frosts. Apricots are a small fruit, about the size and texture of a plum, yet with the sweetness and flavor of a peach. Apricots are best eaten fresh and don't store longer than a few days. They dry easily, holding all their nutrient value and remaining juicy and sweet.

How to Plant & Grow—Plant bare-root transplants or containers as soon as ground can be worked in early spring. Plant into compost-enriched, well-draining soil. Water deeply and mulch, then water once or twice a week during summer and spring (in the low deserts). Cut back watering in fall after fruiting; don't water in winter unless a month goes by with no rain or snow.

Care & Problems—Prune young trees to develop open canopies and structure. Keep height as short as possible for ease of harvest, and cover with frost protection and bird netting. Fertilize each spring with a low-nitrogen fertilizer. Apricots are susceptible to verticillum so don't plant in areas previously planted with tomatoes, berries, peppers, eggplants, or potatoes.

Harvest & Best Selections—Harvest June to July when apricots are fully colored and their flesh gives slightly when squeezed. Some good selections are 'Tilton', 'Mormon', 'Sungold', 'Floragold', 'Dwarf Garden Annie', 'Gold Kist', and 'Katy'.

ASPARAGUS
Asparagus officinalis

Why It's Special—Asparagus is a long-lived, drought-tolerant perennial, spreading naturally year after year. After picking the spears in early spring, its feathery foliage grows tall and billowy, adding interest to the garden through the summer. When the weather turns cold, the ferny growth turns golden amber, providing winter interest until you remove foliage in spring.

How to Plant & Grow—Plant crowns in fall or spring in compost-amended, deeply worked, well-draining soil. Plant in trenches, cover with 3 inches of soil, water deeply once or twice a week (in low-desert climates) through its first season.

Care & Problems—When plants are 4 inches tall, cover with a few more inches of soil. Add soil every two weeks until at ground level, then top with 2 to 3 inches of straw mulch. Water once a week through the growing season if there's no rain, no winter watering unless there's no moisture for a month. It's susceptible to crown rot; don't overwater once it's established. Top-dress with compost after harvest. To grow white asparagus, as soon as spears break the soil (after the second harvest year), cover them with a dark plastic tub that completely blocks the sun and moonlight. Lift the tub a bit at night for airflow.

Harvest & Best Selections—Harvest in its third year. Try the 'Jersey' series. 'Millenium' is cold tolerant and 'Mary Washington' is an heirloom.

BASIL
Ocimum basilicum

Why It's Special—Basil is a vegetable and herb garden mainstay, but it performs equally well in the edible landscape as a border plant. There are small, mounded basils; taller, branching, flowering basils; and large, tropical-leaved basils. Smaller-leaved types are the chef's choice since no chopping is required. Refrigerate or use immediately after picking. Interplant with peppers and tomatoes to thwart pests.

How to Plant & Grow—Sow seeds in flats four weeks before planting outdoors, when ground is warming in spring. Direct sow into well-composted soil that drains well. Keep the seedbed continually moist until germination, spraying once or twice a day. Water new transplants deeply. When plants are 4 inches tall, add a couple of inches of straw mulch.

Care & Problems—Water daily unless it rains. Fertilize with an organic, water-soluble fertilizer if plants appear stunted or hungry. Pinch to promote bushy plants and to prevent plants from blooming.

Harvest & Best Selections—Pinch off foliage to encourage bushiness as the plant grows, then cut the leaves whenever you need them. Small-leaved basil is summer-tough in the Southwest, still requiring regular water but less than large-leaved types. Try 'Pestou' and 'Genovese Aroma 1'. 'Christmas' is taller and branching with purple-red blooms. There are flavored basils with hints of lemon, lime, cinnamon, cloves, or licorice. Ornamental types grow to 3 feet tall and wide, with ruffled or fuzzy foliage in purple, red, and green.

BEAN
Phaseolus vulgaris

Why It's Special—There are bush-type beans and vining-type beans. Some beans are eaten green, while others are left to mature on the vine until crispy yellow for dried shell beans. Grow vines vertically in the garden, to save space, and interplant with squash at their feet. Use bush beans in the edible border for green, lush foliage, abundant blooms and the beans. They are legumes, so their roots fix nitrogen in the soil. Beans are a multipurpose plant in the summer garden.

How to Plant & Grow—Direct-sow innoculated seed when soil temperatures are at least 60 degrees Fahrenheit into well-worked, compost-amended soil. Water well, then allow soil to dry a bit between waterings. When seedlings are 4 inches tall, mulch with straw.

Care & Problems—Relatively drought tolerant while putting on foliage, beans require regular watering once they start flowering. Do not fertilize with nitrogen. If establishment seems slow or plants are not vigorous, apply an organic fertilizer with phosphorus and potassium.

Harvest & Best Selections—Harvest green beans when they're plump with beans; harvest shell beans when the pods are completely dried on the plant, before first frost. Try these: green: 'Speedy'; pole: 'Kentucky Blue'; dried: 'Missouri Wonder'. Heirlooms: Lazy Housewife pole beans, a stringless type brought to the U.S. by German immigrants. Anasazi, grown by cliff dwellers, is a burgundy/cream pinto bean substitute. Blue speckled tepary beans (*Phaseolus acutifolius*), native to the Sonoran desert, were grown without irrigation.

BLACKBERRY
Rubus spp.

Why It's Special—Blackberries are disease and pest free, not picky about soil, long-lived, and are drought tolerant once established. Thornless types make picking and eating them off the vine painless and pleasant. There are seedless types that offer the sweet/tart taste, but without the pesky seeds. Types are available as trailing, erect, or semi-erect; early, midseason, late, and everbearing (which set berries in summer and fall), and some have disease resistance. There is a blackberry for every tastebud and garden in the Southwest.

How to Plant & Grow—Plant bare-root transplants in late winter to early spring. Plant container grown in fall or winter (low desert) or early spring when the ground can be dug. They grow in any well-drained soil, but love more acidic soils. If soil is very alkaline, amend backfill with 50 percent of the volume in peat. Support upright types with wire or fencing. Water deeply.

Care & Problems—Water once a week during growing season, no water in winter. Top-dress each spring with a balanced, timed-release fertilizer. In the fall, prune canes that produced that year.

Harvest & Best Selections—Pick July to August when berries turn dull black. 'Rosborough', 'Navaho', 'Black Satin', and 'Thornless Logan' are good picks. Doyle Thornless Blackberry™, yielding 20 gallons per plant, was discovered by Tom Doyle who found the vine in his garden in 1970. It is reported to be garden friendly in all 50 states.

BROCCOLI & CAULIFLOWER
Brassica oleracea

Why It's Special—Cool-season crops broccoli and cauliflower fill a void in the garden when other crops are waiting for the heat to mature. Packed with vitamins and minerals, they store well and freeze for use for up to a year.

How to Plant & Grow—Germinate seeds in flats or packs six to eight weeks before planting outdoors. Plant starts outdoors six weeks before last frost for a spring crop when soil temperatures are at least 50 degrees Fahrenheit; plant eight weeks before first frost for a fall crop. Plant into deeply worked, compost-rich, well-draining soil. Mulch with straw when plants are 6 inches tall. Water deeply.

Care & Problems—Water regularly throughout the growing season. Apply fertilizer high in nitrogen and phosphorus if stunting of plants or heads is evident. Pests include caterpillars munching on foliage, aphids, cabbage loopers, and moths. Use organic controls or floating row covers, which also protect plants from freezing if you want to get in one final harvest.

Harvest & Best Selections—Harvest broccoli when the heads are dark green and tight; pick cauliflower when curds are firm, compact, and relatively smooth. 'Packman' and 'Belstar' are early, heirlooms 'Snow Crown', 'Amazing' cauliflower types. Broccoli 'Romanesco Italia' is a latecomer (1988) from Italy, a cross between broccoli and cauliflower. 'Veronica' cauliflower looks like a sea urchin with chartreuse spires. Purple of Sicily, an heirloom, is insect resistant with brilliant purple-and-white heads.

CARROT
Daucus carota ssp. sativus

Why It's Special—Homegrown carrots are as sweet as candy, can be interplanted with tomatoes to save space, and their feathery tops are a good accent in the foreground of an edible landscape. Plant where they are easy to dig when they are matured.

How to Plant & Grow—Direct-sow seed in fall in lower-desert climates, in early spring elsewhere. Sow into deep, organically enriched, well-draining soil, between 60 to 75 degrees Fahrenheit. Sow as thinly as possible or use seed tape or pelleted seed to reduce thinning later. Keep seedbeds moist until germination, two to three weeks.

Care & Problems—When carrots reach 4 inches tall, thin to final spacing (if needed). Be ruthless; you will only thin once. Water after thinning, then mulch with 2 inches of straw. Keep seedbed moist, watering daily using drip irrigation or soaker hose. There are no pests to worry about. Interplant with onions to discourage carrot maggots and you can harvest both at the same time.

Harvest & Best Selections—Dig carrots when they are the color and reach the size you want. Harvest every other carrot to allow others to gain size, or harvest all at once and preserve. Try 'Little Finger', 'Nantes', 'Apache', 'Danvers 126'. Carrots come in all colors: white, 'Lunar White'; red, 'Atomic Red'; purple, 'Cosmic Purple'; yellow, 'Amarillo'. Seed tape: 'Danvers'; pelleted seed: 'Napoli' F1 Hybrid.

CILANTRO
Coriandrum sativum

Why It's Special—Cilantro is a star in a container, as filler or groundcover in the edible landscape, and as a self-sower in the garden. With the heat, it sends out long willowy flower stalks covered in tiny white flowers that are pollinator magnets. Cilantro is a mainstay for Mexican dishes; its little bit of pungent spice goes a long way. Some love it; some don't care for it. Use sparingly!

How to Plant & Grow—Sow seed four weeks before the last frost, as soon as the ground can be worked, or sow in late summer for winter growth in frost-free areas. Sow thickly into well-worked soil that is drains well. Keep seedbeds moist until germination.

Care & Problems—When plants have a few sets of leaves, deeply water, but allow the soil to dry a bit between waterings. There are no pests. Fertilize with an organic balanced fertilizer two weeks after germination.

Harvest & Best Selections—Start harvesting by thinning plants with scissors, cutting in swaths each time to allow uncut portions to leaf out; those sections become the swath for harvesting the next time. Cut frequently to prevent plants from bolting. After it sets seed and plants turn brittle, dry and harvest the seed for coriander or planting next season. Try 'Long-standing', 'Slo Bolt', and 'Santo'. Biodegradable seed discs fit right into pots for easy container growing.

CUCUMBER
Cucumis sativus

Why It's Special—Cucumber vines can be grown vertically for a green screen, up a fence or trellis, or trailing for a groundcover in the edible landscape. There are bushier types that grow in containers. Cucumbers love our hot Southwestern summers, but turn to mush at the first signs of frost.

How to Plant & Grow—Sow seeds directly in the garden after all danger of frost is past. If you are in short growing season areas, sow in peat pots three weeks before the last frost. Sow into compost-enriched, well-worked soil with good drainage. Keep seedbeds evenly moist for germination.

Care & Problems—After plants are 4 inches tall, mulch with straw. Drip irrigation is best; water deeply, daily if there's no rain. When vines start to run or climb, side-dress with a balanced organic fertilizer. Cucumber beetles can be deterred by interplanting radishes, which are allowed to flower to attract pollinators. Look for disease-resistant types.

Harvest & Best Selections—Harvest cukes when they're small. If allowed to grow large they'll lose all their character and flavor. 'Burpless' doesn't contain cucurbitacin, the element that causes bitterness and that makes you burp after eating. 'Lemon' is an heirloom, the size of a hard ball, thin skinned, and lemon-yellow. 'Raider' is disease resistant. 'Patio Snacker' is good for containers. 'Spacemaker' is disease resistant, only 6 to 8 inches tall, and good for hanging baskets.

CITRUS
Citrus spp.

Why It's Special—Temperatures below 32 degrees Fahrenheit damage citrus, although some survive short bursts of 15 to 20 degrees Fahrenheit. Citrus blooms are deliciously scented, while glossy evergreen leaves are a perfect complement to blooms and fruits. Generally, the more sour the fruit, the less summer heat needed to grow them. If you live in cooler summer areas, lemons and limes will provide you with all the juices you need. Sweet and juicy naval oranges, tangerines, and mandarins bask in the heat of summer, so desert gardeners who enjoy frost-free winters can pluck these fruits from their own trees.

How to Plant & Grow—Plant in moistened, compost-amended, well-draining soil in spring. Make a large berm and basin, extending beyond the drip line; deeply water. Install drip irrigation for best deep watering. Mulch to within 3 inches of the trunk.

Care & Problems—Water-blast aphids and scale or treat per pesticide label instructions. Fertilize each spring with a balanced, timed-release fertilizer or top-dress with compost; refresh mulch. Water deeply, weekly, to a depth of 3 feet (checked with a soil probe), allowing soil to dry between waterings. Prune suckers only.

Harvest & Best Selections—Harvest when fruit slips easily from a tree, late fall to early spring. Cold-tolerant types include Changsha kumquat, Meyer lemon, and Satsuma mandarin. Heat-lovers include Redblush and Rio Red grapefruit. A "fruit bowl" grafted citrus tree can produce lemons, limes, grapefruit, tangerines, mandarines, pumelos, and oranges, flowering and fruiting over a long season.

GARLIC
Allium sativum

Why It's Special—Garlic can be grown in the same spot every year, unlike other alliums that prefer to be moved about. Freshly dug garlic carries the classic, rich garlic aroma on a higher level than what you buy and the bulb is juicy when you slice into it. Grow a few to try and you will be growing more every year to fulfill your garlic needs. With garlic, more is always better!

How to Plant & Grow—Plant organically produced cloves in fall into well-draining, compost-enriched soil. In frost-free areas, deeply water once a week for the first four weeks; in colder climates, deeply water to 6 inches, then cover with 4 inches of straw mulch.

Care & Problems—Maintain regular watering in lower desert areas, allowing soil to dry between waterings; otherwise, no winter watering. Resume weekly, deep watering in spring when there is new green growth. If soil is compost enriched, no additional fertilizer needed. Otherwise, side-dress once with an organic, balanced fertilizer when plants are actively growing. No pests or diseases bother *Allium*.

Harvest & Best Selections—Foliage starts to fade in early spring in low deserts, usually, or in June to July elsewhere. When garlic tops are completely dry, dig with a fork or trowel. 'Texas White', California Early', and 'Susanville' are soft neck types, good for growing in our climate and soil. They produce small, tight cloves with thick skins, and are good for storage.

GRAPE
Vitis spp.

Why It's Special—Grapes can be grown throughout the Southwest. Choose types recommended for your area. They are not particular to soil, love sun, and are drought tolerant once established. European type 'Thompson Seedless' is the most familiar, thriving in summer heat. American grapes like 'Concord' are the most cold-tolerant types. American hybrids are more cold tolerant, carry some characteristics of European grapes and disease resistence, and are mostly used for wine.

How to Plant & Grow—Plant bare-root vines in late winter or early spring; container plants anytime except in the heat of summer. Plant into well-worked, well-draining, unamended soil. Provide supports at planting. Water deeply and don't water again until after last frost, then water deeply twice a week through the summer into fall. When leaves show fall color, stop watering for winter dormancy.

Care & Problems—Look for disease-resistant vines recommended for your area. Fruiting begins at year three. Prune to specific instructions for grape type and use. Stop watering fruiting grapes to minimize splitting. Grapes are not hungry feeders. Fertilize only upon recommendations following soil test results.

Harvest & Best Selections—Harvest table grapes when they have good color and taste. Heat-lovers are 'Thompson', 'Concord', 'Muscadine', 'Cardinal'. The plants are available bare root. Grapes grow wild at forest edge in full sun and in dappled shade of tree canopies where they climb 60 to 100 feet, but will be controlled in your garden.

KALE
Brassica cultivars

Why It's Special—Kale is famous among foodies for its flavor and health benefits, but when planted for its curled, ruffled, crinkled green to gray-green to blue foliage in the edible landscape, it becomes multipurpose. Pick when it's small for a salad green. Allow it to grow into its large sized leaves, and it is excellent in stir-fry combinations, steamed, or added to soups and stews in the last few minutes to soften it just a bit.

How to Plant & Grow—Sow seed for starts six weeks before planting outdoors; direct-sow as soon as ground can be worked in early spring when soil temperatures are 45 degrees Fahrenheit or higher. Plant 6-packs in late winter or early spring; kale tolerates mild frosts. Sow or transplant into a compost-enriched, well-draining soil. Keep seedbeds moist until germination.

Care & Problems—When kale is 4 inches tall, mulch with straw. Deeply water regularly if there's no rain. Side-dress with an organic timed-release fertilizer, high in nitrogen, monthly during the growing season. Aphids move in at season's end, treat these and pick off cabbageworms and caterpillars.

Harvest & Best Selections—Harvest whenever you want. Small leaves are good in salads, larger leaves are used for cooking. Pick from the bottom. 'Blue Knight', 'Dwarf Siberian', 'Toscano' are good options. Georgia Southern, an heirloom (pre-1880), is a good producer in cold and heat.

LETTUCE
Lactuca sativa

Why It's Special—Leaf lettuce comes in so many colors and textures and types, it replaces head lettuce by its appeal and in ease of growing. Grow a lettuce bowl in a sunny warm window in winter, sow a trough in the cold frame while frosts prevail, or plant lettuce as companion plants in the vegetable garden as filler in open spaces. Sow seed every few weeks during the cooler months for a salad every night.

How to Plant & Grow—Direct-sow into well-worked, composted soil that drains well in late winter or early spring after last frost, with successive sowings every two weeks to prolong harvest until heat causes bolting; part sun-/shade-locations can produce lettuce into summer. Sow six weeks before first frost for fall harvest. Keep seedbed moist. Pelleted seed makes sowing easy and thinning a thing of the past.

Care & Problems—Water lettuce daily. Use netting until germination, if birds eat the seeds. Side-dress with composted chicken manure or an organic fertilizer once a month. Mulch between the rows with straw. Use organic controls for slugs.

Harvest & Best Selections—Start harvesting leaf lettuce thinnings, then trim with kitchen shears in swaths, alternating strips to fill in for cutting the next time. Some to try are 'Red Salad Bowl', 'Fleshy Trout', and 'Simpson'. Mix seed for leaf lettuce, spinach, kale, and Oriental greens and sow densely for a cut-and-come-again baby greens garden.

MELON
Cucumis melo

Why It's Special—Melons are not difficult to grow in the Southwest, loving sun and summer heat. Small cantaloupes and muskmelons can even be grown vertically to save space, keeping fruits off the ground and forming a lovely fruiting green screen with all that tropical-looking foliage.

How to Plant & Grow—Direct-sow seed in early spring, after the last frost, into compost-enriched soil. Melons need 70 to 80 days days to produce fruit, so adjust the planting schedule accordingly. Keep seeds well watered. When seedlings are 4 inches tall, mulch with 3 inches of straw. Sidedress with a timed-release fertilizer after vining begins.

Care & Problems—Use drip irrigation or soaker hoses for irrigation to minimize wetting foliage that leads to mildew. To combat pests, cover melons with row cover until they're vining and flowering, then remove the cover for two to four hours daily for pollinators to gain access. Interplant with radishes which repel cucumber beetle. Allow the radishes to flower to attract pollinators.

Harvest & Best Selections—Harvest when a melon slips easily off the vine. You will be able to smell a cantaloupes' sweetness when it's ready. Look for short-season types with some disease resistance. Try 'Athena', 'Ambrosia', 'Edista', and 'Sugar Baby' watermelons. A newer watermelon, grafted onto a squash rootstock, is stronger, has deeper growing roots, carries disease-resistant characteristics, and produces more fruit per square foot on compact vines.

OREGANO
Origanum spp.

Why It's Special—As a mainstay herb, oregano can't be beat. It is perennial (hardy to USDA Zone 5) in colder winters, where it makes a scented, mounding groundcover in the herb garden. In early spring, it resumes growing, when its succulent new foliage is perfect for picking and drying. In the heat of summer, it sends out stems holding white blooms above the foliage, a bee magnet. It can be container grown overwintered indoors for fresh oregano in winter.

How to Plant & Grow—Plant starts in spring as soon as the ground can be worked, anytime in low-desert regions. Plant in a well-worked, well-draining soil; no amendments are needed. Water deeply, then mulch with straw or shredded bark.

Care & Problems—No pests or disease bother oregano. Water deeply, once a week after establishment. Oregano is drought tolerant and can survive short periods of drought. Where it's winter dormant, don't water. Cut plants back in spring to the point where you see the flush of new growth.

Harvest & Best Selections—Clip anytime. When plants are coming out of dormancy, harvest new tender growth in spring before flowering. Greek type 'Hopleys Purple' is very ornamental, growing to 2 feet tall and has rich green foliage, covered in deep lavender blooms. 'Hot and Spicy' tastes as it sounds; it's very pungent. 'Turkish' is a bit milder, not as hot, but spicy.

PEA
Pisum sativum

Why It's Special—Peas are rapidly growing annual vines whose flowers form into plump pods. Grow dwarf types in a pot; grow climbers on a trellis or along a fence for an early-season, edible, green screen. Edible and ornamental, peas also fix nitrogen in the soil.

How to Plant & Grow—In hotter summer climates, direct-sow peas September to October, 8 to 10 weeks before first frost. Otherwise, sow in spring as soon as soil temperatures reach 60 degrees Fahrenheit. Sow into well-worked, unamended, well-draining soil. An inoculant speeds up germination and enhances its nitrogen fixing capabilities. Keep seedbeds moist.

Care & Problems—Drip irrigation applies water slowly and directly to the roots for regular watering. When plants are 4 inches tall, provide supports for vining types, and mulch with straw. No fertilizer is needed. No pests or diseases bother it. Peas dislike freezing or triple-digit temperatures and being rooted in cold, soggy soil.

Harvest & Best Selections—Harvest edible pod peas about 70 days after sowing, when pods are crisp and juicy and the peas are the size of BBs. 'Oregon Sugar Pod' and 'Sugar Snap' are good ones. Harvest shelling peas when pods are plump and dark green, try 'Wando'. For the color enthusiast, grow heirloom Blue Podded Blauwschokkers, which blooms in purple. The purple-blue pods can be harvested early as a snow pea or left on the vine for shell peas.

PEACH
Prunus persica

Why It's Special—Nothing beats biting into a just-picked fresh peach straight off the tree from your backyard. Peach trees are self-fruitful so you need only one. They're available in dwarf sizes for small gardens, and provide interest all year whether they're blooming, displaying fall color, or dormant.

How to Plant & Grow—Plant bare-root trees in late winter or containers in spring or fall. Site in well-draining soil amended with compost. Stake if high winds are common; remove stakes after its second year. Water deeply, weekly during the growing season. No winter watering is needed once it's established.

Care & Problems—Choose disease-resistant types. Consult your local Cooperative Extension for insect pest controls. Foraging squirrels steal the fruit when it is green; birds wait until it is perfectly ripe—protect accordingly. Late frosts can eliminate fruiting; choose late-blooming types, plant on a mound, and provide frost protection. Fertilize each spring with a balanced timed-release fertilizer or top-dress with aged compost.

Harvest & Best Selections—Harvest in July when peaches have turned color, give slightly when gently squeezed, and you catch their sweet scent. Peaches will not ripen off the tree. Try 'Elberta', 'Hale Heaven', 'Belle of Georgia', 'Eden', 'Reliance', 'Red Haven', 'Bicentennial', and 'Dixie Red'. 'Peachcot' is a cross between a peach and apricot. Late-season blooms may make it more likely to miss late-season frosts. The taste is, well, between a peach and an apricot!

66

PEPPER
Capsicum annuum

Why It's Special—Peppers take the heat, don't care for drought, dislike the cold, barely tolerate high winds, and are worth every bit of their picky selves come harvest time. The plants perform well in containers, and enjoy companionship with basil in the vegetable garden. Grow sweet bells separate from hot peppers. They have been known to cross-pollinate.

How to Plant & Grow—Sow seeds eight weeks before last frost; plant starts when soil temperatures exceed 65 degrees Fahrenheit. Plant into well-worked, compost-amended, well-draining soil. Water deeply to seal in roots and top with 2 inches of straw mulch. Stake young plants, and shelter them from high winds.

Care & Problems—Keep peppers evenly and regularly watered to avoid blossom end rot. Add 2 or more inches of mulch as plants begin to branch. Then, side-dress every three weeks with an organic, timed-release fertilizer. If sunscald appears, cover with shade cloth to shelter. There are no pests, other than foraging rodents and birds.

Harvest & Best Selections—Harvest peppers when they are the "right" color; the longer they stay on the plant, the thicker their walls and the sweeter (or hotter) they become. 'California Wonder' and 'Big Bertha' are sweet. Sweet Banana is mildly hot. 'Felicity' is a jalapeño. 'Ancho' is hot when picked red. 'King Arthur' is a sweet bell hybrid; its extra-large, thick-skinned fruits grow on stout plants, and it has some disease resistance. Try it from seed alongside a grafted plant to compare them.

PLUM
Prunus salicina

Why It's Special—Plums are easier to grow than peaches and apricots because they bloom later, so they're not as susceptible to late-season frosts. Plums are self-fruitful and produce up to 20 years. There are dwarf types available, only growing to 8 feet tall, which are good for small gardens and container-growing. Plums dry well and retain their delicious juicy flavor.

How to Plant & Grow—Plant bare-root trees in early winter or containers in spring or autumn into any well-draining soil. Make a large berm and basin, water deeply, mulch, and deeply water once a week through the growing season. Water monthly during winter if there's no rain or snow.

Care & Problems—Like all fruit trees, plums attract pests from aphids to birds and ground foragers. Ask your local Cooperative Extension about local problems and controls. Fertilize each spring with a balanced, slow-release fertilizer or top-dress with aged compost. Prune to encourage an open canopy, good air circulation, and strong scaffolding.

Harvest & Best Selections—Harvest August through September when fruit turns its final color and has a white, waxy coating. Self-fruitful types are 'Methley', 'Santa Rosa', and 'Satsuma'. 'Alderman' is cold hardy to Zone 4. Mirabelles are a species plum having small red or yellow flavorful fruits that are just a bit bigger than a cherry. Eat mirabelles fresh or use in preserves or brandy or other spirits. They are hardy and self-fruitful.

POMEGRANATE
Punica granatum

Why It's Special—Train pomegranate as a tree, grow it as a bushy shrub for an edible screen, or put it in a pot and overwinter indoors if you live outside Zone 6. Glossy green foliage in spring is followed by a floral show in white, apricot, red, or orange blooms. Its delicious red, globed fruits adorn trees into fall, accompanied by golden yellow autumn foliage.

How to Plant & Grow—Plant in early spring into any well-draining soil. Make a berm and basin, fill with water, and mulch to within a few inches of the trunk. Deeply water 2 to 3 times a week for the first three weeks, then once a week through the first season. Water twice monthly in winter if there's no rain.

Care & Problems—No pests or diseases. Fertilize in early spring and fall with slow-release or organic fertilizer. Water deeply every 10 days during the growing season, more in hot-summer climates. Prune to a tree form while trees are young. Otherwise, allow pomegranate to grow naturally into a dense rounded shrub.

Harvest & Best Selections—Harvest when the fruit is fully colored in autumn. 'Early Wonderful' is hardy to 10 degrees Fahrenheit; 'Salavatski' and 'Utah Sweet' to Zone 6. Texas Agrilife Research & Extension Center rated 'Pecos' and 'Sal' as the best-tasting pomegranates in a trial. 'Texas Red' was ranked as having the highest sugar content. How sweet it is!

POTATO
Solanum tuberosum

Why It's Special—Potatoes bought at a store are entirely different from ones you dig from your own garden. Silken, earthy, sweet, creamy, buttery goodness comes to mind when I think about freshly dug spuds. They take less growing space than you think, can be grown in (deep) containers, don't require much care at all, and store for months.

How to Plant & Grow—Plant seed potatoes in early spring as soon as the soil can be worked. Deeply work and organically amend the soil. For a space- and labor-saving potato-growing method: Plant closely together, 12 inches apart, 3 inches deep. Water well.

Care & Problems—When you see green growth, start mounding up straw around the stems. Every week or so, when you see the potato's top peeking through, add more straw until it is 12 to 18 inches thick. Water deeply, but irregularly, allowing the soil to dry a bit between waterings. Constantly wet, cool soil causes rot.

Harvest & Best Selections—Harvest a few early "baby" potatoes when plants begin to flower, being careful not to disrupt the root growth. Or wait until top growth turns yellow to harvest an entire crop. Good ones include 'La Ratte' (fingerling), 'Yukon Gold', and 'Red Lasoda'. 'Ketchup n Fries' is a grafted tomato/potato plant. Both belong to the same genus; the potato produces under the soil, the tomato fruits on the plant above.

RADISH
Raphanus sativus

Why It's Special—Sow radish seeds at each end of parsnip rows as markers; interplant with cucumbers, melons, and squash as pest deterrents; allow plants to flower to attract pollinators; and plant in containers. Daikon radishes grow in the summer heat and are not as hot and spicy as the round red globes we are accustomed to.

How to Plant & Grow—Sow seeds as soon as ground can be worked in spring after the last frost, six weeks before first frost, or in fall in frost-free zones. Site in well-worked, unamended, well-draining soil. Successive sowings every two weeks gives a longer-lasting crop. Seeds are large enough to sow to final spacing. If you have to thin, do so three days after germination, then water well to heel-in the disrupted soil. Keep the seedbed moist.

Care & Problems—After plants are 4 inches tall, mulch with straw. Water deeply, but irregularly, allowing the soil to dry out between waterings. No pests or diseases. There's no need to fertilize.

Harvest & Best Selections—Harvest radishes when they're young, three to four weeks after germination. Daikon can stay in the ground longer. Try 'Cherry Bell', 'French Breakfast', and daikon 'Minowase Summer'. Asian radishes are more like a beet (they are related), a bit sweeter and meatier. Try Rat's Tail, an heirloom from the 1860s; instead of eating the root, you eat the delicious, sweet, edible pods when they are about the diameter of a pencil. It has pretty lavender flowers too.

ROSEMARY
Rosmarinus officinalis

Why It's Special—Rosemary is drought and heat tolerant, upright or sprawling, evergreen, scented, and trainable. It doesn't run out of control if allowed to grow naturally. You only need one rosemary plant to supply the family with enough of the herb for fresh use, to dry, or freeze. Very high in oils, a little bit goes a long way. Use it singly in a pot to bring indoors in colder winters for fresh rosemary year-round.

How to Plant & Grow—Plant from containers in spring after the last frost into well-worked, well-draining, unamended soil. Water deeply; mulch. Deeply water every few days, allowing soil to dry between waterings, for a couple of weeks to establish. Drip irrigation is best.

Care & Problems—Water deeply once a week during its first summer. It's cold hardy and perennial to Zone 6 if mulched; otherwise, overwinter indoors. Water established container plants when the soil is dry down to a couple of inches. Water established outdoor plantings once a month if there's no rainfall; twice monthly in sandy soils or extreme temperatures. No fertilizing or pests to worry about.

Harvest & Best Selections—Harvest rosemary anytime. Try 'Arp', 'Tuscan Blue', and 'Mrs. Howard's Creeping'. 'Goriza' reaches 30 inches tall, and carries some mildew resistance. For a drought-tolerant, aromatic hedge, try 'Salem', which has classic rosemary scent infused with pine and a rounded form to 3 feet tall.

SPINACH
Spinacia oleracea

Why It's Special—Plant spinach in trough gardens in the greenhouse for winter use or interplant in the vegetable bed with lettuce, kale, and chard for a colorful, ready-made salad. Spinach likes the cool of spring and fall, but you can blanch and freeze it for use when you can't grow it fresh in the garden. If it is thoroughly dry when refrigerated, it lasts longer.

How to Plant & Grow—Sow outdoors into well-worked, compost-amended soil six weeks before last frost, as soon as soil warms to 45 degrees Fahrenheit. Soften seeds by soaking overnight. Sow a fall crop six to eight weeks before the first frost. Keep seedbeds moist until germination.

Care & Problems—Drip irrigation is best to avoid wetting the leaves. When plants germinate, use the thinnings in salads. Space waterings to allow the soil to dry a bit between them, and to toughen up the plants. Apply an organic side-dressing a month after sowing if you see signs of deficiency. Watch for aphids, caterpillars, and leaf miners. The best defense is healthy plants.

Harvest & Best Selections—Harvest baby leaves from the outside of the plant, always leaving six leaves for health of the plant. Or wait until spinach matures (40 days) and harvest the entire plant. 'Regatta', 'Olympia', and 'America' are ones to try. Grow New Zealand spinach (*Tetragonia expansa*) through summer. It's best cooked, but fills the spinach void during the heat.

SQUASH
Cucurbita pepo

Why It's Special—Summer squash is sweet and juicy with thin, edible skin, making it good for fresh eating but not good for storage. Winter squash grows large with thick, tough skins, making it good for long-term storage. It is sweet, more pulplike, making it the squash of choice for pie! If it has good supports, summer squash can be grown vertically in the garden to save space. Winter squash can be grown at the feet of corn as a living mulch.

How to Plant & Grow—Sow seeds of summer and winter squash outdoors into compost-enriched, well-worked, well-draining soil after the last frost, when soil temperatures have warmed. Sow seed in hills if you have poorly draining soils. Keep seedbeds moist until germination.

Care & Problems—When plants reach 6 inches, mulch with 3 inches of straw. Water deeply and regularly, but allow the soil surface to dry a bit before watering. Avoid wetting the leaves. If you notice deficiencies, side-dress with an organic, timed-release fertilizer when plants begin to trail. Squash bugs are a nuisance; interplant with nasturtiums or radishes or pick off.

Harvest & Best Selections—Harvest summer squash while it's small, still holding its blossoms; harvest winter squash when the rind is hard and the tendril closest to the squash is dried. Winter squash to try are 'Delta' (also mildew resistant), 'Carrrizo', and 'Hunter'. Try these summer squash, 'Lemon', 'Chayote', and 'Early White Bush'.

THYME
Thymus spp.

Why It's Special—Thyme is a hardy (some to Zone 4), drought-tolerant, perennial herb that can be grown in containers, in sweeps in herb garden borders, spreading between pavers in hardscapes, and interplanted in the vegetable garden for its pest repellant and pollinator magnet attributes. Its tiny leaves carry a big flavor that is tempered when the herb is dried, so you need more dried thyme than fresh to bring it to the attention of the eaters of the turkey stuffing!

How to Plant & Grow—Plant from containers in spring, after the last frost, into well-worked, well-draining soil. Plant at same level as plants were in the pot; water deeply to settle. Keep moist for a few weeks to establish.

Care & Problems—Thyme is pretty carefree. After establishment, water deeply, weekly during summer and twice monthly in spring and fall. No watering is needed in cold-winter areas when it's dormant. Thyme likes lean soil; if you want to apply a timed-release fertilizer in spring, just one application will do it. No pests, but root rot occurs in soggy, cold soil. Cut back to new green growth in spring if it's winter dormant.

Harvest & Best Selections—Harvest thyme leaves at the flush of new growth in spring or anytime, about midday when the oils are at their peak. There are lemon, lime, mint, coconut, caraway, and lavender "flavors."

TOMATILLOS
Physalis ixocarpa

Why It's Special—Tomatillos are excellent in containers and there are bushy types that don't require staking, growing stoutly with some branches trailing on the ground, same as their relatives, the ground cherries. Tomatillos don't taste anything like a tomato, having a tartness that, when added to a scorching hot salsa, brings the heat down. Tomatillos grow in a protective husk, which gives them an extended storage life in the refrigerator for up to three weeks, allowing time to collect enough to make delicious salsa verde.

How to Plant & Grow—Sow seed in packs six to eight weeks before planting outdoors in spring or plant starts in the garden after the last frost. Plant deeply into well-composted and well-worked, well-draining soil. Keep seedbeds moist until germination. Water transplants deeply and apply 3 inches of straw mulch.

Care & Problems—Maintain evenly moist soil and regular watering. After seedlings are 4 inches tall, mulch 2 inches. Cage or stake at that time as well. No additional fertilizer is needed. Tomato hornworms love tomatillos. Hunt them down in early morning or evening when they forage.

Harvest & Best Selections—Harvest tomatillos when their husks are papery dry and you can feel the hardened tomatillo through the husk. Try 'Tomatillo Verde', 'Rio Grande', and 'Mexican Strain'. Tomatillo Purple is an heirloom, purple from the outside in, and sweet enough to eat right off the plant.

TOMATO
Lycopersicon esculentum

Why It's Special—Tomatoes come in every color imaginable (even purple), grow tall, short, bushy, or sprawling. No longer relegated to the vegetable garden, grow tomatoes in pots so you can move them to late afternoon shade when the temperatures heat up. Some are sweet as candy and good for snacking. Others are more acidic and good for canning. Some have less meat, more seeds, and make wonderful sauces. Others have fewer seeds. Tomatoes are good dried as is and easily reconstituted to their full flavor years later.

How to Plant & Grow—Sow seed in packs 8 to 10 weeks before planting out in spring, after the last frost. Plant into well-draining, compost-amended, deeply worked soil. Water deeply; apply 4 inches of straw mulch. Install caging or supports.

Care & Problems—Tomatoes need regular, deep watering throughout their growth. Irregular watering can cause blossom end rot and fruit splitting. Apply supplemental fertilizers if soil test warrants it or if stunting occurs, but use a low-nitrogen fertilizer. If tomatoes in your area are disease prone, look for resistant varieties. Seek out and destroy tomato hornworms.

Harvest & Best Selections—Harvest as soon the fruit ripens to its final color. 'Jujube' is an heirloom cherry type. Try all the colors—green: 'Emerald Evergreen' (stays green, very sweet); orange: 'Dad's Sunset' (uniform, keeps well); yellow: 'Roman Candle' (paste type); pink: 'Pink Icicle' (high producer); black: 'True Black Brandywine' (earthy, acidic); purple: 'Indigo Rose' (newer).

EDIBLES MONTH-BY-MONTH

JANUARY

- In temperate-winter areas, prepare the asparagus bed for planting. Asparagus remains in the same spot for years. Site carefully so it can grow and produce without disruption. Install drip lines directly in the trench after the first backfill is completed. After filling in the trench, cover the entire bed with a 4-inch layer of straw mulch.

- Sow bulb onions seed indoors. They take a long summer season to grow to size, so beginning with starts gives you an edge on producing the plumpest onions. The plumper the onion, the longer its shelf-life. They germinate in a cool soil so no heat mat is needed. Sow up to 100 seeds into a 6-inch pot. Cover lightly; set in bright sunlight. Keep moist. When seedlings reach 5 inches tall, give them a crew cut to encourage root development. Repeat the process until they're planted outdoors.

- Cool-season crops can be planted in frost-free areas. Plant broccoli, green onions, carrots, lettuce, Swiss chard, peas, spinach, and kale in the garden.

FEBRUARY

- In cold-winter zones, if you have a greenhouse and a heat mat or a bright indoor area for seed sowing, sow pepper, tomato, and tomatillo seeds. Starting them early requires transplanting to larger containers and adhering to a weekly water-soluble fertilizer regime for four to six weeks. It is worth the effort to set out established, flowering plants in spring. It makes for a tougher, hardier, pest-resistant plant that produces fruit sooner in the season.

- In warm, low-desert climates, you can plant tomato starts into deeply worked and amended garden soil. Plant them deeply, up to their second set of leaves, run drip lines, then mulch with an inch of straw. Water 6 to 8 inches deep and regularly to avoid blossom end rot and fruit splitting. Add straw mulch as the plants grow, until you have a 4-inch layer.

- Plant bare-root fruit tree and berry vines as soon as the soil can be worked. Keep bare-root plants in a shady, cool spot.

Set them in an opened plastic bag or moistened burlap, entirely covering the roots with moistened peat, sand, or sawdust, then loosely close the bag or wrap the burlap. Check daily to make sure the medium is moist (but not soggy) until planting before leaves start to form.

MARCH

- In cool-winter climates, sow basil, chamomile, oregano, and marjoram indoors on heat mats. They like warm soil and light to germinate. Basil, after transplanting, enjoys a bit of fertilizer. Use an organic, water-soluble fertilizer at half rate. Perennial herbs prefer lean soils, and may burn with added nitrogen, so it's best not to fertilize.

- Plant broccoli, Swiss chard, spinach, kale, green onions in the garden. Swiss chard will grow throughout the season, as will kale if you give it part shade and water it regularly. Broccoli can be interplanted with aromatic herbs, dill, sage, rosemary, and chamomile to deter aphids and beetles.

- In warmer areas, the asparagus beds will be completing the harvest. If you need to use the space, then interplant tomatoes in the bed between the plants. Near the end of the month, plant cantaloupe, melons, cucumber, and winter and summer squashes.

APRIL

- In colder climates, pick asparagus spears in established beds daily. To protect newly emerging spears from munching pests (my dog loves asparagus!), cover them with an empty inverted 1- or 5-gallon pot with a rock on top to hold in place. The spears will continue to form, but the critters can't see them or get to them to munch. This method is easier than having to fence or cage the area.

- Flowering fruit trees are subject to late-season frosts. String holiday lights through the canopies. A few degrees might make the difference to protect the flowers from freezing and losing the fruit.

- In low-desert areas, plant cucumbers and melons to have time to ripen before summer heat sets in.

- Cucumber and melons can be grown vertically. Tie the vines to supports as soon as they begin trailing. Support larger fruits with slings made of netting and tied to the support. The fruits stay clean, get greater sunlight exposure, and are easier to harvest.

MAY

- After the last frost, it's safe to plant out all starts in the garden. Maximize the space, soil, and water resources by interplanting veggies, herbs, fruits and flowers. Tomatoes and carrots, basil and peppers, cosmos and melons, oregano in the basin of fruit trees, squash, corn, and beans make good companions.

- Garlic may set scapes before it's time to harvest the heads. They look like small garlic heads, but form at the top of long stalks. Cut off the scape, stalk and all, to send the energy to the bulb below. Use scapes as you would garlic. They are high in oils.

- Make an easier chore out of thinning carrots. Use seed tape and avoid thinning all together. Or sow as thinly as possible, but wait until the plants are 4 inches tall, then thin ruthlessly to final spacing so you only thin once. Use the tiny carrot thinnings in salads.

JUNE

- Tomato hornworms like tomatillos and sweet bell pepper plants (they stay away from hot peppers and chilis) too. They are camouflage artists, blending in so well you can look right at them and not see them. The best time to capture and feed them to the chickens is early morning and late evening. Look for stripped stems, then find them just beneath or above the damage.

- As the heats sets in, prolong spinach and lettuce plants by covering with shade cloth and picking small juvenile leaves often.

- Sow seeds of New Zealand spinach (*Tetragonia expansa*) into bolting lettuce beds, interplanted with pepper plants and in the landscape for a groundcover. It produces thick, soft fuzzy leaves on long trailing stems. Use the smaller leaves for salads, the larger for sautéing, soups, and stir-fries. They reseed, but not in a bad way.

JULY

- Corn is ready to pick in low elevations. Look for tassels that have turned brown and crispy. A second crop can be planted to harvest before first frost. Look for short-season varieties. These same areas can plant a fall crop of peppers and tomatoes if established plants are set out.

- Herbs like perennial sage, oregano, and thyme send roots deep and are fairly drought tolerant once established. In the summer heat, they appreciate a deep, slow drink of water a couple of times a month.

- Peach fruit ripens and the birds watch and wait. The trees should be netted if birds lurk. Peaches are ready to harvest when they have a blush, give just a bit when squeezed, and you catch that heavenly peach scent. They bruise easily. Twist off the branch and set gently into the basket. Salvage all that you can. Cut off the bird-pecked or bruised portions and enjoy the rest!

AUGUST

- Blackberries are irresistible when they turn shiny black, but they will pucker you up with the tartness. Wait to pick until they turn dull black.

- Direct sow cool-season crops now. Lettuce, kale, broccoli, and spinach like warm soil to germinate and cool weather to establish. Net lettuce crops until they germinate if you have visiting birds. Once the plants are 3 inches tall, remove the netting and apply an inch of straw between the rows of leafy crops; add mulch around broccoli plants as they grow until it is 3 inches deep.

- Leave tomatoes on the vine as long as you can resist. The longer they stay on the plant, the higher their sugar content, and the better their fruit. Pick cherry tomatoes as soon as they color to keep the plants producing. Heirloom 'Jujube' cherry tomatoes begin ripening midsummer and produce fruits through a couple of light frosts.

SEPTEMBER

- It is difficult to know when to harvest winter squash, but they must be brought in before the first hard frost. Thumping on the shell to make sure it is hardened is one way. A woody looking stem and a squash that slips gently away from it is another. I found that when the first tendril closest to the stem shrivels and turns brown, the squash is ready to pick.

- Table grapes are ripening. The best way to tell if they are ready is to pick one off the cluster and eat it. When they are just right, pick the entire cluster. All clusters may not ripen at the same time, so continue with the taste test.

- Begin digging potatoes as the plants flower, but for a bountiful harvest with sizable spuds, wait until the tops turn yellow and die back. Leave the potatoes in the sun for two hours, then store in burlap or paper bags (not plastic) in a cool, dark space, away from onions or apples. Leave as much soil on the spuds as you can, it protects the skin. Wash just before use.

OCTOBER

- Plant garlic. It can grow in the same spot year after year and can be planted wherever there are a few inches of space in the landscape. Plant a ring of garlic around the drip line of apple trees to thwart borers. Interplant it in sweeps, meandering in the rose garden to discourage aphids.

- As fruit is harvested from trees and vines, stop watering so they can prepare for winter dormancy.

- As peppers finish up, pull the plants, throw them into the compost pile, and cover the bed in compost or straw for winter. The space will have to be occupied by a different crop next season, as peppers must be rotated year to year.

- Use the last ripened heirloom tomatoes to collect and save the seed. Cut the fruit open and scrape the seed onto a couple of layers of paper towel. Label the seeds with the name of the tomato and the year, writing the information on the towel with a marker. Set the seeds out of direct sunlight to dry. When completely dried, fold the towel and store in a plastic bag in a cool, dark location. In spring, cut the paper towel into small bits, each holding a few seeds and plant the paper bit directly into the container, covering with a bit of soil. Keep moist until germination.

NOVEMBER

- Asparagus plants have lovely golden fall color. Allow the foliage to stay on the plant until spring.

- Root vegetables grow well throughout winter in low-desert elevations or in areas where the ground doesn't freeze. Beets, carrots, radishes, and turnips can be overwintered in colder-winter climates by covering them with a foot-thick layer of straw or creating a grow tunnel with heavy plastic and PVC pipe.

- Lettuce, spinach, and kale can be interplanted in one bed for an easy-picking mixed salad. In cold-winter climates, sow seed in troughs or deep pots in the greenhouse or sunny window garden for midwinter fresh salad greens.

DECEMBER

- In cold-winter areas, water lines must be drained and shut off where pipes freeze. Hoses crack and split if they're left out, so bring them to the garage for winter, store under the house, or cover with layers of burlap and leave in a sunny spot for warmth.

- Rosemary, thyme, oregano, savory, and sage can all be container grown, overwintered indoors, or greenhouse grown. Wait until the soil dries out before watering and give them as much light as possible. There is no need to fertilize these hardy herbs.

- Order tomato, tomatillo and pepper seeds now for January sowing indoors. Heirloom tomatoes are often more productive, stronger, and more resilient plants if grown from second-generation seeds, collected from the ripened fruits the previous season. Pepper seeds are difficult to collect and grow from prior crops as they can cross-pollinate and won't come back true to seed.

GROUNDCOVERS
&VINES
for the Southwest

Whatever job you need done, there is a groundcover or vine that steps up to the task, doing what they do best, naturally. Groundcovers cover the ground and vines climb, but vines cover the ground too. Some we grow because they have lush, beautiful foliage at all times of the year. Others we choose for profuse blooms blanketing the plant, for their heavenly scent, or because the flowers attract bees, butterflies, and hummingbirds. There are vines that grow so fast in one season, it seems they are out of our control. But come winter, they fade quietly into dormancy, reigning in the rampant growth and beginning their climb again in spring. Sprawling, boisterous vines climb a trellis, an arbor, or fence. When they run out of space, they grow up the trees or crawl at their base, filling both horizontal and vertical spaces. Ground-hugging plants, only inches tall, seem to be delicate things as they creep along the surface, but they create a dense mat that can stand up to being trod upon.

RIGHT PLANT, RIGHT PLACE

While selecting a groundcover or vine, consider its mature size so the plant can grow into its allotted space without continual pruning. A vine that may be declared invasive and rampant in one situation might be just the plant for your garden. My son and his wife were forced to remove an enormous stand of ivy from their garden in southern California. It grew, unchecked and thriving in the temperate climate, until it swallowed a fence, pulling it down with its weight, then proceeded to cover the ground, shading out the lawn with its foliage.

At the home in Utah where I live with my husband, ivy grows under the canopy of a native juniper, covering the bed and discouraging weeds that might grow, but allowing the daffodils and mums to grow tall and flower. 'Midas Touch' ivy intertwines with needlepoint ivy, creeping and attaching to the peeling, shredded bark of a juniper tree. Evergreen throughout our cold and snowy

Pyrostegia venusta (aka *Bignonia venusta*)

winter, but slowed in growth and water needs, it thrives with occasional watering the rest of the year, needing no fertilizing, and sending out new foliage during triple-digit summer heat. It creeps out of the flowerbed and is allowed to climb as far as it wants up the tree, as it is not parasitic.

SUN, PART SUN/PART SHADE, FULL SHADE

There are many sun-loving vines and groundcovers that create microclimates with their shady foliage, making spaces at their feet to plant part- to full-shade plants, building a cool, shady retreat. Some prefer part sun/part shade in the afternoons when the sun and heat are at their highest. Those types are perfect choices to use under deciduous trees. They get the sun they need in early spring, but by the time summer heat sets in, they are cooled by shady tree canopies. Groundcovers and vines that prefer full shade fill spaces that otherwise might be dark and dreary. Brightly colored, climbing or crawling foliage brings color and texture to these areas, intermingling with other shade-loving plants, turning a design challenge into a welcoming vignette.

GIVE THEM A JOB

If you have an unsightly storage area (every gardener has at least one), vines create a green screen and draw the eye to their show, while putting the area out of sight by hiding it with their dense foliage. Want to create a shady retreat? Look for vines that need some tying to the arbor or pergola. They are less apt to wander off. Vines that grow freely and attach themselves to a fence or wall do double duty as groundcovers. Self-anchoring to the ground, they choke out any weeds that get in their way, and can cover a slope to bring texture and color to the landscape.

Groundcovers fill spaces, some creeping slowly, forming tidy mounds and allowing other plants to live with them. Planted in drifts, they meander in and out of shrub beds, tree canopies, and serve as fillers in color borders and perennial gardens, tying the landscape together, defining and organizing the space. Others cling to the ground, barely inches tall and can take some foot traffic. Those types work between pavers, soften a pathway, or serve as a turf alternative. Flowering groundcovers blanket the ground with color, bringing the wow factor when planted *en masse* on hillsides, lining an entrance drive or path, filling a meridian strip or drifting around a specimen tree or shrub.

HEIGHT X WIDTH = PRUNING

Consideration of maximum size of a groundcover or vine affects the pruning you may need to do later. If a vine grows 20 feet at maturity or within a growing season, and an arbor is 8 feet tall, then a midseason clipping keeps it in check. But if you plant the same vine along a fenceline, you may not need to prune, other than eliminating a few errant branches. Some vines go dormant in winter, so any hard pruning can be done then or before it leafs out in spring, a much easier chore while the foliage is gone. Winter damage may occur on evergreen vines and sometimes winter burn alone keeps evergreen vines controlled.

Groundcovers are more forgiving in their growth. Matching their mature height and width to a garden space eliminates continual pruning to contain them. Buying fewer plants to fill the space and mulching between the plants gives the bed a finished look while you are waiting for these plants to fill their space. For those groundcovers that insist on extending their growth beyond the bed, some pruning may be required whenever they disobey. But always consider before you cut. If the intrusion isn't a tripping hazard or a threat to nearby plants, then just let it be. You may be delighted with a lush, blooming groundcover creeping into the garden path, softening a border, or spilling over a wall.

SHARING SOIL, NUTRIENTS, AND WATER

Most groundcovers and vines, if given well-worked, well-draining soil, have no other needs (beyond deep watering) and they grow vigorously. Turning the soil, sifting, and breaking up clods will fluff it up and add airspaces, which allow water and nutrients to percolate through the soil to reach the roots. These airspaces assist the roots in their growth, eventually developing into deep-reaching, healthy root systems. Strong roots anchor the plant and go deep into the soil to absorb any moisture that might be there. Healthy root systems absorb nutrients available in the water, thriving with no additional fertilizers.

Groundcovers and vines have a place in our gardens. If we give them the conditions they require, they grow, flower, and thrive, doing their jobs, filling the spaces with beauty for years to come, all on their own.

Wisteria floribunda

ARCHANGEL
Lamium maculatum

Why It's Special—Shade-lover archangel brightens dark corners or entryways, trails over basket edges, and provides contrast to shady perennials. Use it in sweeps along a shady drive or drifting in and out of broad tree canopies. Planted *en masse*, archangel makes quick, dense cover on a slope; its network of rhizomes and stolons control erosion.

How to Plant & Grow—Plant from containers or divisions in early spring after the last frost, into well-worked, compost-amended, well-draining soil. Archangel needs afternoon shade, at minimum, preferring full shade in areas of hotter summers. Water deeply and top with 3 to 4 inches of mulch.

Care & Problems—No supplemental fertilizer is needed if the soil was well prepared with amendments. If stunting occurs, fertilize with water-soluble fertilizer at half rate. Cut back by half in midsummer to encourage new growth. Scale and sunscald are its worst problems.

Water Needs—Provide deep, regular watering except where it's winter dormant, then only in extended periods of no moisture.

Bloom Color—White, pink

Peak Season—Spring to early summer

Mature Size (H x W)—8 to 10 inches x 36 inches

BOUGAINVILLEA
Bougainvillea spp. and hybrids

Why It's Special—Bougainvillea offers thornless, dwarf types for containers and hanging baskets; trailing types to cover slopes with color year-round; and climbers for a trellises, arbors, or pergolas. Or grow it naturally as a large, dense, sprawling shrub.

How to Plant & Grow—Plant in spring after last frost, into moistened, deeply worked native soil. Prepare the planting hole to exact size and depth. Carefully plant, with minimal disruption to the roots. Water deeply, adding a 3- to 4-inch mulch layer. Provide supports for bougainvillea to climb or remove stakes so it can trail.

Care & Problems—Prune frost-damaged stems to new growth in spring. Fertilize the first three years with slow-release fertilizer in spring or fall; thereafter, don't feed.

Water Needs—It's drought tolerant, but water deeply every 10 days in summer; twice monthly otherwise.

Bloom Color—Magenta, pink, white, salmon, orange, red, purple

Peak Season—Spring through winter

Mature Size (H x W)—1½ to 30 feet x 6 to 20 feet

Hardiness—Zones 9 to 11; established bougainvillea tolerates mild frosts, but suffers root damage below 20 degrees Fahrenheit. In colder zones, overwinter indoors.

BOSTON IVY
Parthenocissus tricuspidata

Why It's Special—Boston ivy (and its relative Virginia creeper, *Parthenocissus quinquefolia*) need no supports, clinging to surfaces on its own or sprawling to blanket ground surfaces with large, green lush foliage in spring. Boston ivy cools through summer, then turns up the color for the fall show. Not finished with its job, Boston ivy's blue-purple berry clusters persist into winter.

How to Plant & Grow—Plant from containers in early spring or fall. The hotter the summer, the more shade it needs. Plant into well-worked, well-draining soil. Water deeply; add 3 to 4 inches of mulch.

Care & Problems—Fertilize its first three years in spring with timed-release fertilizer; then, no fertilizing is needed. It's carefree in shade. Watch for leaf skeletontonizing caused by striped caterpillar; treat with *Bacillus thuringiensis*. Prune to control growth.

Water Needs—After three years, water deeply every two weeks; no water is needed during its winter dormancy.

Bloom Color—Insignificant; blue winter berries

Peak Season—Fall foliage in red, orange, yellow

Mature Length—20 to 40 feet

CAROLINA JESSAMINE
Gelsemium sempervirens

Why It's Special—Carolina jessamine thrives in summer heat, quickly and densely covering slopes, arbors, pergolas, or fences with shiny evergreen foliage. Its yellow, scented blooms are magnets for bees and hummingbirds. Site where you can watch their show and catch its scent.

How to Plant & Grow—Plant in spring after last frost into well-worked, well-draining, native soil. The hotter the summer, the more shade it requires. Water deeply, keeping soil moist the first season. Apply 3 to 4 inches of mulch.

Care & Problems—Carolina jessamine needs room to grow, but no pruning is necessary. You can hard prune by one-fourth every three or four years to generate new soft growth. Fertilize the first three years in spring with timed-release fertilizer, then nothing. No pests bother it.

Water Needs—After three seasons, deeply water weekly during summer, twice monthly in spring, once a month in winter if there's no rain or snow.

Bloom Color—Yellow

Peak Season—Early spring

Mature Length—20 feet long

Hardiness—Zones 6 to 9. Plants come back from their roots after a hard freeze.

CARPET BUGLE
Ajuga reptans

Why It's Special—Carpet bugle is at home in every landscape. Plant drifts under deciduous trees, mass-plant as a bulb bed foil, in containers to accent other plants, spilling over the edges of rock gardens, plant singly into crevices of a rock wall, to cover slopes, tuck into terrace gardens, in the shady spots, and to fill window boxes.

How to Plant & Grow—Plant in early spring or fall into well-draining, deeply worked, compost-amended soil. Water deeply and keep moist its first season. Add 2 inches of mulch.

Care & Problems—Fertilize with a water-soluble fertilizer in spring for the first three years; thereafter no fertilizer is needed. Non-aggressive mats will spread and creep out of their confines; dig up and replant. No pests bother it, but root rot occurs in cold, constantly wet soils.

Water Needs—Though drought tolerant once established, water deeply and regularly during sprin and summer, allowing soil to dry the touch between waterings. Don't water during winter dormancy.

Bloom Color—Blue

Peak Season—Spring

Mature Size (H x W)—3 to 8 inches x 12 to 24 inches

CLEMATIS
Clematis spp.

Why It's Special—Clematis likes its head in the sun, but must have its feet in the shade. Interplant these beautiful vines with groundcovers, sweeps of annuals, low-growing perennials, or clumping herbs at its base. Allow clematis to climb over arbors, up trellises, along fences, and over pergolas.

How to Plant & Grow—Plant in spring into well-worked, well-amended, well-draining soil. Water deeply; mulch 3 to 4 inches.

Care & Problems—Fertilize hybrids monthly from April through August with slow-release fertilizer. Maintain a thick layer of mulch to keep the roots shaded and cool. Prune Jackman (*Clematis × jackmanii*) and virgin's bower (*C. tangutica*) in fall, others in spring. No diseases or pests bother clematis. Given its desired environment, it's a considerably tough plant.

Water Needs—Do not allow soil to dry. Maintain regular, deep watering once or twice weekly in summer (depending upon air temperatures and wind); every two weeks in spring and fall. Water once a month during winter.

Bloom Color—Pink, purple, red, yellow, white

Peak Season—Spring, summer

Mature Size (H x W)—6 to 15 feet x 4 to 6 feet

CREEPING DALEA

Dalea greggii

Why It's Special—Creeping dalea can cover a slope or a hot, sunny area, fill a strip along hot pavement, grow against a building in reflective heat, tumble over container edges, or form a mass of blooms for an informal border or small hedge. It does it all and, once established, requires little water to do it.

How to Plant & Grow—Plant in spring into well-worked, unamended, well-draining native soil. Water deeply and maintain regular watering for two seasons until establishment. After planting, add 3 to 4 inches of mulch.

Care & Problems—No supplemental fertilizing is needed. Give dalea space to grow and avoid pruning. As it loses its mounding habit, shear back into older wood to about ankle height to rejuvenate. As it establishes, no mulching is needed; its habit shades the roots and cools the soil. No pests or diseases affect it.

Water Needs—Deeply water twice monthly through summer, once a month in spring, and as needed in winter.

Bloom Color—Indigo to purple

Peak Season—Spring through summer

Mature Size (H x W)—1 to 2 feet x 2 to 4 feet

CREEPING JUNIPER

Juniperus spp.

Why It's Special—Creeping juniper adds color and texture to slopes, garden borders, rock gardens, interplanted with other conifers, in dry or wet streambeds, in sweeps along a drive, in containers, or as a drought-tolerant lawn substitute. Many types exist including tiny, feathery, spiked, dense foliage on low-growing, sprawling shrubs in light to dark green, yellow, chartreuse, gray-green, green-blue, silver-blue, or plum.

How to Plant & Grow—Plant in spring or fall into deeply worked, well-draining native soil. If it's rootbound, cut off a few inches of root mass from the bottom and make three vertical slices on the remaining rootball before planting. Water deeply and mulch.

Care & Problems—Water once a week the first year, allowing the soil to dry down a few inches between waterings. Spray plants in early in the morning to keep them clean and mite free. No pruning is needed.

Water Needs—Give established plants occasional supplemental deep watering during droughts.

Bloom Color—Insignificant

Peak Season—Blue-purple berries in summer

Mature Size (H x W)—1 to 2 feet x 3 to 10 feet

CREEPING FIG

Ficus pumila

Why It's Special—Creeping fig makes a lush green screen, hides an unsightly wall, creates a visual barrier, creeps for a groundcover, fills a topiary form in no time, spills over a hanging basket (and can even grow as a houseplant). It attaches freely, so give it a wide berth and it will take care of itself.

How to Plant & Grow—Plant in early spring after last frost into well-worked, compost-enriched, well-draining soil. Water deeply; apply 3 to 4 inches of mulch.

Care & Problems—Fertilize with a timed-release fertilizer every two months during the growing season. Prune to direct growth or control size; cut back to the ground in spring to minimize woody growth and encourage new soft foliage. Don't allow it to climb other plants, as it will shade them. No pests bother it.

Water Needs—Water deeply, three times a week in summer, once monthly in winter, allowing soil to dry a bit between waterings.

Bloom Color—Insignificant

Peak Season—Evergreen

Mature Length—40 feet long

Hardiness—Zones 8 to 9; overwinter in zones below 8.

HOSTA
Hosta hybrids

Why It's Special—Hosta is grown primarily for its large, boisterous, multicolored foliage. Its tubular flowers add yet another feature to the summer border, container, or shade garden, rising on tall, delicate, branching spikes. Hybrids sport foliage in blue, green, burgundy, blue-gray, golden-yellow, and chartreuse, some outlined in white create color and drama in shady entryways, drifting in the understories of shade trees, clumping at the base of conifers, or intermingling with hardy ferns.

How to Plant & Grow—Plant in early spring into well-worked, deeply amended, and well-draining soil. Water deeply and apply a 3- to 4-inch layer of mulch.

Care & Problems—Fertilize in spring with a timed-release fertilizer. Maintain a thick layer of mulch. Slugs and snails will visit; control with bait, following application directions, applying under the mulch where they hide out. No pruning or dividing is needed.

Water Needs—Water deeply every other day during summer, less frequently in spring, fall, and winter.

Bloom Color—White, blue

Peak Season—Summer

Mature Size (H x W)—2 to 3 feet x 3 to 5 feet

IVY
Hedera spp. and hybrids

Why It's Special—Ivy is tough and carefree, but languishes in shady gardens. In sunny spots, let it drift among groves of mature trees, blanket a slope, cover a fence for a green screen or an arbor for year-round shade, and cascade out of hanging baskets. Interplant hybrids for textural, colorful effects.

How to Plant & Grow—Plant container-grown or rooted cuttings in spring, early summer, or fall into well-worked, compost-amended, well-draining soil. Water deeply and mulch.

Care & Problems—Ivy doesn't require supplemental fertilizing unless you notice deficiencies; then water well afterward, washing fertilizer off the leaves to avoid burn. Prune to control size, but it's best to plant it where it can grow freely or confine it to a container. It's not a parasite, so it can be allowed to climb mature trees as long as it doesn't block the tree's foliage from the sun.

Water Needs—Ivy is drought tolerant, but it grows lushly with deep watering once a week.

Bloom Color—Insignificant, berries in maturity

Peak Season—Evergreen foliage

Mature Length—Up to 20 feet

KINNIKINNICK
Arctostaphylos uva-ursi

Why It's Special—Kinnikinnick is a heat, cold, wind, and drought workhorse, providing all-season interest with shiny evergreen foliage, clusters of pink flowers in spring, red fall foliage, and bright red berries through winter. It provides a dense, green cover on slopes and in open areas, an accent in rock gardens, and is a reliable, compact grower in the dry border or as a filler in the shrub bed. It roots along its stems as it grows, providing a weed barrier.

How to Plant & Grow—Plant in early spring into well-worked, well-draining soil. Kinnikinnick prefers afternoon shade in hottest desert areas. Water deeply, add 3 to 4 inches of mulch, allow soil to dry, then water deeply. Repeat through the first season.

Care & Problems—Though slow to establish, kinnikinnik is carefree and drought tough after a couple of seasons. No pruning or supplemental fertilizing is needed. No pests or diseases affect it.

Water Needs—After establishment, water deeply but infrequently, allowing soil to dry between waterings.

Bloom Color—Pink

Peak Season—Mid-spring

Mature Size (H x W)—1 to 2 feet x 2 to 4 feet

HYACINTH BEAN
Lablab purpureus

Why It's Special—Hyacinth bean is grown as an annual in areas that receive frost, but there's plenty of time for it to cover a fence, climb a trellis or arbor, make a green screen, or to tumble down a slope. It quickly creates a dense green foliar vine or groundcover with sweet pea-like blooms covering the plant, followed by showy purple pods. Hyacinth bean carries the show all through the growing season until frost, all for such little effort on the part of those planting it.

How to Plant & Grow—Direct-sow seed in spring after the last frost into well-worked, well-draining soil. Keep the seedbed moist for germination.

Care & Problems—Hyacinth bean is a legume, so it doesn't require any additional fertilizer. When plants are 6 inches tall, provide climbing supports and top with 3 inches of mulch. Prune to stay within boundaries. When seedpods shrivel and turn brown, pull them from the vine; harvest seed for sowing next year.

Water Needs—Provide regular, deep watering.

Bloom Color—Lilac to purple

Peak Season—Midsummer

Mature Length—6 to 20 feet

MONEYWORT
Lysimachia nummularia

Why It's Special—Moneywort forms a dense mat of evergreen foliage, covering the ground quickly, rooting along the ground as it travels, making it a good groundcover for slopes and open areas to control erosion and choke out weeds. Plant this shade-lover in drifts in tree understories; its roots won't interfere with a tree's roots and the plant creates a living mulch. If you can't allow it to grow with abandonment, use it in hanging baskets or in containers trailing over the sides.

How to Plant & Grow—Plant in spring, summer, or fall, unless temperatures are above 95 degrees Fahrenheit, into a well-draining, deeply worked soil. Mulch just after planting. Water deeply.

Care & Problems—Plant where its spreading habit is not restricted or you will be pruning to control. Fertilize to encourage quick growth if necessary, in spring or fall, with a balanced, timed-release fertilizer. No pests or diseases affect it.

Water Needs—Water deeply and regularly.

Bloom Color—Yellow

Peak Season—Spring

Mature Size (H x W)—2 to 4 inches x 12 to 24 inches

MOSS PINK
Phlox subulata

Why It's Special—Moss pink is an aptly named mounding groundcover that is covered in profuse flowers during bloomtime, growing above its evergreen foliage as thickly as moss. When not in bloom, plants hug the ground with their needlelike foliage, shading plant roots and cooling the soil beneath, both attributes that make it drought tolerant.

How to Plant & Grow—Plant container-grown plants or divisions in spring after the last frost into a deeply worked, well-draining soil. Part-sun to part-shade sites are best in hot-summer-desert climates, but too dense shade will sacrifice blooms. Water deeply and keep soil moist until transplants overcome transplant shock and put out new growth. Mulch after planting.

Care & Problems—Cut back plants by half after blooming to encourage bushiness and repeat bloom in fall. No fertilizing is needed. Divide plants after blooming if they outgrow their space. Occasionally, spider mites occur in summer drought.

Water Needs—Water deeply, infrequently, allowing soil to dry down a few inches between waterings.

Bloom Color—Pink, white, red, blue, lavender

Peak Season—Spring

Mature Size (H x W)—6 inches x 24 inches

PACHYSANDRA
Pachysandra terminalis

Why It's Special—Pachysandra is an evergreen to semi-evergreen groundcover that adds more texture than the usual groundhuggers. Whirled foliage gives it a lush appearance, especially when planted in drifts under deciduous trees or *en masse* along a shady drive. Interplant with other shade-loving perennials in a shady entryway; it remains green year-round in temperate climates.

How to Plant & Grow—Plant in spring into deeply worked, compost- or peat-amended, well-draining soil. Pachysandra prefer acidic soils, so amend alkaline soils or plant in containers with a heavy percentage of peat incorporated into potting mix. Water deeply and regularly, once a week if no rainfall, until established.

Care & Problems—Pachysandra doesn't need pruning, staying within its boundaries. Drought-stressed plants might show mites and scale while deep shade, poor drainage, or extended wet weather can bring on fungal disease. Mulch to keep soil cool and retain moisture.

Water Needs—Water deeply during extended droughts; otherwise, wait until the soil dries a bit before watering.

Bloom Color—White

Peak Season—Spring

Mature Size (H x W)—6 to 8 inches x 12 to 18 inches

PASSION FLOWER
Passiflora spp.

Why It's Special—Passion flower is drought tolerant once established, despite its appearance with large, waxy, tropical-looking blooms on vines with deeply lobed, lush foliage. It branches and climbs if given support, surpassing great heights by summer's end or it can crawl upon the ground, giving foliage and floral cover in a large area throughout the season.

How to Plant & Grow—Plant after danger of frost is past in spring into well-worked, well-draining soil. If your soil drains poorly, plant in deeply enriched, amended soil or in raised beds. Water deeply and top-dress with 3 to 4 inches of mulch.

Care & Problems—No pests or diseases will bother *Passiflora*. Prune just to control size, but it goes dormant in early winter so Mother Nature does the job. Remove dead vines and foliage in spring, cutting to the point of new growth.

Water Needs—Apply deep, infrequent watering in periods of extended drought; don't water in winter dormancy.

Bloom Color—Pale to pinkish lavender, blue, yellow, purple

Peak Season—Summer

Mature Size (H x W)—6 to 20 feet

Hardiness—Zones 6 to 9

PERIWINKLE
Vinca minor

Why It's Special—Periwinkle is a tough groundcover that tumbles over walls, climbs a slope, spills over a container edge, and sweeps in and out of dappled shade of evergreen trees. Its foliage makes it a star and continuous flowering throughout three seasons is a bonus.

How to Plant & Grow—Plant into well-drained, deeply worked soil in spring after the last frost. Periwinkle handles early morning sun, but needs shade in hot summer areas. Water deeply and top-dress with 3 to 4 inches of mulch.

Care & Problems—Occasional aphids or snails prove problematic. Mow plantings every few years to refresh them if winter freezes don't do the job for you. Use a square-point shovel and make vertical cuts to control rooting stems. Prune errant branches. After establishment, they cool their roots and the soil beneath as their own mulch. No fertilizer is needed.

Water Needs—Water deeply once a week if temperatures exceed 90 degrees fahrenheit; otherwise, water as soon as wilt occurs.

Bloom Color—Blue

Peak Season—Spring to fall

Mature Size (H x W)—3 to 10 inches x 12 to 24 inches

PLUMBAGO
Ceratostigma plumbaginoides

Why It's Special—Plumbago is a three-season groundcover with shiny, oval green foliage in spring and blue flowers until fall, followed by red fall foliage. Slow-growing and noninvasive, plumbago makes a great foreground border plant, a companion for other shade plants, or a plant for drifts to meander in and out of shade canopies.

How to Plant & Grow—Plant in spring after last frost into well-worked, compost-amended, well-draining soil. Water deeply. Top-dress with 3 to 4 inches of mulch. In elevations above 5,000 feet, plumbago can take full sun, but it prefers afternoon shade or full shade. Maintain regular, deep, weekly watering to establish.

Care & Problems—No pests or diseases bother it. No pruning is needed but rejuvenate it after a few years by cutting it to the ground in early spring. No fertilizing is needed.

Water Needs—When temperatures exceed 90 degrees Fahrenheit, water deeply weekly; otherwise, every two weeks, but no winter watering.

Bloom Color—Blue

Peak Season—Summer to fall

Mature Size (H x W)—8 to 12 inches x 12 to 24 inches

Hardiness—Zones 6 to 9

QUEEN'S WREATH
Antigonon leptopus

Why It's Special—Queen's wreath thrives in summer heat and is drought tolerant after establishment—a good combination from a plant that flowers in abundance through the hottest months. You can even sit under its dense, cool shade canopy to enjoy the show. Let it climb over an arbor, pergola, trellis, or anywhere you need shade.

How to Plant & Grow—Plant in spring when soil has warmed. Plant into well-worked, well-draining native soil. Incorporate a timed-release fertilizer into the backfill. Water well and add a 3- to 4-inch mulch layer. Provide supports at planting.

Care & Problems—When new growth emerges in spring, ferilize with a slow-release or organic fertilizer. Maintain a thick layer of mulch, adding each fall to protect roots during winter. Prune in spring to remove winter-damaged stems and to shape. No pests or disease bother it.

Water Needs—Deeply water weekly during the hottest summers; otherwise, water twice monthly. Don't water in winter.

Bloom Color—Pink, white, rose-red

Peak Season—Summer

Mature Length—Up to 40 feet long

Hardiness—Zones 9 to 11

SILVER LACE VINE
Fallopia baldschuanica

Why It's Special—All you need is one silver lace vine to cover an arbor, fill a trellis, screen a view, sprawl on a bank, or climb a pergola. Neither thirsty nor hungry, this sun-loving and quick-growing vine is the solution to dry, lean, infertile areas. In summer, it features lush foliage and profuse blooms; in fall, the plant turns golden brown. It even attracts beneficial insects.

How to Plant & Grow—Plant container grown, rooted cuttings, or root divisions into warm soil in spring, summer, or early fall. Site in well-worked, unamended, well-draining soil. Water transplants every few days until they're over transplant shock. Mulch 3 inches. Provide support and keep it away from other plantings that it will quickly overtake.

Care & Problems—No fertilizer is needed, nor do pests or diseases bother it. If given the space to grow, no pruning is needed but a rejuvenation pruning promotes soft growth.

Water Needs—Water deeply to 2 feet, once a month in summer in low deserts; otherwise, no supplemental watering is necessary.

Bloom Color—White

Peak Season—Summer to frost

Mature Length—Up to 40 feet long

SNOW-IN-SUMMER
Cerastium tomentosum

Why It's Special—When it's blooming, snow-in-summer looks like snow—in the desert—in summer! It'll cover a slope for erosion control, fill a hanging basket, brighten a night garden planted in drifts along a path, make other plants pop with color in the flower border, provide a foil for bulb beds, and can be used as a lawn substitute for hot spaces that need to be cooled down (but which are rarely walked upon).

How to Plant & Grow—Plant anytime into deeply worked, amended, well-draining soil. Incorporate a timed-release fertilizer into the backfill. Water deeply; top with 3 to 4 inches of mulch.

Care & Problems—Fertilize in spring with a timed-release granular fertilizer, watering in well. Mow to the ground in spring to encourage lush growth. Replace any aged, thinning plants. It has no pests or diseases. Refresh mulch as needed.

Water Needs—Twice weekly, water 1 inch deep in summer in low-desert areas; otherwise, water only in extended drought.

Bloom Color—White

Peak Season—Summer

Mature Size (H x W)—6 inches x 36 inches

STAR JASMINE
Trachelospermum jasminoides

Why It's Special—Star jasmine covers a slope with green foliage and brilliant white blooms while controlling soil erosion. With support, it climbs a wall, trellis, arbor, or pergola, creating shade and a floral show. Put it in a container, sited close to seating areas, and it will spill over the sides, filling the air with its scent.

How to Plant & Grow—Plant in well-worked, well-draining soil amended with compost. Water deeply and apply 3 inches of mulch. Water three times a week until new growth appears. In low-desert climates, plant it where it gets afternoon shade. Lower than Zone 7, plant in containers and overwinter in the greenhouse.

Care & Problems—Prune to control its size or if you want a bushier plant. Fertilize each spring with a slow-release fertilizer. No pests or disease bother it.

Water Needs—Water deeply once a week in summer; monthly in winter if there's no rain.

Bloom Color—White

Peak Season—Spring

Mature Length—10 to 30 feet

Hardiness—Zones 8 to 11

SUNROSE
Helianthemum spp. and cultivars

Why It's Special—Sunrose is a sun lover and fairly drought tolerant once it's established. Planted *en masse*, it makes a good slope or groundcover in large areas, a tidy filler in the perennial border, a heat-tough rock garden plant, a foreground grouping in the xeric shrub bed, and a long-blooming container plant. Primarily evergreen, it is never without foliage or color, always having a few blooms spring through summer.

How to Plant & Grow—Plant in spring into well-draining, deeply worked, unamended soil. Water deeply to establish, add 3 inches of mulch.

Care & Problems—Too much fertilizer or too rich soils causes weaker growth and fewer blooms. Do not overwater. Shear after blooming to keep compact and flowering. No pests or disease affect it.

Water Needs—Deeply water weekly in summer, monthly in winter. Allow the soil to dry between waterings.

Bloom Color—White, red, apricot, pink, yellow, rose

Peak Season—Spring to summer

Mature Size (H x W)—6 to 8 inches x 3 feet

Hardiness—Zones 6 to 8; in Zone 6, cover with mulch for winter protection.

TRAILING LANTANA
Lantana montevidensis and hybrids

Why It's Special—Trailing lantana and 'New Gold' lantana are heat and sun lovers, but also tolerate part sun to part shade. They cascade freely with profuse blooms blanketing their stems throughout the season. Use them *en masse*, interplanted for a colorful slope cover, sweeping along a driveway, bordering a path, in hot meridians, and in containers.

How to Plant & Grow—Plant in spring after last frost into well-worked, well-draining, but unamended soil. Water deeply every two weeks, allowing the soil to dry between waterings, until plants establish. Apply 3 inches of mulch.

Care & Problems—Overwatering in high humidity causes chlorosis. Too much fertilizer and water equals fewer blooms. Prune frost-damaged branches in spring, cutting back to new growth; prune in summer to control size and increase branching. Refresh mulch.

Water Needs—Water deeply once a week in summer; monthly in winter if no rain.

Bloom Color—Lavender, purple, white, gold, yellow

Peak Season—Spring to fall

Mature Size (H x W)—I to 2 feet x 2 to 6 feet

Hardiness—Zones 7 to 10; use as annuals in colder zones.

TRUMPET VINE
Campsis radicans

Why It's Special—Trumpet vine is a winter- and heat-hardy carefree vine or groundcover that emerges in early spring. Its divided leaves quickly sprawl along the ground or climb a support, filling a slope, creating a dense covering over an arbor, fence, or pergola. The large, tropical-looking trumpet blooms attract hummingbirds.

How to Plant & Grow—Plant in early spring as soon as the soil can be worked. Plant into well-draining, well-worked native soil. Water deeply three times a week until new growth appears. Top with 3 to 4 inches of mulch.

Care & Problems—Prune in winter or early spring to promote bushiness and new growth. Prune errant branches in summer. No pests or disease attack trumpet vine. Fertilize only if deficiency symptoms occur. It's drought tolerant once established. It climbs and attaches itself freely and spreads with sucker growth.

Water Needs—Deeply water twice per week in summer in low-desert areas; otherwise, water once a month. Don't water during winter dormancy.

Bloom Color—Red, red-orange, yellow

Peak Season—Summer to fall

Mature Length—30 to 40 feet

VERBENA
Verbena spp.

Why It's Special—Verbena is drought and heat tolerant, blooming throughout the seasons in frost-free zones. A mounding or trailing plant, depending upon the species, verbena is reliably tough and low maintenance. Use it for color on slopes, in sweeps along a path, as borders in perennial beds, in pots, and in hanging baskets.

How to Plant & Grow—Plant in spring or summer in well-worked, well-draining, native soil. Water deeply and regularly to establish. Apply a 3- to 4-inch mulch layer.

Care & Problems—Fertilize *Verbena canadensis* with timed-release fertilizer in early spring; *V. pulchella* needs no supplemental fertilizer. Prune spring and summer to control size or to refresh. It suffers no pests or diseases other than occasional powdery mildew.

Water Needs—Water deeply every 10 to 14 days in summer; otherwise, once a month if no rain.

Bloom Color—Purple, white, pink, red

Peak Season—Late fall to summer in frost-free zones; summer otherwise

Mature Size (H x W)—4 to 8 inches x 2 to 5 feet

Hardiness—Zones 7 to 9; grow in containers or as annuals in cold zones.

WINTERCREEPER
Euonymus fortunei

Why It's Special—Wintercreeper is a heat- and cold-hardy evergreen plant that thrives with minimal water or attention. Give it room to grow and it covers slopes, fills open areas, drifts in and out of tree canopies, sweeps along drives, fills meridians, and climbs walls, trellises, or fences. Multipurpose wintercreeper is tough and always green, even in the coldest of winters, the hottest of climates, and the driest of soils.

How to Plant & Grow—Plant spring, summer, or fall into well-worked, well-draining soil. No amendments are needed. Water deeply once a week until new growth appears. Mulch 3 to 4 inches deep.

Care & Problems—Prune to keep within bounds. Top-dress with timed-release fertilizer its first spring, then no fertilizer is needed. Sometimes scale or powdery mildew occurs in dense cool shade. After establishment, it creates its own mulch, cooling the soil and thwarting the efforts of weeds.

Water Needs—Water deeply once a week in summer in desert sites; otherwise, water monthly if there's no rain or snow.

Bloom Color—Inconspicuous

Peak Season—Evergreen

Mature Size (H x W)—20 feet x 2 to 8 feet

WISTERIA
Wisteria sinensis

Why It's Special—Wisteria's sweetly scented blooms hang in clusters on bare scaffolding in spring, followed by a shady canopy in summer, large ornate purple-red pods in autumn, and golden yellow fall foliage. It's a drought-, heat-, and cold-tolerant vine that climbs to 40 feet at maturity making wisteria a much sought-after plant.

How to Plant & Grow—Plant in early spring into well-draining, well-worked, unamended soil. Tie vines to stakes and scaffolding. Water deeply, once a week when temperatures exceed 85 degrees Fahrenheit; every two weeks between 70 to 85 degrees Fahrenheit; monthly in winter if there's no rain or snow. Add 3 to 4 inches of mulch.

Care & Problems—Prune to train throughout its growing season; root prune dormant plants to stimulate bud formation. In early spring as buds form, cut back to 4 or 5 buds per stem. No pests or disease bother it. No fertilizer is needed.

Water Needs—Deeply water to a soil depth of 2 feet twice monthly in summer; once per month in fall, spring; no winter watering.

Bloom Color—Purple, white, rose

Peak Season—Spring

Mature Length—25 to 40 feet

YELLOW BUTTERFLY VINE
Mascagnia macroptera

Why It's Special—Yellow butterfly vine flowers profusely, followed by ornate chartreuse pods forming fans as they mature, resembling a butterfly. The vine is a strong grower, though not out of control, climbing a trellis, fence, or arbor with some assistance and spilling freely over the edge of a large pot.

How to Plant & Grow—Plant in spring after all danger of frost is past into well-worked, well-draining, unamended soil. Water deeply every two to three days for two weeks, then, every five to seven days through its first summer.

Care & Problems—Prune winter-damaged branches or to shape in spring; rejuvenate prune by cutting to 1 foot tall in spring. No pests or diseases bother this plant. Fertilize the first spring with slow-release fertilizer; no supplemental fertilizer after establishment.

Water Needs—Water deeply once per week in summer; monthly in winter.

Bloom Color—Yellow

Peak Season—Spring

Mature Length—10 to 15 feet

Hardiness—Zones 8 to 10; hardy to 15 degrees Fahrenheit, it goes briefly dormant in winter, leaving time to prune before its early spring show.

GROUNDCOVERS & VINES MONTH-BY-MONTH

JANUARY

- Bougainvillea cannot be grown outdoors year-round below Zone 8, so treat it as an annual or pot it up and bring indoors in winter. Put it in a sunny window, apply water-soluble fertilizer, and it may flower through winter, quite an uplifting sight.

- Water overwintering vines and groundcovers when the soil is dry down to a couple of inches. Do not allow them to sit in standing in water. Set them in the bathtub or sink, water until you see water pouring out of the bottom of the pot, let them drain completely, then return to their locations.

- In warmer-winter areas, you might not need to water at all if you have had rain or snowfall in the past month. Deciduous plants are not actively growing and evergreens slow their growth.

FEBRUARY

- While it may be warming in lower elevations, it's still too early to fertilize. Encouraging new growth in cooler months subjects tender leaves and stems to cold damage.

- Prune wisteria and trumpet vine now before they bud or send out foliage. If they have gotten out of control, hard prune them to the ground to rejuvenate and retrain. Root pruning wisteria encourages more blooming. Make vertical slices with a spade around the rootball, taking care not to slice too close to the trunk or main stem.

- This is a good month for planning new groundcovers and vines. Groundcovers require area for top and root growth, so account for their mature width when calculating how many plants to buy. Vines require more vertical space, but may only need 1 to 3 feet of growing space for their roots. Incorporating vines into existing landscape may require removing nearby plants, but usually you can just tuck them in without disturbing other plantings.

MARCH

- Wait to cut back winter damage or old growth until you see new green growth, then cut back just to the point of the new foliage.

- When you purchase already leafed-out deciduous vines in containers, the plants may have been forced out of dormancy and grown in greenhouses for early spring sales. Soft tissues are not able to stand up to wind, late season frosts, or cooler soil and air temperatures. Set them in a shady, protected spot for a few days and nights, pulling them indoors if frost threatens. Then set them, still in their containers, for a few days in the location where they will be planted to see how they like their future home before planting.

- If you are replacing turf with a drought-tolerant groundcover, then remove the turf while it is dormant or slowed in growth. Stoloniferous lawns may require a dose of systemic herbicide to completely kill their roots. Remove what lawn you can with a sod cutter, and water the remnants so they are green and healthy before spraying. The herbicide is absorbed into the growing tips of the plant, then translocated through the active vascular system to kill a plant from the roots up.

APRIL

- April is the last killing frost for some gardeners, signaling time to plant, sow, prune, and fertilize.

- Water all the landscape and new planting areas deeply and slowly to bring the soil moisture content up. Extend the soaker hose or drip line to at least 1 foot beyond the planting zone to ensure that the water doesn't wick to the drier surrounding soil after planting. If soil drains slowly, then apply water until it puddles, shut off the flow, allow water to percolate into soil, then water again until water has penetrated to 18 to 24 inches deep. Deep watering leaches out any salt accumulations, gets water to deeply growing roots, and prepares the soil for cultivation and fertilizing.

- Fertilize only moist soil, when you see new green growth, and when you have researched the plants to determine if they even need fertilizer. Some groundcovers and vines prefer lean soils. Fertilizing them when they don't require it can lead to root or leaf burn or kill the plant due to toxicity.

MAY

- When you plant a vine, provide the supports it needs as soon as you install it. It may be too small to tie to the support, but come back in a few weeks when it has sent out new growth. Tie it as soon as you can without bending the plant or bruising the stem.

- Flats of groundcovers are the best buy for planting large areas. When you remove the mass from the flat, use a sharp knife and cut the flat into 2-inch sections, just as if you were cutting a cake. Don't worry about damaging the roots; you will likely be stimulating them to grow.

- It is easier to run drip tubing in a new groundcover bed before you plant. Anchor the lines in place and run the system for at least 10 minutes to see how the flow distributes and to gauge the run times needed to get the water to at least 6 inches deep to accommodate new young roots.

JUNE

- Check the mulch between young groundcover plants and around vines after some growth has occurred, then top off the mulch. Depending upon the maximum height of the plant, mulch at least 2 inches for groundcovers, 3 to 4 inches for vines. As groundcovers grow, they shade their own roots, thereby forming their own mulch.

- If you compost vine clippings and prunings, then use jute twine to tie them to supports. Plastic ties do not break down; they just become brittle and break into teeny-tiny pieces so you will find yourself picking them out of the compost forever.

- If you plant new vines and groundcovers this month, maintaining soil moisture is key to getting them through transplant stress and actively growing before heat sets in. If they are interplanted with other landscape plants that need less water, then supplement them by handwatering, adding emitters to the drip line, or running a temporary soaker hose.

JULY

- When temperatures heat up, the real damage is the effects of rising soil temperatures on roots. When plants wilt, it may be because the soil is dry or the roots are hot. Deeply water the plant (if soil is dry) and make sure it has mulch. If a plant is not regaining turgidity by the end of the day, rig up some temporary shade. Do not hose off the leaves to cool the plant. Heat accelerates the rate of evaporation from the leaves, causing tip burn.

- Weeds not only look unsightly, they are also water hogs and are a magnet for pests. If the area is mulched, the weeds will slide out easily. If they are annual weeds, just cut them off at ground level. They will die without completing their life cycle or setting seed.

- Use a light hand when fertilizing groundcovers and vines when temps heat up. Containers receive water once or twice daily and are planted with soilless mixes, so nutrients leach out quickly. Apply water-soluble fertilizers once each week to containers or use a timed-release fertilizer as a topdressing. Fertilize only damp soil.

AUGUST

- Some vines seem to grow before your eyes. As you travel around the garden, take your clippers and loppers to trim errant growth as you see it. This eliminates major pruning when they get out of hand.

- Wind is common in August. Leaning supports, insufficient ties, branches loaded with foliage and/or blooms are subject to blowing over, broken or damaged branches, dehydration, and loss of flowers in heavy winds. Check supports, add ties, and keep the soil moist. Check plants after winds to see what repairs are needed. Plants you watered that morning may need water again after a windstorm.

- Clinging groundcovers that spread by surface roots can creep into adjacent areas without an invitation. How rude. Contain them by taking a spade and making sharp vertical cuts to sever the roots. Then pull up the invading parts and plant elsewhere, gift to friends, or compost.

SEPTEMBER

- Cooling temperatures make groundcovers and vines (and humans) happy. They will require less water now so check the soil before you water. Use your index finger to dig through the mulch and into the soil. If the soil is dry beyond your second joint, water deeply.

- Less watering and lush growth brings pests, especially if there are no summer monsoons to wash them off. Try hosing off the undersides of the plant leaves (aphids) and stems (mealybugs and scale) to control. Syringe foliage in the early morning hours so it dries before the heat of the day.

- Plant vines and groundcovers so they're established before cold weather slows them down or freezing temps push them into dormancy. Container plants purchased at this time of year are most likely potbound. Before planting, cut off the bottom inch of root mass and make four vertical cuts with clippers around the rootball. Otherwise, the roots will continue to wrap, eventually girdling (strangling) the plant and new root growth will be stunted.

OCTOBER

- Vines and groundcovers that give fall foliage color are better performers if the water is cut off when they start showing color. The plants are headed into dormancy at the time and need to toughen up for winter, so just sit back and enjoy the show.

- Start weaning plants for winter. Cut back on watering, allowing the soil to dry between waterings. Evergreen groundcovers and vines only need watering every couple of weeks. Deciduous types can be shut off completely.

- Newly planted vines and groundcovers may need deep watering once a week in warmer-winter zones until they start sending out new growth. Make sure they have plenty of mulch and if no freezing weather occurs in your area, a dose of timed-release fertilizer will get them growing through the warm winter months.

NOVEMBER

- Check supports for vines before the snow flies. While it is too late to prune dense branch works, added supports, wires, or cross beams can save the plant from breaking under snow load.

- If you chose vines and groundcovers that are on the fringes of your USDA cold hardiness zone, then cover them with a thick 6- to 12-inch layer of mulch for winter protection. If you can get the plant to maturity, then it will be more likely to acclimate to your zone. Pull the mulch off to expose the green growth in spring, leaving 4 inches of mulch for the growing season.

- In low-desert areas, you still need to water, but with less frequency. If the soil is moist and the night brings a freeze, then the moisture keeps the plant turgid. Damp soil holds heat longer than dry soil, effectively insulating the plant roots.

DECEMBER

- Evergreens in cold winter climates need less water than during the growing season. If you go without rain or snow for over a month, then wait for the sun to warm the soil, water deeply and slowly. If the ground is frozen, then wait until spring thaw to water. If the plant is established, it will most likely be able to make it through winter without supplemental watering.

- Warm winter gardens require less water now too. Water established plants monthly if no rain, and new plantings every two weeks. Don't fertilize and maintain a thick layer of mulch to protect the plants from cold and occasional frosts.

- Overwinter vines and groundcovers in containers in a cool room or greenhouse. As long as the storage space doesn't fall below freezing and the air is moving, then the plants should survive. Water deeply with room temperature water when the soil dries to a few inches deep. If single-digit night temps are forecast for outdoors, then wrap the pots in burlap or blankets to protect the roots from freezing. Keep a fan running day and night for air movement.

PERENNIALS
for the Southwest

Perennials are a diverse group, some filling spaces as clumping plants in the flower garden and the same plant serving as a groundcover in the bulb bed. For example, my yarrow plants began as a small grouping, but now are colonized, forming many plants that softly creep along the surface of the soil, meandering under a juniper tree, and serving as foil to the spring-blooming bulbs. Yarrow that is mowed makes a soft, walkable lawn substitute. Planted *en masse* on a slope, it anchors the soil. The many cultivars now available bring mixed colors to the cut flower bed. Think outside of the box when designing with perennials. They are the ultimate multi-purpose plant.

Perennials begin in spring as small tufts of green, barely visible to a passerby, but with your gardener's nose to the ground, you can see them almost the very minute they poke up through the mulch. Growing all season, they put on as much as 5 feet of growth in just a few months. In warmer-winter areas, perennials are a presence in the garden year-round, filling spaces with green leafy foliage that forms a backdrop to other bloomers or adding continuous colored blooms during the growing season. They slow in growth during winter or summer, barely noticed except by the gardener tending them, but after this brief period, they come back refreshed and vigorous.

PERENNIALS TALK TO YOU

If they are given a well-draining soil, water, and summer and winter mulch protection, they thrive. I have planted perennials in dappled shade even though they prefer full sun, but they tolerate part shade in hot summer areas (which is what we have in Utah). Years later, that dappled shade turned to full, dense shade and while the plants still sent out new growth in spring and grew, they were lanky things, with few to no flowers. Perennials send signals when they are not happy in their environment. Not enough water (wilting, no new growth), too much sun (leathery, burned leaves), no wind protection (defoliation), too lean soil (stunting, nutrient deficiencies) are some of the ways they communicate. Rather than expend efforts in trying to make the situation right, move them to a better spot more to their liking.

Make the change in spring or fall, so you are not uprooting them in triple-digit heat or when frost threatens. Using a round-point shovel, dig around where you think the rootmass might extend, pry it up and carry it, soil and all, to its new location. Dig a hole in the new home before the transport, plop the perennial into it, burying it at the same level it was before. Leave the hose to trickle into the area while you do something else, so the water seeps slowly into the soil, reaching the entire root mass. Then top with 3 to 4 inches of mulch and cut back the foliage by half. The perennial that's been moved will most likely send out new growth right away, its way of giving a nod of approval for the move. If you still note signs of struggle, leave it there for a season to see if it acclimates. If it doesn't, then you can move it again.

Perennials are most often available in containers at your local garden centers and home-improvement stores. Spring offerings are released earlier than the last frost date and are shipped directly from the production greenhouse to the garden centers. While they are lush with foliage and blooms, the growth is soft, so they need a few weeks of getting used to still-cool days and nights and barely warming soils before planting in the ground. Mail-order plants increase your options for trying new types and hybrids not available locally and they usually are timed to ship after your last frost date.

GROWING PERENNIALS FROM SEED

Some perennials grow easily from direct-sown seed, which is an option to grow new types and to grow a lot of them inexpensively. Direct-sow *Rudbeckia*, *Gaillardia*, *Aurinia*, *Coreopsis*, and *Echinacea* into the garden in fall. They naturalize and reseed freely. Some perennials are a bit more challenging, requiring sowing seed in flats indoors or in a greenhouse. They need a grow mat for bottom heat, a very lightweight soil mix, grow lights or bright natural light for most of the day, and then transplanting to pots and hardening off before planting outdoors. Unlike annuals that need only four to six weeks to grow from seed to plant, perennials need eight to twelve weeks due to a longer germination window, slower growth, and transplant establishment. Agastache, oregano, globemallow, and candytuft are just a few to try. If you can fulfill their needs, then sowing perennials from seed is gratifying, as well as a substantial money saver.

PERENNIALS ARE UNDEMANDING

Outside of a seasonal pruning and occasional deadheading, perennials really grow on their own. In warm-winter areas, prune old growth to shape or to revitalize in fall. In cold-winter areas where perennials go dormant, prune old stems to new green growth in spring. Don't be impatient and prune early, as new soft growth is subject to freeze burn in late season frosts. Wait until the plant has a good 4 inches or so of new growth before you prune.

Always mulch right after planting, refresh in spring, create a thicker layer in cold-winter areas or when you are trying a perennial on the edge of your cold hardiness zone. If you can get it established and growing through three seasons, then it will acclimate to its new zone. That's one more notch in your seasoned gardener's cap!

A well-draining soil is key to perennial health and if they have that, then most obtain all the nutrients they need from the soil. A few like a boost in spring, so time the fertilizer application and the type of fertilizer so you can feed adjoining or companion plants at the same time. Balanced, timed-release fertilizers work for most garden plants. As it is with with all plants, if you notice deficiency signs that are not corrected by deep watering, mulching to cool the soil, protection from the elements or pests, then fertilize. If all seems right in the garden, then don't change anything.

PLANTING

Plant them singly in beds or containers, serving as a focal point with their foliage or blooms. Repeat them throughout the landscape. The repetition of form, foliage, and flower brings continuity and flow to the garden. Perennials are easy to grow, versatile in their uses, not picky in their demands, congenial with bedfellows, cooperative with their caretakers, and not adverse to change.

Need I say more?

Sow perennial seed directly into packs or cells for easy transplanting later.

To hold in moisture, cover the seed flats at night until germination.

ARTEMESIA
Artemisia spp.

Why It's Special—Low-growing, mounding, and sprawling artemisia covers slopes; shrubby types, with gnarled woody trunks, crawl over boulders and rock walls; upright types draw the eye to the midground in shrub beds with foliage that makes all other colors pop!

How to Plant & Grow—Plant in spring or summer in warmer climates; otherwise, plant in spring or early autumn. In extreme summer heat locations, site for afternoon shade. Plant in well-worked, well-draining soil. No amendments are needed but mulch 3 to 4 inches. Deeply water two to three times a week for a month to establish, allowing soil to dry between waterings.

Care & Problems—Stem rot and mildew occur in high humidity or slow-draining soils, but no pests bother it. No fertilizer is needed. Prune to the ground in spring to rejuvenate. It's drought tolerant when established.

Water Needs—Water deeply, weekly when it's over 90 degrees Fahrenheit; otherwise, twice monthly. No winter watering except in extended droughts.

Bloom Color—Insignificant

Peak Season—Silver-gray, blue, white, icy green evergreen foliage

Mature Size (H x W)—1 to 4 feet x 1 to 5 feet

BARRENWORT
Epimedium spp. and hybrids

Why It's Special—Barrenwort is notable for its heart-shaped, pink-tinged leaves that emerge in spring, turning lime to dark green, and finally bronze-red in fall, persisting into winter. Loose clusters of small, delicate blooms grow profusely, adding color and texture to this beautiful plant. Use in understory plantings, *en masse*, or in drifts.

How to Plant & Grow—Plant in early spring into a peat-, humus-, or compost-amended, slightly acidic, well-draining soil. Water deeply two to three times a week for a month to establish. Add 2 to 3 inches of pine or bark mulch.

Care & Problems—Prune only to remove winter-damaged foliage in spring, cutting almost to the ground. Fertilize after bloom to encourage foliage growth. Use a timed-release fertilizer; water afterwards to avoid foliage burn. No pests or diseases bother barrenwort.

Water Needs—Water deeply twice weekly in summer, once week in spring, fall. Water as needed to maintain moisture in winter unless it's dormant.

Bloom Color—Yellow, white, pink, red

Peak Season—Spring

Mature Size (H x W)—8 to 18 inches x 24 to 36 inches

BASKET-OF-GOLD
Aurinia saxatilis

Why It's Special—Basket-of-gold makes showy hanging baskets. Even when it's not covered in golden-yellow blooms, its gray-green foliage adds contrast to the garden. Plant in drifts under the dappled shade of a trees, *en masse* along an entranceway or lining a foot path, grouped in the foreground as filler in the perennial bed, in rock gardens, and along the edge of dry streambeds.

How to Plant & Grow—Plant in spring or early fall into well-worked, well-draining soil. In the hottest summer regions, it appreciates part shade in the afternoon. Water deeply; add 3 to 4 inches of mulch. Allow the soil to dry a bit, water deeply once a week until sending out new growth.

Care & Problems—No pests or diseases bother it. After blooming, cut back plants by half to encourage bushy growth. No fertilizer is needed. It's drought tolerant once established.

Water Needs—Water deeply, infrequently, allowing soil to dry between waterings.

Bloom Color—Yellow

Peak Season—Late winter to spring

Mature Size (H x W)—9 to 12 inches x 12 inches

BEAR'S BREECHES
Acanthus mollis

Why It's Special—Tropical-looking foliage and dramatic tall flower spikes make bear's breeches a good choice for brightening a dark entryway, interplanting with ferns, drifting under the dappled shade of tree canopies, covering an open sunny area with foliage, or filling an urn in an interior plantscape.

How to Plant & Grow—Plant in spring into well-worked, well-draining soil. It grows in any soil, but quickly establishes in compost-amended soil. Site in part sun to part shade, or in full shade in low-desert regions. Water deeply, weekly for its first season to establish. Add 3 to 4 inches of mulch.

Care & Problems—Snails and slugs hide under dense foliage. If a plant completely dries in summer, it may go dormant. This plant can invade other beds so allow plenty of room to grow or use a weed-barrier fabric or edging to contain.

Water Needs—Water deeply and regularly through the growing seasons, less in winter.

Bloom Color—Spring through summer

Peak Season—White, purple

Mature Size (H x W)—4 to 5 feet x 3 feet

Hardiness—Zones 6 to 10

BEEBALM
Monarda didyma

Why It's Special—Beebalm is aptly named but it is also beloved by hummingbirds and butterflies. Site it where you can watch the show while it blooms for two months. Plant groupings in the perennial garden at midground so nearby plants provide interest when beebalm is not blooming. Use it singly or in combinations in container gardens, in the herb garden, or drifting in and out of the shrub bed.

How to Plant & Grow—Sow seed in packs six to eight weeks before planting in spring or plant container-grown seedlings into deeply worked, amended, well-draining soil. Water deeply and frequently to establish. Apply 3 to 4 inches of mulch.

Care & Problems—Beebalm is prone to powdery mildew; plant disease-resistant cultivars. Give it room to grow to accommodate invasive tendencies or plant in lean, dry, unamended soil to restrict its spread. In temperate climates, it is short-lived. Deadhead to encourage blooming.

Water Needs—Provide deep, regular watering if there's no rain or snow.

Bloom Color—Pink, rose, purple, white

Peak Season—Summer

Mature Size (H x W)—1 to 3 feet x 2 to 4 feet

BERGENIA
Bergenia cordifolia

Why It's Special—Bergenia is favored for its foliage with some cultivars showing brilliant maroon and bronze fall color. When it blooms, bright flower clusters stand above mounded foliage, forming a living bouquet. Use in containers, in sweeps along a drive, and in the foreground of borders.

How to Plant & Grow—Plant in spring as soon as ground can be worked. In hot-desert climates, plant in fall in part-sun to part-shade sites. Bergenia goes dormant in cold winters. Plant in any deeply worked, well-draining soil. Amend the site with compost for better performance. Water deeply, and top with 3 to 4 inches of mulch.

Care & Problems—Watch out for slugs and snails. Cut bergenia back yearly to promote bushiness; divide only when it's overcrowded, in late winter or early spring, before or after bloom. Fertilize in early spring with a timed-release fertilizer.

Water Needs—Water deeply, twice a week in summer; water once weekly otherwise.

Bloom Color—Red, lilac, pink, purple, white

Peak Season—Midwinter, late spring, early summer

Mature Size (H x W)—18 to 20 inches x 18 to 20 inches

BLANKET FLOWER
Gaillardia × grandiflora

Why It's Special—Blanket flower is native to the Southwest, a sign of its durability. This long-season bloomer partners well with other flowering plants in containers, provides loads of flower's when planted in drifts at meadow edges, in sweeps in perennial beds, or in groups in the foreground of xeric gardens.

How to Plant & Grow—Sow seed or plant seedlings in spring after the last frost into well-draining, well-worked, unamended soil. Incorporate a timed-release fertilizer into the backfill. Keep the seedbed moist until germination. Mulch 3 to 4 inches deep. Water plants deeply, once a week through the first summer to establish; allow soil to dry a bit between waterings.

Care & Problems—Choose mildew-resistant types in humid areas. If plants grow slowly or lack vigor, apply a water-soluble fertilizer in spring. No pests or diseases bother it. Deadhead to encourage blooming. It's drought tolerant.

Water Needs—Water deeply every two weeks in summer; monthly in fall and spring. Don't water in winter if it's dormant.

Bloom Color—Yellow, red

Peak Season—Spring to frost

Mature Size (H x W)—1 to 2 feet x 1 to 2 feet

BRITTLEBUSH
Encelia farinosa

Why It's Special—Brittlebush does have brittle branches, but its bushy, open habit allows wind to pass freely through it and the sun to reach its branches, contributing to profuse blooms. Grow *en masse* and in sweeps, on slopes, hillsides, in open areas interplanted with other xeric plants. Mimic nature in your landscape and it will thrive.

How to Plant & Grow—Plant in fall into well-draining, well-worked, unamended soil. Water deeply every two to four days for two to three weeks, then every four to seven days until established. Apply a 3- to 4-inch layer of mulch.

Care & Problems—Overwatering and constantly wet soil lead to root rot and plant stress. After blooming, prune back by one-third to encourage bushiness. Occasionally aphids bother it, but otherwise no pests or diseases. No fertilizer is needed.

Water Needs—Water weekly in fall and spring, except when temperatures exceed 90 degrees Fahrenheit, water twice weekly. Water monthly then in fall and winter if there's no precipitation.

Bloom Color—Yellow

Peak Season—Late fall to early spring

Mature Size (H x W)—3 to 4 feet x 3 to 4 feet

CALIFORNIA FUCHSIA

Zauschneria californica

Why It's Special—California fuchsia resembles the thirsty fuchsia hybrids, but only in its prolific tubular blooms, as it is very drought and heat tolerant. Plant singly in pots or as focal point; planted *en masse* it puts on a big show.

How to Plant & Grow—Plant in spring into well-worked, well-draining, lightly compost-amended soil. Site in partly shaded locations in hotter deserts. It's hardy to Zone 7. Water deeply every two to four days for two to three weeks, then every four to seven days until established. Add 3 inches of mulch.

Care & Problems—Prune hard to a few inches tall in late winter in frost-free, warm-winter areas; in spring in cooler climates. Apply a timed-release fertilizer in early spring and in fall. No pests or diseases, although mildew may occur with overhead watering.

Water Needs—In hot summer climes, water deeply once a week. In cooler summer areas, water every 10 to 14 days; intermittently otherwise.

Bloom Color—Orange, red

Peak Season—Summer to fall

Mature Size (H x W)—1 to 2 feet x 2 to 3 feet

CANDYTUFT

Iberis sempervirens

Why It's Special—Candytuft is evergreen in temperate zones, semi-evergreen elsewhere. Its real show is in the pure, bright white flowers. Use this feature to highlight container plantings, in the foreground of color borders, *en masse* to outline perennial gardens, or to line a path in night gardens.

How to Plant & Grow—Plant in early spring or fall, into well-worked, compost-amended, well-draining soil. Incorporate timed release fertilizer into the backfill. Sow seed in flats or direct sow when air temperatures are 60 degrees Fahrenheit or warmer. Water deeply and regularly until established. Mulch 3 inches.

Care & Problems—Candytuft grows more lushly and requires less water in part-sun to part-shade locations where plants can grow in the same spot for a long time. After blooms fade, cut back by two-thirds to encourage bushiness. It doesn't suffer from any pests or disease. No fertilizer is required.

Water Needs—When temperatures exceed 95 degrees Fahrenheit, water weekly. Otherwise, water deeply every two weeks or monthly in cooler temperatures.

Bloom Color—White

Peak Season—Spring

Mature Size (H x W)—4 to 6 inches x 18 inches

CARDINAL FLOWER

Lobelia spp.

Why It's Special—Cardinal flower, *Lobelia cardinalis*, is suited for moist, woodland sites, and Mexican lobelia, *L. laxiflora*, for xeric sites. Both are native to their specific regions, making them tough, durable plants if their natural habitats are duplicated. Use cardinal flower in drifts as background shrubs in bog plantings. Plant Mexican lobelia along dry streambeds that meander through the dappled shade of a grove of trees.

How to Plant & Grow—Plant after danger of frost is passed into deeply worked, compost-enriched, well-draining soil. Water deeply until established. Cover with 3 to 4 inches of mulch.

Care & Problems—No fertilizing is needed. Deadhead to encourage blooming. Prune old growth in spring as plants come out of dormancy. *L. laxiflora* is subject to root rot if installed in cold, wet soils. No pests or diseases bother *Lobelia*.

Water Needs—Maintain deep, regular watering for moist soil; weekly in summer; twice monthly in spring and fall; monthly in winter.

Bloom Color—Orange, yellow, red, pink, white, scarlet

Peak Season—Late spring to midsummer; summer to autumn

Mature Size (H x W)—3 feet x 2 to 3 feet

CATMINT
Nepeta × faassenii

Why It's Special—Catmint thrives in drought, heat, wind, poor soils, and is cold hardy. This sterile hybrid is a compact, tidy mound made up of small silver leaves that fill garden borders and perennial beds with texture and contrast. The continuous blooms, except when temperatures soar consistently above 90 degrees Fahrenheit, bring nonstop color garden from spring to frost.

How to Plant & Grow—Plant in spring or summer into well-worked, well-draining, unamended soil. Choose a site in afternoon shade in hot, humid locations. Water deeply, allowing soil to dry between waterings. Mulch 3 to 4 inches.

Care & Problems—Pinch back midseason to encourage rebloom if catmint falters in the heat. Cats will roll on plantings, so protect new plantings for about two years until established, and protect new spring growth. It isn't bothered by pests and doesn't need fertilizer.

Water Needs—Water deeply every two weeks if temperatures exceed 70 degrees Fahrenheit; monthly in cool weather. Don't water during winter dormancy.

Bloom Color—Violet-blue, pink

Peak Season—Summer to fall

Mature Size (H x W)—1 to 4 feet x 2 to 3 feet

CHOCOLATE FLOWER
Berlandiera lyrata

Why It's Special—Chocolate flower is a hardy perennial with tidy tufts of deeply divided foliage that stay low to the ground, holding delicate flowers that release its heavenly chocolate aroma. It's the perfect filler for tiny crevices in rock gardens, containers sited closely to seating areas, natural drifts in meadow or scented gardens, or naturalized among the wildflowers in a xeric landscape.

How to Plant & Grow—Plant in fall or early spring in well-draining, deeply worked, native soil. Water deeply every two to four days for two to three weeks; then, every four to seven days to establish.

Care & Problems—Deadhead to encourage blooming. No fertilizer is needed. It suffers from no pests or diseases. It may reseed freely; transplant or let seedlings grow. They are not invasive.

Water Needs—Deeply water every four to seven days in hot, dry summers; otherwise water only to supplement in drought. Water every two months if there are no winter rains.

Bloom Color—Yellow

Peak Season—Spring through summer

Mature Size (H x W)—1 to 2 feet x 1 to 2 feet

COLUMBINE
Aquilegia spp.

Why It's Special—There is a columbine for every garden; many are native to our local regions. Woodland gardens with moist soils and full shade are home to freely reseeding *Aquilegia formosa*; you barely notice the three- to four-year-old mother plants fading away. Heat-tough *A. chrysantha* thrives in low deserts. *A. coerulea*, from the Rocky Mountains, grow at high elevations, reappearing after winter dormancy.

How to Plant & Grow—Plant in fall in temperate winters or spring into compost-amended, deeply worked, well-draining soil. Water deeply every two to four days for three weeks; then, water every four to seven days until new growth appears. Add 3 to 4 inches of mulch.

Care & Problems—Deadhead to discourage reseeding. Cut back old growth in spring when new growth appears. No fertilizer. Columbine has occasional aphids or scale on hybrids.

Water Needs—Water deeply, regularly weekly during blooming; every two weeks other times, monthly in cool weather, none if dormant.

Bloom Color—Blue, yellow, red

Peak Season—Spring to fall

Mature Size (H x W)—2 to 4 feet x 1 to 2 feet

COREOPSIS
Coreopsis spp. and hybrids

Why It's Special—Coreopsis is drought, heat, cold, sun, and wind tolerant; adapts to any soil; comes in clumping, spreading or colonizing forms; blooms profusely throughout the season; and needs little attention once established. Use the many *Coreopsis* species and hybrids to cover slopes, fill beds, accent containers, add a spot of color to xeric gardens, or permit them to self-sow in the meadow garden.

How to Plant & Grow—Plant in spring after last frost into deeply worked, compost-amended, well-draining soil. Water deeply every few days until established. Apply 3 to 4 inches of mulch.

Care & Problems—Deadhead in summer to encourage blooming; cease in fall to permit reseeding. Cut back old foliage in spring when new growth appears. Watch out for spittlebug. Use water-soluble fertilizer in spring. Divide naturalizing, spreading types every three to four years in fall. Refresh mulch in spring.

Water Needs—Water deeply, infrequently, allowing soil to dry in-between.

Bloom Color—Yellow, white, pink, rose

Peak Season—Spring through fall

Mature Size (H x W)—1 to 3 feet x 1 to 2 feet

CRANESBILL
Erodium spp.

Why It's Special—Cranesbill is a geranium relative, but unlike *Pelargonium*, *Erodium* species are cold and heat hardy, growing in Zones 4 to 9. Cranesbill are low-growing, mounding plants with beautiful foliage from gray-green and deeply divided to dark green and scalloped. They're excellent choices for tucking into rock gardens, along dry streambeds, and into containers. All species offer profuse blooms that persist throughout the season, blanketing the plants in color, making them perfect for color borders, perennial bed fillers, and hanging baskets.

How to Plant & Grow—Plant in spring into well-worked, well-draining soil amended with compost. Water deeply and regularly until established. Top with 2 inches of mulch.

Care & Problems—Stem rot occurs in cool, wet soils, but no pests or diseases otherwise. Fertilize in early spring with a water-soluble fertilizer. Divide overgrown plants in spring.

Water Needs—Deeply water, allowing the soil to dry a bit between waterings. Water monthly in winter.

Bloom Color—Pink, white, lavender, yellow

Peak Season—Spring to fall

Mature Size (H x W)—6 inches x 12 inches

CUP FLOWER
Nierembergia linariifolia

Why It's Special—Cup flower is heat, drought, and humidity tolerant. It adds texture to the perennial garden with its foliage, and its profuse cup-shaped blooms bring color to the garden during the heat of summer. Plant singly in container gardens or window boxes and in the rock garden; plant in drifts along a path or in groups as a border.

How to Plant & Grow—Plant in spring or summer in well-draining, well-worked soil. Amendments spur vigorous growth. Deeply water, regularly, until it sends out new growth.

Care & Problems—Provide supplemental timed-release fertilizer in spring when plants are growing vigorously. Cut back old growth in spring when new growth appears. Mulch in fall for extra winter protection. Watch for spider mites in dry weather.

Water Needs—Deeply water weekly in summer; twice-monthly spring and fall. No watering in winter.

Bloom Color—Purple, white

Peak Season—Summer

Mature Size (H x W)—4 to 15 inches x 8 to 15 inches

Hardiness—Zones 6 to 10. It's cold hardy with protection to Zone 6. Use it as an annual in colder climes.

DALMATIAN BELLFLOWER
Campanula poscharskyana

Why It's Special—Dalmatian bellflower loves the shade, adding it to the short list of shade-loving perennials. It flowers over a long season and takes a few years to establish, but its foliage and flowers brighten dark entryways, courtyards, and form broad sweeps under dappled shade canopies.

How to Plant & Grow—Plant into well-worked, compost-enriched, well-draining soil. Plant in full shade in hot summer locales. Water deeply. Add 2 to 3 inches of mulch. Maintain even moisture until it's established.

Care & Problems—If planted in compost-enriched soil, no fertilizer is needed. Deadhead to encourage more blooms. Cut to the ground in fall or early spring to keep plants compact and tidy. No pests or diseases bother it. Foliage yellows if it's planted in a too-dry, hot location. Divide in autumn or early spring to control size.

Water Needs—Water deeply, weekly when temperatures exceed 80 degrees Fahrenheit; twice-monthly at 60 to 80 degrees Fahrenheit; monthly in cool weather if there's no rain.

Bloom Color—Blue-purple, white

Peak Season—Spring to summer

Mature Size (H x W)—6 inches x 18 inches

DESERT MARIGOLD
Baileya multiradiata

Why It's Special—Desert marigold is native to Nevada, making it heat and drought tolerant. It is a heavy, long-season bloomer, which leads to reseeding and colonizing but it's not invasive. It is a compact, mounding plant with marigold-like blooms, flowering in early spring and may give year-round blooms if given a drink of water occasionally in winter. Use singly in containers, *en masse* in meadow plantings or hillsides, and in drifts in the perennial garden.

How to Plant & Grow—Plant in spring into well-worked, well-draining soil. No amendments are needed. Water deeply. Add 3 to 4 inches of mulch. Sow seed in spring or fall, rake to lightly cover, water until germinated. Add an inch of mulch when plants are 4 inches tall.

Care & Problems—Don't fertilize. Deadhead or leave seed to self-sow. If plants have lanky growth, prune close to the ground in fall.

Water Needs—Water deeply, weekly in summer; twice-monthly otherwise.

Bloom Color—Yellow

Peak Season—Spring through winter (in temperate zones)

Mature Size (H x W)—1 foot x 1 foot

DIANTHUS
Dianthus spp.

Why It's Special—Dianthus is lush, flowers profusely, and is deliciously scented. One would think it would guzzle water, fizzle out early, and only be available from a florist, but dianthus is heat, drought, and cold tolerant, adding texture with gray-green foliage and color from its blooms on strong stems. Use in containers, borders, rock gardens, perennial beds, and cutting gardens.

How to Plant & Grow—Plant in spring or early fall into well-worked, amended, well-draining soil. Water deeply, allowing soil to dry between waterings, until established. Direct-sow seed in spring when temperatures reach 60 degrees Fahrenheit. Keep seedbeds moist until germination. Mulch when plants are 4 to 6 inches tall.

Care & Problems—Don't fertilize. There aren't any pests, but it's susceptible to fusarium wilt and powdery mildew; avoid overwatering. Deadhead to encourage bloom. Cut back winter damage in spring.

Water Needs—Water deeply weekly when temperatures exceed 85 degrees Fahrenheit. Water every two weeks otherwise; monthly if it's not dormant in winter.

Bloom Color—Pink, white, yellow, orange, red

Peak Season—Spring to fall

Mature Size (H x W)—6 to 15 inches x 8 to 24 inches

ECHINACEA
Echinacea hybrids

Why It's Special—Echinacea is prized for its blooms by gardeners, butterflies, bees, and birds. Tall, strong flower stalks persist even in windy conditions. Use groupings at meadow edges, midground in cut flower or perennial gardens, and in drifts among shrubs in xeric landscapes.

How to Plant & Grow—Plant into unamended, well-worked, well-draining soil. Deeply water. Add 3 to 4 inches of mulch. In the hottest summers, plant in part sun to part shade. Water deeply every two to four days for two to three weeks, then every four to seven days until established.

Care & Problems—If plants show deficiencies, apply slow-release fertilizer in spring before refreshing mulch. Overfertilizing causes legginess. Powdery mildew occurs in full shade. Divide in spring if needed, every five years. Cut back stalks in early spring to new green growth.

Water Needs—Water deeply twice a week in low-desert areas; weekly or every two weeks in cooler summer areas. Don't water in winter if it's dormant.

Bloom Color—Purple, pink, yellow, white, orange

Peak Season—Spring to fall

Mature Size (H x W)—2 to 4 feet x 2 to 3 feet

ELDERBERRY
Sambucus canadensis

Why It's Special—Elderberry are grown for their foliage, flowers, and fruit. Many cultivars offer variously colored foliage, larger blooms, brilliant red fruits, and fall colors. Grow elderberry as a bushy shrub in the landscape, as background plantings, screens, outdoor room enclosures, and hedges. For better fruiting, grow cross-pollinators.

How to Plant & Grow—Plant in spring or early summer in slightly acidic, moist soil. *Sambucus* tolerates slightly alkaline soils; amend with peat or compost before planting. Water deeply. Add 3 to 4 inches of mulch. Keep moist until established.

Care & Problems—Prune to the ground each spring for bushy growth for ornamental use; for fruiting, prune older, weakened canes, avoid cutting previous season growth. If plants are stunted, slow-growing, or lack fruit, fertilize with timed-release fertilizer in spring. Too much nitrogen or water-soluble fertilizer causes legginess. Refresh mulch. Watch for aphids and spider mites.

Water Needs—Deeply water every two weeks in summer, less often in spring and fall, and none in winter.

Bloom Color—Greenish white

Peak Season—Summer

Mature Size (H x W)—8 to 12 feet x 6 to 8 feet

FALSE INDIGO
Baptisia australis

Why It's Special—False indigo is a prairie native, making it at home in meadow plantings. It's also used in perennial borders, grouped as a focal point, and in drifts along a sunny drive. It is a colonizing plant-it-and-walk-away perennial that never needs dividing. Its deep taproots anchor it to the ground and also make it drought tolerant, and it is a legume so never needs fertilizing.

How to Plant & Grow—Plant in late spring or early summer into any soil that is well draining and well worked. Do not amend or incorporate fertilizer. Water deeply, regularly just to establish. Add 3 to 4 inches of mulch.

Care & Problems—No pests or disease bother *Baptisia*. Cut plants back in late spring to new green growth. Stake if they topple over in too-fertile soils or dense shade. Don't fertilize. Refresh mulch in spring. Deadhead to encourage longer bloom period.

Water Needs—Water deeply, irregularly in drought conditions, then only when soil is dry or plants wilt.

Bloom Color—Purple, yellow, white

Peak Season—Spring, summer

Mature Size (H x W)—3 to 5 feet x 3 to 5 feet

GARDEN MUM
Chrysanthemum spp. and hybrids

Why It's Special—Hardier than related florist's mum, garden mums tolerate cold winters, going dormant after fall bloom and hot summers if given water and afternoon shade. Plant in drifts in the dappled shade of trees, *en masse* to line driveways or paths, in groups in perennial borders, and in containers.

How to Plant & Grow—Plant in early spring, late summer, or fall into compost-amended, well-worked, well-draining soil. Stick cuttings directly into the garden in late spring into warm soil. Dappled or afternoon shade is fine, but dense shade is not. Water deeply. Add 3 to 4 inches of mulch. Maintain regular, deep watering until established.

Care & Problems—Provide water-soluble fertilizer monthly during the growing season or add timed-release fertilizer in spring. Pinch back by half in late spring for bushiness. Deadhead to encourage blooms. Aphids may occur, but no diseases. Keep mulched.

Water Needs—Water deeply once or twice per week to maintain even moisture.

Bloom Color—All except blue

Peak Season—Summer to winter

Mature Size (H x W)—1 to 2 feet x 1 to 2 feet

GAURA
Gaura lindheimeri

Why It's Special—Gaura is a reliable, long-blooming, heat-loving, drought-tolerant perennial that grows wild along undisturbed roadsides. It is a prolific bloomer, open and airy with little foliage, so its blooms are the stars. Many cultivars offer fragrant blooms, variegated foliage, or compact growth. Plant it singly in pots, in drifts in meadows, perennial beds, and in cut-flower gardens.

How to Plant & Grow—Plant in spring or summer in low elevations, in fall or spring in higher elevations into well-worked, well-draining, native soil. Deeply water every two to three days for two to three weeks, then every four to seven days until established.

Care & Problems—Do not fertilize. Prune in spring to remove winter damage. Deadhead to encourage blooms. It has no pests or diseases. Gaura is short-lived in too-rich soils or low-desert climates. Leaf spot will occur in too-shady locations. Refresh mulch in spring.

Water Needs—Water deeply weekly in hot summers; elsewhere twice per month. Water monthly in winter if there's no rain.

Bloom Color—White, pink

Peak Season—Spring to fall

Mature Size (H x W)—2 to 4 feet x 3 to 5 feet

GLOBEMALLOW
Sphaeralcea spp.

Why It's Special—Native to Utah, globemallow grows and reseeds easily once established, but it's not invasive. When not blanketed in flowers, the almost-white foliage brings contrast to other plants. Use in drifts throughout the garden, colonize it for a natural look, and combine it with perennials and grasses.

How to Plant & Grow—Plant in early spring or summer to establish before winter dormancy. Plant into well-worked, well-draining native soil. No amendments or fertilizer is needed. Water deeply, and mulch with 3 to 4 inches. Allow soil to dry slightly between waterings until established. After establishing, it is drought tolerant. It doesn't propagate easily from seed.

Care & Problems—Too rich soils, too much fertilizer, and too much water create lanky growth and rot. Cut back stems to new green growth in spring. No pests or diseases bother it.

Water Needs—In hottest summer regions, water deeply once every three to four weeks if there's no rain. Do not water in winter.

Bloom Color—Orange, coral pink

Peak Season—Spring, late summer, fall

Mature Size (H x W)—3 to 4 feet x 3 to 5 feet

HELLEBORE
Helleborus spp.

Why It's Special—Hellebores come in many bloom colors and range in form from shrubby evergreens to clumping deciduous types. Tolerant of alkaline or slightly acidic soils, they're best planted in groups in perennial borders, in drifts under dappled shade trees, *en masse* in shaded woodland gardens, and singly in rock gardens. The more hellebores, the bigger the show, so plan accordingly.

How to Plant & Grow—Plant in spring into compost-amended, well-worked, and well-draining soil. Incorporate a timed-release fertilizer. Water deeply and keep moist until established. Add 3 to 4 inches of mulch.

Care & Problems—Fertilize twice yearly with timed-release fertilizer. There's no need to divide and they don't like to be disturbed once established. Move volunteers in early spring. Watch for slugs and snails.

Water Needs—Water deeply once or twice per week in summer. Water weekly if there's no rain in spring, fall, or winter.

Bloom Color—White, pink, red, green, purple

Peak Season—Winter (in mild-winter areas) to spring

Mature Size (H x W)—12 to 36 inches x 18 to 36 inches

HOLLYHOCK
Alcea rosea

Why It's Special—Hollyhocks are cherished for their boisterous blooms. The old-fashioned types have single blooms on taller plants and are biennial, but some cultivars offer double blooms on stalky, branching plants that are long-lasting perennials. Grow them *en masse*, in sweeps, or in clumps for a big show.

How to Plant & Grow—Sow seed in fall or midspring when temperatures are 65 degrees Fahrenheit or more. Plant seedlings in spring into well-worked, well-draining, compost-amended soil. Keep seedbeds moist until germination; water plants deeply two to three times a week for a month. Protect from wind. Mulch 3 inches.

Care & Problems—Prune flower stalks to the ground before they scatter seeds to discourage self-sowing. Fertilize only in very sandy soils with timed-release fertilizer in spring. There are no pests, but rust is common. Slugs and snails may feed in moist areas.

Water Needs—Water deeply weekly while it's blooming; otherwise water twice monthly. Water in exended drought if it's winter dormant.

Bloom Color—White, yellow, pink, apricot, rose, red, lavender

Peak Season—Summer

Mature Size (H x W)—2 to 8 feet x 2 to 3 feet

HUMMINGBIRD MINT
Agastache spp.

Why It's Special—*Agastache* attracts hummingbirds by the droves and its foliage has a minty scent, yet it has no invasive tendencies like mint. Choose from many species, bloom colors, and growth habits to fill small spaces singly or to make bold statements planted in threes and fives in a bed, as midground plantings in shrub beds, and in scented and perennial gardens.

How to Plant & Grow—Sow seed 10 weeks before transplanting outdoors. Plant seedlings in spring after last frost into well-worked, well-draining, native soil. Water deeply every three to five days until establishment. Mulch 3 to 4 inches.

Care & Problems—Root rot occurs in cold, heavy soils. Don't fertilize. Cut back old stems to new green growth in spring. Dense shade causes lanky growth, no flowers. No pests or diseases.

Water Needs—Water deeply; weekly when temperatures exceed 85 degrees Fahrenheit, every two weeks otherwise. Water monthly if there's no rain in winter, none if it's dormant.

Bloom Color—Rose-pink, coral, lavender, yellow, violet-blue, red

Peak Season—Midsummer to frost

Mature Size (H x W)—2 to 3 feet x 1 to 3 feet

INDIAN PAINTBRUSH
Castilleja indivisa

Why It's Special—Gardeners love challenges, especially if success leads to colonies of native Indian paintbrush. It is hemiparasitic, needing host plants close by to thrive. Grasses and penstemons in meadow, prairie, or native gardens are perfect hosts, so Indian paintbrush will colonize naturally.

How to Plant & Grow—Sow seed in late summer to early fall into well-worked, moistened, well-draining soil. Sow seed in the meadow or native garden after cutting host plants very short so light can penetrate to the seed. Press seed into soil but do not cover. Keep seedbeds moist until germination, three or four months.

Care & Problems—Indian paintbrush is hard to establish as a colonizing perennial. When just a few plants have germinated and are growing, do not deadhead or prune; allow it to reseed and naturalize. Sow more seed in the area each autumn until the colony matures. Don't fertilize. No pests or diseases.

Water Needs—Supplement with overhead watering in extended drought to simulate summer rains.

Bloom Color—Red-orange

Peak Season—Spring to summer

Mature Size (H x W)—8 to 24 inches x 4 to 6 inches

JUSTICIA
Justicia spp.

Why It's Special—Justicia is favored for its year-round, prolific blooms, which it does with minimal water (once established) and even less attention. Many species, from low-growing to round, upright, and bushy, make justicia useful as a flowering groundcover on slopes, a midground landscape shrub, and grouped as nonstop bloomers in perennial beds.

How to Plant & Grow—Plant in fall or spring into lightly amended, well-worked, well-draining soil. Water deeply, twice weekly until established. Add 3 to 4 inches of mulch.

Care & Problems—Don't fertilize after its first year. To reduce size and rejuvenate, shear to 12 inches in early fall or early spring. Refresh mulch each summer. No pests or diseases bother it. Most species won't tolerate extended cold temps below 45 degrees Fahrenheit, so grow them as an annual. *Justicia californica* is cold hardy to USDA Zone 5.

Water Needs—Water deeply every week in summer; every other week in spring and fall, and monthly in winter.

Bloom Color—Red, orange, yellow, white

Peak Season—Year-round

Mature Size (H x W)—2 to 4 feet x 2 to 4 feet

LANTANA
Lantana hybrids

Why It's Special—If your site is too cold in winter (extended temperatures below 25 degrees Fahrenheit), grow as an annual. Hybrids are available in new colors and varying forms from wide spreading, trailing types for hanging baskets and groundcovers, to broad, mounding midground shrubs for drifts in perennial beds, to taller types for borders or hedges.

How to Plant & Grow—Plant in spring after the last frost into well-draining soil. Incorporate compost deeply into the soil. Mulch 3 to 4 inches. Water deeply every two to four days for two to three weeks, then every four to seven days until established.

Care & Problems—Prune winter-damaged stems to new green growth in spring. Occasionally whiteflies or aphids attack, or powdery mildew develops in humid or shady locations. Feed slow-release fertilizer in spring, late summer. Refresh mulch in spring.

Water Needs—Deeply water every three to five days in summer; weekly in fall, spring; monthly in winter if there's no rain.

Bloom Color—Yellow, orange, white, red, pink, purple

Peak Season—Spring to fall

Mature Size (H x W)—1 to 5 feet x 3 to 5 feet

LAVENDER
Lavendula spp.

Why It's Special—Scented, serrated, feathery, green, gray-green, and almost-white foliage lends texture and contrast to color borders, perennial gardens, and xeric shrub beds. Blooms range from tall and willowy to short and spiky and there are compact cultivars and taller lavenders that serve as small shrubs. Varied species handle the desert heat or slow growth in cold winters.

How to Plant & Grow—Plant in spring after last frost into well-worked, unamended, well-draining soil. Water deeply and mulch 3 to 4 inches. Water regularly its first season, but allow the soil to dry a bit between waterings.

Care & Problems—Trim back old growth by half in spring. Root rot occurs in too much shade, wet soil, or humid conditions, but there are no pests or diseases. Don't fertilize.

Water Needs—Deeply water weekly when temperatures exceed 90 degrees Fahrenheit; twice per month if it's 60 to 90 degrees Fahrenheit. Water monthly if there's no winter rain or snow.

Bloom Color—Purple, lavender, pink, white

Peak Season—Spring, summer

Mature Size (H x W)—1 to 4 feet x 1 to 3 feet

LUPINE
Lupinus argenteus and hybrids

Why It's Special—Lupine, native to many Southwestern states, varies in growth habit. Dwarf lupines grow in low-desert gardens, slowing their growth in summer heat. Dry meadows, in higher elevations, are home to perennial lupine, whose lushly foliaged mounds grow in drifts, sending out tall floral spikes in spring. Part-shade mountain locations find lupine thriving in acidic, moist soils. Newer hybrids offer longer lifespans, sturdier stalks, and mildew resistance.

How to Plant & Grow—Plant in spring into well-worked, amended, well-draining soil. Sow scarified seed and keep moist until germination. Water deeply and regularly, maintaining soil moisture until establishment.

Care & Problems—Powdery mildew is lupine's biggest issue; space plants for air movement. Don't prune. It's a legume, so no fertilizer is needed, but refresh its mulch.

Water Needs—Water deeply, once or twice a week in summer to keep soil moist; less often spring, fall. Don't water if it's winter dormant.

Bloom Color—Blue, pink, white, maroon, red, orange, yellow

Peak Season—Spring, summer

Mature Size (H x W)—15 to 24 inches x 10 to 16 inches

ORNAMENTAL OREGANO
Origanum laevigatum

Why It's Special—Don't confuse it with edible oregano, but they're definitely related as you discover when you brush against its foliage or catch the scent of its blooms. While you may not want to eat this oregano, it carries similar drought-tolerant, low-maintenance characteristics and contributes to the xeric landscape, planted in drifts along a drive, in clusters in the perennial garden, or singly in containers or as a focal point shrub.

How to Plant & Grow—Plant hardened off container plants in spring into well-worked, well-draining native soil. Amend heavy clay soils for better drainage. Water deeply. Add 2 inches of mulch.

Care & Problems—Trim plants back to 6 inches tall in spring. Deadhead to prevent self-sowing. No pests, disease, or fertilizers. It can colonize so give it room to grow.

Water Needs—Water deeply, weekly when temperatures exceed 85 degrees Fahrenheit. Water every two weeks when they're above 65 degrees Fahrenheit, and monthly if cooler.

Bloom Color—Purple

Peak Season—Midsummer to frost

Mature Size (H x W)—12 to 30 inches x 24 to 36 inches

PENSTEMON
Penstemon spp.

Why It's Special—Penstemon grow naturally in every state featured in this book. They grow in lean, rocky, sandy, loamy, and clay soils. They grow in full sun, but love dappled shade in hot summer locations. They reseed, popping up where you least expect them, a testimonial to their vigor. Use them singly as focal points. Mix differing species, planted in drifts for a knock-your-eyes-out colorful, textural display.

How to Plant & Grow—Plant into well-worked, well-draining soil in spring. No amendments. Water deeply. Add 3 to 4 inches of mulch. Water every two to four days for two to three weeks, then every four to seven days until established.

Care & Problems—Overwatering leads to root rot; overfertilizing causes excessive leaf growth and no flowering. Deadhead to encourage repeat blooming. No pests or diseases bother penstemons.

Water Needs—Water deeply every 7 to 10 days in summer; twice-monthly in fall and spring; winter only if no rain; none if it's dormant.

Bloom Color—Lavender, pink, red, blue, purple, white

Peak Season—Spring through fall

Mature Size (H x W)—2 to 4 feet x 1 to 2 feet

PEONY
Paeonia hybrids

Why It's Special—Gardeners pursue peonies for love of challenge and for their huge, showy, and often heavenly scented blooms. They need cold for winter dormancy, can take the heat if sited in dappled sun and mulched. They're remarkably easy care after establishment, and worth all the babying in the beginning. They take a few years to bloom but they are long-lived so you'll have years of bouquets.

How to Plant & Grow—Plant bulbs in autumn, eight weeks before frost; plant container grown in spring when available. Plant into well-worked, compost-amended, well-draining soil. Water deeply and add 3 to 4 inches of mulch.

Care & Problems—Peonies don't like to be moved; site where they can remain. Fertilize in spring with triple super phosphate (0-45-0); they show toxicity to nitrogen. Peonies are subject to botrytis in cool, humid climates, but no pests. Keep foliage dry, site where they get good air movement.

Water Needs—Water deeply, twice weekly in the growing season. Don't water during winter dormancy.

Bloom Color—Red, yellow, pink, white

Peak Season—Spring to summer

Mature Size (H x W)—2 to 4 feet x 3 to 5 feet

PHLOX
Phlox paniculata

Why It's Special—Phlox provides nonstop flowers in summer's heat and some are candy-scented. They're remarkably tough, colonizing in well-draining soils. Plant a drift and in a few years it's a hardy stand. Plant singly in containers or as focal points, at meadow edges, on hillsides, in perennial beds, and in cutting gardens.

How to Plant & Grow—Plant in spring as soil warms. Lightly amend and deeply work well-draining soil. Mulch 3 to 4 inches. Water deeply every two to four days for two to three weeks, then every four to seven days until established.

Care & Problems—Avoid overhead watering, which causes mildew and collapsed stems. Plant mildew-resistant types. Apply timed-release fertilizer in spring; cut back to new green growth in spring. As phlox colonize, their centers thin out. Cut the plant down to the ground (I use a string trimmer) in spring to rejuvenate.

Water Needs—Water deeply, weekly in summer; intermittently when there's no rain otherwise. Don't water in winter dormancy.

Bloom Color—Pink, red, white, lavender, purple

Peak Season—Summer

Mature Size (H x W)—3 to 5 feet, 2 to 3 feet

PRINCE'S PLUME
Stanleya pinnata

Why It's Special—Prince's plume is special because it doesn't require any special treatment. When it blooms, it is boisterous. At other times, it prefers to be left alone. The ease of growing it at the fringes of the hot garden, in dry spots where nothing else will grow, and in lean, gravelly soils make it a must-have plant.

How to Plant & Grow—Sow seeds in well-prepared, unamended, warm (70 degrees Fahrenheit) soil. Rake seeds into the soil, and keep it moist until germination, 7 to 10 days. Plant in spring into well-worked, well-draining, native soil. Water deeply. Top with 3 to 4 inches of gravel mulch.

Care & Problems—The less attention you give it, the better. No fertilizer, no pests, no diseases. It's a real drought- and heat-tolerant plant once established. It doesn't even care to be in company of a fussed-over landscape.

Water Needs—Water deeply every two to three weeks in summer until second year, then no watering.

Bloom Color—Yellow

Peak Season—Spring, summer

Mature Size (H x W)—30 inches x 12 to 18 inches

RED HOT POKER
Kniphofia hybrids

Why It's Special—Red hot poker can take hot sun, but to grow it in low-desert gardens requires part shade, thicker-than-usual mulch, and more water. In spring, it forms dramatic, clumping, grassy leaves. Planted in drifts, it makes a good xeric garden border. In summer, when it sends out tall "poker" spikes of blooms, it deserves center stage as a focal point.

How to Plant & Grow—Plant in spring into well-draining, well-worked, compost-enriched soil. Water deeply every two to four days for two to three weeks, then every four to seven days until established. Add 3 to 4 inches of mulch.

Care & Problems—Divide overgrown clumps in spring, and apply timed-release fertilizer. Don't fertilize established plants. Remove faded flower stalks. Clean out dead or damaged leaves by cutting near its base in fall. Add thicker winter mulch. No pests or diseases bother it.

Water Needs—Deeply water every 7 to 14 days. Don't water during winter dormancy.

Bloom Color—Yellow, red, orange

Peak Season—Summer

Mature Size (H x W)—2 to 6 feet x 2 to 3 feet

RUDBECKIA
Rudbeckia spp.

Why It's Special—Rudbeckia is a heat and drought workhorse. It's a short-lived perennial, but you won't detect its decline because it's a self-sower. Plant singly in containers, in drifts in perennial beds, and at meadow edges. Be welcoming if it chooses to grow throughout your garden.

How to Plant & Grow—Plant in spring into well-draining, deeply worked soil. Sow seed in fall; keep soil moist. Seed germinate quickly in warm-winter areas; elsewhere, in spring. When plants are 6 inches, add 3 inches of mulch. Water deeply every four to seven days for three to four weeks to establish.

Care & Problems—No pests or disease affect *rudbeckia* but powdery mildew occurs in high humidity. Deadhead to encourage blooming. Remove old foliage to new green growth in spring. Cut back ragged foliage and it bounces back.

Water Needs—Water deeply, weekly when temperatures exceed 90 degrees Fahrenheit; as needed in extended drought. Don't water if it's winter dormant.

Bloom Color—Yellow, orange, mahogany

Peak Season—Summer to fall

Mature Size (H x W)—2 to 6 feet x 1 to 2 feet

RUELLIA
Ruellia brittoniana

Why It's Special—Ruellia is fickle. It's drought tolerant once established, yet grows with abandon in boggy soils. You only need one to colonize, so plan for sweeps along a drive, on dry slopes, or *en masse* in back of the perennial bed.

How to Plant & Grow—Plant into compost-amended, well-worked, well-draining soil. Mulch 3 to 4 inches. Water deeply every two to four days for three to four weeks to establish.

Care & Problems—Cut back winter damage to new green growth in spring. To control legginess, prune to a few inches tall in spring. No fertilizer needed. No pests or diseases. Ruellia can run amok in soggy soils.

Water Needs—Water every 7 to 14 days, allowing soil to dry down 1 inch before rewatering. Water monthly or less in winter if there's no rain or it's dormant.

Bloom Color—Purple, pink, white

Peak Season—Spring to fall

Mature Size (H x W)—1 to 3 feet x 1 to 3 feet

Hardiness—Zones 7 to 11. It's cold hardy (with mulch) to Zone 7, or is a summer-blooming annual in xeric gardens.

RUSSIAN SAGE
Perovskia atriplicifolia

Why It's Special—Cold-hardy Russian sage has pungent, silver-gray feathery foliage and is very deep-rooting, attributes that make it drought, heat, and wind tolerant. You don't need many to make a big statement as a focal point, background plant, container specimen, or to anchor a hillside. New dwarf cultivars offer brighter foliage and blooms.

How to Plant & Grow—Plant spring to summer into well-draining, unamended soil. Allow ample spacing between plants, as they colonize by runners and can become quite dense. Water deeply, allowing the soil to dry between waterings, weekly for a month to establish. Apply 3 to 4 inches of mulch.

Care & Problems—Shear to new growth if it's winter dormant or cut back to 3 inches in spring to encourage bushiness. No pests or diseases bother it. Don't fertilize. Refresh mulch.

Water Needs—Water deeply every two weeks when temperatures exceed 85 degrees Fahrenheit; then, only when soil dries out. Water monthly in winter if it's not dormant or if there's no rain.

Bloom Color—Lavender-blue

Peak Season—Summer to frost

Mature Size (H x W)—3 to 4 feet x 3 to 4 feet

SALVIA
Salvia spp.

Why It's Special—There are over 900 salvia species and an unknown number of hybrids, ranging in size and growth habit from groundhugging to linear, thriving in varied soils from dry to boggy. Select salvias for your cold hardiness zone. Grow in pots, borders, as fillers, midground, groundcovers, as focal points, in sweeps, and *en masse.*

How to Plant & Grow—Plant anytime; water more in summer to establish. Work well-draining soil deeply, incorporating a thin layer of compost. Add 3 to 4 inches of mulch. Water plants deeply every two to four days for two to three weeks, then every four to seven days until new growth.

Care & Problems—Cut back winter dormant plants to new green growth in spring. Deadhead, cutting stems the ground. No pests or diseases. Don't fertilize. Hybrids take a bit more fuss.

Water Needs—Water deeply twice monthly when temperatures exceed 70 degrees Fahrenheit; monthly when it's cooler. Don't water during winter dormancy.

Bloom Color—Red, purple, lavender, blue, pink, white

Peak Season—Spring to fall

Mature Size (H x W)—4 to 36 inches x 6 to 24 inches

SCABIOSA
Scabiosa columbaria

Why It's Special—Scabiosa loves the heat and blooms right through it until first frost. Its compact growth habit makes it amenable to any garden setting. Use it in containers, as a perennial border or foreground planting in the color bed, in drifts in the cut flower garden, and *en masse* as a clumping, flowering groundcover.

How to Plant & Grow—Plant in spring into well-worked, compost-amended, well-draining soil. Plant in part sun to part shade in the hottest summer climates. Incorporate timed-release fertilizer, water deeply, and mulch 3 to 4 inches. Divide spreading clumps in spring or fall (optional). It suffers no pests or diseases. It's drought tolerant once established, but avoid water stress.

Care & Problems—Deadhead flower clusters as they fade to keep plants tidy. Feed timed-release fertilizer in spring to encourage lush growth.

Water Needs—Water deeply, weekly in summer; every 10 days in spring, fall; monthly in winter. Don't water if it's dormant.

Bloom Color—Pink, yellow, white, purple, lavender

Peak Season—Spring to frost

Mature Size (H x W)—12 to 18 inches x 12 to 18 inches

SHASTA DAISY
Leucanthemum × superbum

Why It's Special—Crystal white blooms make Shasta daisy a good accent plant, bringing pop to other perennials, shrubs, and trees, as well as making it a star in the cutting, night, or white garden. Grow from seed for new types in dwarf forms, yellow blooms, or spiderlike blossoms.

How to Plant & Grow—Plant into well-worked, compost-amended, well-draining soil in early spring or fall. Sow seed in early spring. Water deeply, keeping soil moist. Add 3 to 4 inches of mulch. Plant in part sun to part shade if your summers are hot and dry.

Care & Problems—Divide established clumps every 3 years in spring. Apply timed-release fertilizer in spring. Deadhead to encourage flowering. Root rot and leaf spots occur in soggy, poorly draining soils, but it has no pests. Refresh mulch, covering root area for cold protection and to retain moisture in hot summers.

Water Needs—Water deeply once or twice weekly in summer; every 10 days in spring and fall; monthly in winter if there's no rain.

Bloom Color—White

Peak Season—Spring to fall

Mature Size (H x W)—12 to 30 inches x 24 inches

VERONICA
Veronica spp.

Why It's Special—There is a veronica for every landscape situation. Low-growing, compact forms are more drought tolerant. Use veronicas as fillers, in rock gardens, and as groundcovers. Mid- to larger-sized branching types fill the midground or background with tall blooms and lush foliage. New cultivars add a plethora of flower colors and forms.

How to Plant & Grow—Plant in spring or summer into well-drained, compost-amended soil. Water deeply and add 3 to 4 inches of mulch. Keep moist with regular watering until established.

Care & Problems—Apply timed-release fertilizer in spring. Cut back to new green growth in spring. Deadhead to encourage bloom, cutting stems to the ground. Divide spreading types in spring to rejuvenate. There are no pests, other than rabbits, which love the foliage, and no diseases. Refresh mulch.

Water Needs—Water weekly, deeply when temperatures exceed 80 degrees Fahrenheit; twice monthly from 60 to 80 degrees Fahrenheit; monthly in cooler weather. Don't water if it's winter dormant.

Bloom Color—Blue, pink, white, purple

Peak Season—Spring, summer

Mature Size (H x W)—2 to 36 inches x 12 to 24 inches

YARROW
Achillea spp.

Why It's Special—Native to arid regions, yarrow is a drought- and heat-tolerant plant. Varied foliage shapes, many bloom colors, and growing habits make it a mainstay in perennial gardens, mass plantings as a foil for bulbs, and as a turf alternative.

How to Plant & Grow—Plant in spring or summer into well-worked, well-draining, compost-amended soil. Water deeply two or three times a week until established. Add 2 to 3 inches of mulch.

Care & Problems—Deadhead to keep plants tidy. Mow or cut down to the ground in early spring to clean up winter foliage. Don't fertilize. It has no pests or disease but there are fewer blooms in dense shade. Divide in fall to control spread if desired.

Water Needs—Water deeply, weekly if temperatures exceed 80 degrees; twice monthly from 60 to 85 degrees Fahrenheit; monthly in winter if there's no moisture. Don't water during winter dormancy.

Bloom Color—White, yellow, pink, red, salmon, purple, lilac

Peak Season—Spring to fall

Mature Size (H x W)—6 to 36 inches x 8 to 36 inches

PERENNIALS MONTH-BY-MONTH

JANUARY

- In frost-free warmer-winter zones, some perennials are blooming. Deadhead to encourage them. Cut back plants that are finished, but check weather first for unusual frosts. Open wounds are susceptible to cold damage. Don't fertilize yet.

- If you have taken some risks and planted perennials that may not be recommended in your cold hardiness zone (good for you!), then cover them with at least 12 inches of straw, shredded bark, wood chips, branches off a discarded holiday tree, or compost if you have it.

- Perennials that are actively growing in your area need winter watering, but less of it. Soil and air temps are cooler, slowing the rate of evaporation. Wilt occurs from water stress, but it also signifies root or stem rot. Dig down through the mulch and push your index finger into the soil. If it is dry a few inches deep, then water deeply. If it is moist, then check again in a week.

FEBRUARY

- Winter-dormant perennials need deep watering once a month, either from Mother Nature or from you. If there is a thick winter layer of mulch, remove half the amount from around the base of the plant before laying a soaker hose. Water during the warmest time of the day. Replace mulch after watering.

- Start perennial seeds indoors. Provide a warm soil, consistent moisture, and light. Acclimate seedlings gradually before transplanting outdoors. Elevate the seedlings when they have four sets of leaves so the roots don't overheat on the mat, yet the soil stays warm.

- Order perennials online now before the selections are sold out. Find suppliers in your USDA Zone. They will offer tried-and-true types for your area. The shipping date is determined by the frost-free date for each zone. If you want to acclimate the plants before planting, request an earlier ship date.

MARCH

- Wait until the perennials start pushing out new green growth and you see a few inches of green before you prune. Their old stems offer protection from late-season frosts.

- You may notice seedlings popping up at the base of native perennials. If they have three sets of leaves, transplant to other spots in the garden. Prepare the soil and planting holes first. No amendments are necessary. Dig as much of the root and surrounding soil as you can. Transplant with as little root disruption as possible, watering deeply with a watering can to avoid soil displacement. Mulch. Keep moist until established.

- Bunnies, rats, mice, squirrels, and chipmunks do not discriminate on what they eat this time of year, as long as it is green. Set traps in the greenhouse or overwintering area. Cage cherished perennials, completely enclosing them. Anchor the cage to the ground with wire pins.

APRIL

- Perennials coming out of dormancy guide you where to prune. Cut old branches down to new green growth. Native perennials take care of themselves, but if you want to help them out, wait until their stems are completely brown before you cut.

- When deciding how many perennials are needed to fill a space, measure the bed area, then account for the space needed to grow the perennials to their mature plant width. Mulch between the young plants, tucking in some annuals until they fill in.

- Water more now than you did last month. Daytime/nighttime temperatures fluctuate. The best method is to check the soil before you water. If it is drying out every few days, then you may need to top off the mulch. Water slowly and deeply.

MAY

- In low-desert areas, choose perennials that like full sun, but tolerate part sun to part shade. Create microclimates. Drive in bamboo stakes and run a length of shade cloth, or install an arbor or pergola for a shady respite. Plant perennials under the dappled shade of trees. If you have evergreens, consult an arborist to see if they can clear out the canopy to allow more light underneath without damaging the tree's scaffold.

- Native yarrow, *Achillea millefolium*, grows tall, but many cultivars are short and can be mowed for a lawn alternative, meadow, path, or groundcover. Set the mower blades high and attach a bag so debris, old growth, and clippings are captured for easy cleanup.

- Although I have not had luck growing globemallow from seed or by transplanting seedlings, it is available in containers by mail order or from growers that specialize in natives. If you buy just one plant, establish it and allow it to seed; it will colonize.

JUNE

- Make sure the drip irrigation system is running smoothly. While it is running, dig down to the drip tubing and emitters to make sure water is coming out where it is supposed to. Rodents love drip tubing for the water or as nesting material. A tiny tooth hole stops the flow from reaching plants down the line. By the time you notice wilting plants, it might be too late. Weekly system checks save your plants.

- If you are watering container gardens more than once a day, move them to a part-shade site. If the perennial is potbound, it may be impossible to keep it moist. Lift it out of the container, cut off the bottom inch to 2 inches of root mass, and shave down the side roots. Put new potting soil in the bottom of the pot, place the plant back in the container, and pack soil around the shaved rootball. Water deeply, topping with mulch. Then it will only need water once a day.

- Chrysanthemums are generating mostly foliage and stems now. Autumn bloomers need to be cut back by half and fertilized with a timed-release fertilizer to prepare them for flowering. If you want more mums, use the clippings as cuttings. Strip off the bottom foliage, cut just at the bottom of the node, and stick the stems directly into the soil. Position them closely together, deep enough to stand on their own, with three to four nodes buried. Water them when you water the mums. Before you know it you will have a drift of mums at a fraction of the cost.

JULY

- Spring-blooming perennials may have set seed. Cut off their stems at ground level. Hang them upside down in a cool, shady spot with newspaper underneath to catch the seed or set them upside down in a large paper bag. When they are completely dry, the seeds will fall out.

- Some native perennials slow their growth, stop blooming, or go into summer dormancy. Let them be and resist watering to perk them up. This is their natural rhythm.

- Rudbeckia love the heat! They are fully blooming now, so cut flowers to bring indoors. They have a long vase life. Allow the blooms to dry on the plant and cut the stems for the remaining black center cone to use for dried arrangements. You can also bag the stems to collect the seed within the cone for direct-sowing in fall.

AUGUST

- To get more show out of perennials, cut them back by about one-third. They will plump up before first frost and may repeat bloom.

- Use those clippings to start cuttings of favorite perennials. The plants should be actively growing, free of pests and disease. Keep cuttings moist until you can plant. If it is a matter of hours, put them in a bucket of water and place in a shady spot. If they have to wait overnight, wrap the stems in wet paper towels, put in a plastic bag, and refrigerate.

- Allow blooming perennials that you want to repeat in the garden to set seed. Stop deadheading and fertilizing. As stalks turn completely dry, bend them over to the ground so their seed can naturally disperse. Leave them in place through winter.

SEPTEMBER

- Plant mums in the garden for blooms from fall to first frost. Purchase them when buds are tight, with few blooms fully opened. Interplant with other perennials, groundcovers, shrubs, and trees. Plant them *en masse* or in drifts for a natural look, with monochromatic groupings fading from one color to another for an organized design.

- In mild-winter areas, September is perfect planting weather. Water deeply or run a soaker hose throughout the entire planting bed, extending the hose 1 foot beyond the planting zone. Wait until the soil dries a bit before planting. If you make a ball of soil and squeeze it, it should hold together but no water should seep between your fingers. Then it is ready to dig.

- Do not fertilize in cold-winter zones where perennials go dormant. Start spacing out the frequency of deep waterings to begin hardening off plants for winter. Don't cut them back as exposed stems can be damaged as fall nights grow colder.

OCTOBER

- Perennials that offer fall colors are slowing their growth in preparation for winter dormancy so it's best to wean them from watering gradually. Water every two to three weeks, allowing the soil to dry between waterings.

- Divide perennials before the ground freezes. A few days before dividing, water the area you are digging and the new planting bed deeply. If divisions are to be planted in the same spot, dig out all the plants first. Deeply work the soil to incorporate 3 inches of compost into the bed. Cut out the old plant sections, then cut the remaining clumps into small portions, each having a mass of healthy roots. Trim the roots all at once by giving a straight cut, clean off dead foliage, and replant.

- Sow seeds of Echinacea and Rudbeckia. They grow naturally in drifts. Rake the area with a heavy tine rake, moving it back and forth a few times to create shallow fissures. Scatter the seed, drifting your hand across the bed as you walk backwards to the end of the area. Walking forward, lightly cover the seedbed with sand or seed starter. As you walk, your footsteps will press the seed into the soil and seal the topper.

NOVEMBER

- In mild-winter areas, water perennials every 8 to 10 days. In colder areas, deeply water perennials once a month if there is no rain or snow. Where the ground freezes and outdoor water is turned off for winter, make sure perennials are heavily mulched to hold in moisture over the long winter.

- Dig and pot up perennials that will not survive winter. Remove mulch. Dig a circle around the plant, beginning at the edge of the drip line (the outer reaches of the branchworks), digging one shovel deep and prying the roots up just a little with each dig. Go around the plant a couple of times to lift out easily. Trim the roots and pot up, using a container that is slightly larger than the rootball. Use fresh lightweight potting soil with some organics. Don't use soil from the garden.

- Move container and non-hardy perennials indoors to overwinter. If they are stored in an unheated garage, wrap the containers with burlap for added protection from freezing temperatures. Cool, wet soils can lead to root rot. Allow soil to dry a few inches deep between waterings. Do not fertilize.

DECEMBER

- It's a good time to shop for some new perennials to add to your collection. Look for traits that make them low water users. Small, narrow, or needlike leaves with waxy, fuzzy, rough surfaces or carrying scent (usually means they have oils) help a plant conserve water. The smaller the leaf, the less evaporation there is, and coatings or oils protect leaves from drying out.

- If the storage area is very cold for overwintering perennials, then run a fan to assure that the air circulates, day and night if temperatures outside are 32 degrees Fahrenheit or below. A fan maintains dry foliage, minimizing condensation that contributes to frost damage.

- If you are making out your wish list for the holidays, add a heat mat, thermostat, and a small grow light for germinating perennial seed indoors. A small heat mat holds one flat. A flat holds fifteen 6-cell packs. That's 90 new perennials for your garden!

ROSES
for the Southwest

When my husband, Steve, and I were newly married, we lived in a fifth-wheel travel trailer in the middle of a wholesale plant nursery where he worked as grower. Right outside our front door were rows and rows of container roses, all blooming at once. The intermingling scents and colors were enough to bring tears of joy to my eyes. We would walk between the rows and bend down to breathe deeply, considering possible candidates to take to our first home. That was over 20 years ago and as I walk through our gardens at our homestead in Utah, I am delighted to see my old rose friends growing here, transported from California and thriving, even though their current home is quite a different place from where they began.

Deadheading keeps roses blooming longer.

ROSES ARE TOUGH

Okay, okay—to be sure, the hotter your summers are, the more challenging it is to grow roses, but it's certainly not impossible and roses are tougher than they appear. Let's take a look:

- If it gets too hot for roses, they stop blooming, extending their efforts to keeping the foliage green and their roots cool and hydrated. When the weather cools, they resume blooming, bringing their heavenly scented or prolific blooms back into the limelight when other plants are finished with their show.
- Truth is, the sun can be brutal in our Southwest gardens, burning foliage, buds, and blooms. Full-sun roses will perform equally as well—and better—if given a part-sun to part-shade site in the afternoon. That means they are not relegated only to full sun, open beds, but those roof overhangs, dappled shade understories, and shady afternoon alcoves are perfect locations.
- Strong winds can cause problems for roses, but if their roots are kept cool, if mulch is

in place to protect the soil from drying, and if they have strong support or shelter from winds, they can stand up to the blasts.

- All roses need regular watering, but if you lay out the drip irrigation lines or soaker hoses, then the water is applied slowly and deeply at their roots where they need it, minimizing foliar diseases since the leaves stay dry.
- Our soils may be alkaline, lean, or rocky, but roses really don't mind the kind of soil as long as it drains well. Their roots will grow deeply to anchor them in and to collect water and nutrients from the soil. As we know, healthy roots equal healthy plants.
- Some roses are hungrier than others, but a once-a-year application of a timed-release fertilizer in spring or adding compost in fall, and keeping a watchful eye for other deficiencies that might pop up, minimizes these issues before the roses suffer.
- A few types may need selective or hard pruning once each season and some deadheading along the way to keep them

blooming, but if you miss that opportunity, they will continue to grow and flower until you can get to them the next year.

- If a rose is unhappy in its situation, it will give you signs. Yellowing foliage, defoliation, lack of blooms, wilting—a rose is very transparent in showing its needs. Wait until it goes dormant or slows in growth in the cooler months, then move it to another, more hospitable home. In spring, you will see results of your efforts at once.

ROSES CAN ADAPT

All these issues considered, roses show their ability to handle whatever we or Mother Nature throw at them. Some roses are easier to grow than others.

Shrub roses are self-deadheading, require little pruning and are prolific bloomers. Mini-roses stay small, require no pruning, and continue to bloom whether you deadhead or not. Species roses require nothing in the way of fertilizer, pruning, or deadheading, and are tough-as-nails plants, able to perpetuate their species through the ages with no help from us.

Some roses don't mind the winter cold, thriving in wind, freezes, snow, and frozen soils. Being the adventurous gardeners we are, it is not unusual for us to push the zonal limits in our gardens. Providing a bit of extra protection in winter by adding a 4- to 6-inch layer of mulch, covering a rose with a sheet or burlap in its first few winters, and making sure it has adequate water and nutrients creates a healthy, strong plant that

This species rose has single-petaled blooms, often has thorns, and requires minimal care.

Roses, when interplanted in the landscape, are garden stars when in bloom. Their foliage and form accent other plants around them so they can shine when at their best.

can beat the odds. If you can get the rose through the first three seasons, then it will make its home permanent in your garden.

The types of roses we grow in our gardens are only limited to the types that grow best in the area. I buy some roses locally, from a small, family-owned nursery that pots up bare-root roses in January. They fill their greenhouses with containers, lined up like soldiers and showing just bare canes. Carefully grouped and labeled with photos of the flowers, we can easily see what colors they will show when blooming. Buying them

already potted up means there are good strong roots with stems holding swollen buds, which will give us gardeners a leg-up on the growing season once we plant them in the ground. Potted roses are available throughout the growing season and they can be planted from spring through fall. Give them a frequent, slow, deep drink of water, a thick layer of mulch, protection from the heat and sun for their first summer, and they will thrive.

Garden centers and home-improvement centers offer tried-and-true roses and new hybrids as bare root in late winter or very early spring.

Bare-root roses are less expensive, and planting at this stage assures a well-acclimated, strong plant. In order to get the best selection, buy early in the season. Bare-root stock is typically available in January and sold out by the end of February. You may need to store bare-root roses outdoors in a cool, protected, shady spot for a few weeks until the ground can be worked in spring. Wrap the bags they come in with additional layers of burlap and check the peat moss that surrounds the roots regularly to make sure it hasn't dried out. Then check the soil in the garden often to see if it has thawed, if you live in an area that freezes. Bare-root roses need to be planted in the ground before they start to bud. It is sometimes a race against time to coordinate both milestones.

DESIGNING WITH ROSES

How you use roses in your garden design is limited only by your imagination. Designated rose gardens are the design of choice for rose purists and botanical gardens. The many different types and forms laid out in a formal garden style make comparisons, evaluation, and maintenance an easier chore by grouping them all together. Home gardeners have the freedom of using them in differing ways as shrubs, hedges, green screens; arbor, pergola, or trellis covers; focal points, groundcovers, *en masse*, drifts, and groups, and in containers as single specimens or in combinations. Roses are good companions to other landscape plants and even to edibles. The diversity created by interplanting roses with other plants can minimize pests and disease. By mingling roses in the landscape, their dormant period will go virtually unnoticed as evergreens or deciduous plants offer winter interest.

Climbing roses can't be beat for covering an arbor or trellis, but combine them with tomato plants and the two growing, flowering, and fruiting in unison makes them a showstopper. Shrub roses make excellent bushy, dense floral hedgerows; serve as background plants in the small garden setting; or act as midground accents in the perennial bed. Heirloom roses take a space as a focal point in the cutting garden. Night gardens glow with blooming grandifloras or floribunda roses, their scents wafting in the night breeze. Groundcover roses make a foreground garden border, fill a hot meridian strip or a bed along the patio edge that gets reflective heat, cover a slope, or flow over the edges of a container. Species roses can be allowed to grow freely, forming large shrubs that make a safety barrier at the property edge (all those thorns!), offering four-season interest with foliage, blooms, and rosehips.

There is a rose for every garden situation and roses like growing throughout our zones. They tolerate our soils, and can take the summer sun, although if they don't like it, you can move them to a partly shaded spot and they will still go on growing. They are content if watered, thrive if fertilized, and even bloom if you forget to prune them in spring. Really, all you need to do is bend over, breathe deeply, and take time out of your busy day to smell the roses.

CLIMBING ROSE
Rosa spp.

Why It's Special—Climbing roses cover (usually with our assistance) arbors, fences, or walls, creating living, green, blooming, often sweetly scented surfaces. Several of note include, 'Lady Banks', which is drought, heat, and cold tolerant. 'Zephirine Drouhin' has shade tolerance, and isn't as prone to mildew. 'Don Juan' has dark red, velvety, heavenly scented blooms.

How to Plant & Grow—Plant bare-root roses as soon as soil can be worked. Plant container grown in spring or summer into compost-enriched, well-worked, well-draining soil. Site in part sun in low deserts. Water deeply, twice weekly, until established. Mulch 3 to 4 inches.

Care & Problems—After first bloom cycle, cut canes to 10 to 12 buds. Then seasonally trim after bloom, allowing long canes to develop blooming laterals. Tie laterals to supports, bending into arches. Fertilize monthly during growing seasons with rose fertilizer. Refresh mulch. Treat pests and diseases upon recommendations.

Water Needs—Deep water one to two times weekly; monthly in winter if there's no rain or snow.

Bloom Color—Red, yellow, white, pink

Peak Season—Spring, summer, fall

Mature Size (H x W)—8 to 20 feet x 4 to 6 feet

FLORIBUNDA
Rosa hybrids

Why It's Special—Floribundas put on quite a floral show, sometimes season-long. Their blooms come in clusters so the stems make an entire flower arrangement in a vase. Considered the landscape shrub rose, floribundas stay compact, requiring less care than other roses. Look for offerings at your local garden centers for the best for your area.

How to Plant & Grow—Plant in spring using well-worked, compost-enriched, well-draining soil. When soil can be worked, plant bare-root roses. Do not fertilize until first bloom. Add 3 to 4 inches of mulch. Water deeply, twice weekly until established.

Care & Problems—While dormant, just before bud break after the last frost, remove one-third of the growth, leaving 8 to 12 healthy canes. Fertilize in spring with a timed-release rose food. Spray off aphids.

Water Needs—Deep water two to three times weekly in low deserts; weekly in summer in other areas. Water twice monthly in winter if there's no rain or snow.

Bloom Color—Red, white, pink, yellow, orange, lavender

Peak Season—Spring, summer, fall

Mature Size (H x W)—2 to 4 feet x 2 to 3 feet

GRANDIFLORA
Rosa spp. and hybrids

Why It's Special—Grandiflora roses grow on a tall shrub, holding blooms on long stems built for cutting, it is a continuous bloomer that deserves to be a focal point in the garden or massed for a dense floral screen at the back of the garden.

How to Plant & Grow—Plant bare-root roses as soon as soil can be worked. In spring, plant container grown in well-worked, compost-amended, well-draining soil. Water deeply every two to three days for three weeks. Add 3 to 4 inches of mulch.

Care & Problems—Remove one-third of a bush while it's dormant, just before budding, after the last frost. Leave three to five strong canes, cutting them to 2 feet to an outward-facing leaf bud. Fertilize in spring with slow-release rose food. Treat pests as they arrive.

Water Needs—In hot-summer regions, water two to three times a week; weekly in milder-summer areas, and fall and spring. Water monthly if there's no rain or snow.

Bloom Color—White, pink, orange, red, yellow

Peak Season—Spring through autumn

Mature Size (H x W)—4 to 8 feet x 3 to 5 feet

HEIRLOOM
Rosa spp. and hybrids

Why It's Special—Also called old garden roses, heirloom roses have withstood the test of time, surviving on their own in old home sites, abandoned lots, cemeteries, and farmsteads. Many have thorns, most have soft, pale tinted blooms, some are heavenly scented and produce hips for teas for people and for birds in winter.

How to Plant & Grow—Plant bare-root roses as soon as the ground can be worked and when available. Plant container grown in spring or fall incorporating a well-worked, compost-amended, well-draining mix. To establish, water deeply every two to three days for three weeks.

Care & Problems—Prune heavily in late winter to early spring to remove dead or damaged wood or to control size. Fertilize in spring with a timed-release rose food. No pests or diseases bother heirlooms. Refresh mulch.

Water Needs—Provide two to three deep waterings weekly in hot summers; weekly otherwise. Water twice monthly in winter if there's no rain or snow.

Bloom Color—Soft white, pink, red

Peak Season—Spring through summer

Mature Size (H x W)—2 to 8 feet x 3 to 8 feet

HYBRID TEA
Rosa hybrids

Why It's Special—It's a sort of gangly, uncoordinated rose, but when a hybrid tea blooms, it becomes a prom queen. Grow it for its large, velvety flowers—some scented. All put on a show on or off the bush.

How to Plant & Grow—When they're available, and the ground can be worked, plant bare-root roses. Plant container grown after the last frost into well-worked, compost-amended, well-draining soil. Mulch 3 to 4 inches. Water deeply every two to three days for three weeks to establish.

Care & Problems—Pruning is variable; prune landscape shrubs in early spring, removing exhausted canes when flower numbers decline. Each stem blooms for six years. For show quality roses, cut to 2 to 3 feet, saving three to five canes for flower production. Fertilize monthly with a timed-release rose food. Treat pests as you see them.

Water Needs—Deeply water two to three times weekly in hot summers; otherwise weekly. Water twice monthly in winter if there's no rain or snow.

Bloom Color—Red, orange, yellow, white, pink

Peak Season—Spring through autumn

Mature Size (H x W)—3 to 6 feet x 2 to 4 feet

MINIATURE
Rosa hybrids

Why It's Special—Miniature roses are aptly named because of their miniature blooms, but most have a more compact growth habit than other shrub roses. Their size, ease of maintenance, and even some tolerance to drought make them excellent as border plantings, in drifts, *en masse*, and in containers.

How to Plant & Grow—Plant in early spring, after last frost and before temperatures climb above 90 degrees Fahrenheit. Deeply work compost into well-draining soil. Water every two to three days for a month until established.

Care & Problems—Cut old flower stems back to a leaf node, and remove twiggy growth and damaged stems in early spring. Remove up to one-third of its growth every three to four years to rejuvenate. Top-dress with timed-release fertilizer in spring; refresh mulch. Few pests or diseases bother minis.

Water Needs—Deeply water two to three times weekly in summer; once weekly fall, spring. Water twice monthly in winter if there's no rain or snow.

Bloom Color—Red, pink, yellow, white, orange

Peak Season—Spring, summer, fall

Mature Size (H x W)—2 to 3 feet x 1 to 2 feet

POLYANTHA
Rosa spp. and hybrids

Why It's Special—Polyantha is a shrub rose, known for its prolific blooms that continue from spring until first frost. Polyantha rose is vigorous growing, covered with small, narrow leaves and tight buds that open in soft shades; some are fragrant. Its size makes it excellent for containers, borders, or as a color bed filler.

How to Plant & Grow—Plant in early spring or fall. Plant bare-root polyanthas as they are available after last frost. Plant into compost-amended, deeply worked, well-draining soil. Water deeply every two to three days for a month to establish. Top with 3 to 4 inches of mulch.

Care & Problems—Prune old stems back to a node in early spring; remove one-third of oldest canes every four to five years. In spring, feed a timed-release rose fertilizer. Watch for pests; some have disease resistance.

Water Needs—Deeply water one to two times weekly in summer; twice monthly fall, spring. Water monthly in winter if there's no rain or snow.

Bloom Color—Orange, pink, yellow, white, red

Peak Season—Spring through autumn

Mature Size (H x W)—2 feet x 3 feet

SHRUB ROSE
Rosa spp. and hybrids

Why It's Special—Shrub roses are the most carefree of hybrid roses, cold hardy and disease resistant. They are a sturdy, bushy landscape rose, blooming early and repeating their show in fall when the weather cools. Use shrub roses for screens, background plantings, in midground drifts, or lining paths or drives. They fit in every garden effortlessly.

How to Plant & Grow—Plant any time, or bare-root plants when they're available and after last frost into well-drained, well-worked soil amended with compost. Water deeply every two to three days for three weeks. Add 3 to 4 inches of mulch.

Care & Problems—Remove dead wood and shape in spring, but don't shear. Fertilize with a balanced, timed-release fertilizer in spring. It's relatively disease and carefree but watch for aphids. Keep mulched.

Water Needs—Deeply water weekly in summer; every two to three weeks spring, fall. Water monthly in winter if there's no rain or snow.

Bloom Color—Yellow, red, orange, pink

Peak Season—Spring to summer; fall

Mature Size (H x W)—3 to 6 feet x 3 to 6 feet

SPECIES ROSE
Rosa spp.

Why It's Special—Species rose include native roses and are the oldest classification of roses. They are "built to last," with ample foliage; strong, sometimes arching stems covered with thorns; scented or unscented blooms that appear at various times during the growing season, some continual, some repeating; followed by rosehips, and if winters are cold enough, golden fall foliage.

How to Plant & Grow—Plant in spring or fall into well-worked, well-draining soil. No amendments are needed. Water deeply twice a week for three weeks to establish. Mulch 3 to 4 inches.

Care & Problems—No pruning is needed, but to cut back errant limbs (wear protective armor). Give it room to grow naturally. Fertilize and cut back to 2 feet tall if a mature bush needs rejuvenation. Otherwise, it's pest tolerant and disease free. Refresh mulch.

Water Needs—Water deeply twice a month in summer; monthly spring and fall. Water rarely in winter (only in prolonged drought).

Bloom Color—Pink, red, yellow, apricot, lavender

Peak Season—Spring, summer, fall

Mature Size (H x W)—4 to 10 feet x 4 to 8 feet

ROSES MONTH-BY-MONTH

JANUARY

- Bare-root roses are available in warmer-winter areas. If you can't plant them right away, put them in a container or in the center of moistened burlap. Cover roots with moistened peat, sawdust, wood shavings, or sand. Dampen again, close the burlap loosely, throw a blanket over the top of the container and store outdoors in a cool, dry, sheltered location. Check its moisture every few days; do not allow the medium to dry out. Plant before buds form.

- Keep overwintering containerized roses clean by pulling off yellowed leaves and picking any fallen leaves out of the pot. Water only when the soil dries to a few inches deep, until water runs freely out the bottom. Avoid leaving them in saucers full of water.

- Container roses purchased now may be budding. If the ground is still frozen or you can't plant them right away, keep the pots in full sun during the day, but bring them into protection if freezes or snow threatens. Hard freezes can damage rootballs in pots. Keep the soil moist.

FEBRUARY

- In low-desert regions where there is no danger of frost this month, resume fertilizing roses with water-soluble, timed-release, rose-formulated food, or top-dress with a 3-inch layer of compost. Make sure the soil is moist before fertilizing. Water after applying granulated fertilizers or topdressing.

- Bare-root roses are available in colder climates. If the favored rose is on your zonal edge, take a chance! Plant it in composted, deeply worked, well-draining soil in an area that is sheltered from wind. If it establishes and survives through a few winters, you have success!

- Prune bare-root canes to 8 to 10 inches above the bud union. Hard prune established roses after the last frost date. Cut a bush back by one-third, removing crossing, diseased, weak, or dead branches.

MARCH

- After planting, build a large basin around the rose that extends a few inches beyond the drip line. Make a berm, 4 to 6 inches tall, from moistened native soil. Fill the basin slowly with water, noting collapses and repair. The basin should be filled to the top of the berm each time you water.

- If you have some roses that have not seemed happy in their locations, then now is the time to move them, while they are just beginning active growth. Dig the hole first, then carefully dig around the rootball, prying up as you go, trim broken roots, then transplant into the new home. Water deeply two to three times a week; add 3 to 4 inches of mulch.

- Grow roses in large containers that you can move to other spots in the heat of summer or cold of winter. After planting, add an inch of mulch to the soil surface. Water daily until water runs out the bottom of the pot. Fertilize (a moistened soil) once a month with a water-soluble fertilizer or once every few months with a timed-release fertilizer. Water-in granular fertilizers.

APRIL

- Deadhead spent flowers. Cut back to the first set of leaves with five leaflets. If you plan to display in a vase, take the blooms indoors, pull off leaves except topmost, cut the stem at an angle, and put immediately in water. Or, cut the flower off its stem and float in a bowl of water.

- Wash aphids off flower buds with a high blast of water, or apply a horticultural soap per instructions. More is not better when applying any pesticide, even an organic or home remedy. Apply according to directions, in the cool of the morning, and never on a water-stressed plant.

- Leave major pruning until after blooming on climbers, but remove winter-damaged limbs. Reattach canes blown off supports in winter. Fertilize with a timed-release fertilizer, low in nitrogen, as buds swell.

MAY

- When temperatures heat up and you are watering container roses more than once a day, move them to a part-shade location or where they receive afternoon shade. Add a layer of mulch. Deeply water in the mornings, until water runs out the bottom of the pot.

- The soil in containers needs to be light enough for good drainage, yet contain some organics for nutrient and moisture retention. If you can't see individual particles of perlite in the mix, then incorporate perlite into the potting soil before filling a container. Never use soil from the garden.

- In hot-summer regions, if you want to get in one more fertilizing before the heat sets in, then do it now. Apply a timed-release fertilizer to damp soil. Use a fan rake to scrape away a few inches of mulch before fertilizing. Water in the fertilizer before replacing the mulch.

JUNE

- If you must water roses in the garden daily, then water is not being applied slowly enough or in the quantity needed to percolate down where the roots are. If you handwater, turn the hose to a trickle, set it inside the basin, and let it slowly fill the basin to the top. If your soil drains slowly, wait for it to soak in, then water again.

- Overhead watering in the heat of the day causes leaf and bud burn. If you must hose-off offending aphids, then do so in the early morning before the sun hits the plant. If you overhead-water in the heat and full sun, the rate of evaporation accelerates, causing the leaves to dry out faster, leading to sunscald.

- Wilting and dropping leaves are not only caused by water or heat stress. Root damage by burrowing or tunneling pests, poor drainage, vascular collapse, root and stem rots, or nutrient deficiencies also cause wilt. If the soil is damp, then don't water and investigate other causes.

JULY

- The hottest month in summer brings out the leaf cutter bees that cut out circles and chunks in the leaves. They are pollinators too, so it's best to let them be. Refresh the mulch, add some perennials to brighten the spot and wait out the month.

- If you use drip irrigation, have alkaline water to match alkaline soil, have poor-draining soil, or regularly fertilize roses, then you may notice leaf burn and a white crust on the soil surface. Soluble salts accumulate in these conditions and leaching may be in order. Run the water longer so salts move beyond the root zone. Fill the basin four or five times, allowing the water to penetrate each time before refilling. Leach once a month.

- Organic mulches are best for roses, mimicking natural conditions where they grow wild. Bark shavings or chips, straw, and chipped tree trimmings decompose, offering nutrient value and organic material to the soil. Gravel, river rock, stones are best used for more xeric plants.

AUGUST

- As the growing season slows, look for sales on roses being cleared from a nursery before winter. They may not be lush and are probably rootbound, so check their root health before purchasing. Pull the rose gently out of its pot. You want to see white or light brown roots. If they are wrapping around the bottom of the pot, but there are no black mushy roots or a foul odor, the rose is still a good buy. The weather is cooling enough and gives roses more time to acclimate before winter.

- Before planting a rootbound rose, cut off the bottom 2 inches of rootmass, then using shears, make four or five vertical slices up the rootball at various spots. If you don't do this (I know its painful for you, but not for the rose!), the circling roots will continue in the same pattern, girdling the plant, preventing it from generating new, healthy roots. After planting, deeply water and apply a thick layer of mulch. Water again after a few days if the soil has dried down a few inches; repeat for a few weeks. Don't cut any canes, only deadhead or trim broken branches. Wait until spring to fertilize. The foliage and top-growth offer extra protection through its first winter.

SEPTEMBER

- As the weather cools this month, resume fertilizing in warm-winter areas. Those gardening in cold-winter climates should not fertilize this month to begin hardening off roses before frost.

- The repeat bloomers will be putting on their last hurrah while the heat subsides. Deadhead regularly to encourage them to continue the show, keep up with regular deep watering, and make sure the layer of mulch is intact. The bushes might look scraggly after going through the hot summer, but resist the urge to prune. Pruning accelerates new growth, which is subject to freeze damage.

- Roses in small pots may need to be overwintered indoors. Move them to a shady location to begin the acclimating process. Water them regularly, but check before watering to verify the soil is dry just a bit. Cooler soils need less water. Overwatering can lead to root rot. Don't fertilize.

OCTOBER

- Large container roses can either be heeled-in by planting the pot, rose and all, deeply into the soil or moving it to a sheltered location, with burlap wrapped around the container and a thick layer of mulch in the pot to protect the roots.

- Start hardening off in-ground roses. Space watering frequency to allow the soil to dry down to a few inches, until you are watering twice monthly in October. Deadhead the last of the rose blooms; there's no pruning.

- If small pots are rootbound, then trim the roots (see August), slice the slides, and re-pot in fresh potting soil. Water-in well, allow them to drain and for the foliage to dry completely before bringing indoors for winter.

NOVEMBER

- To give roses a jumpstart in spring, move the mulch aside and apply a 2-inch layer of compost around the rose, keeping it a few inches away from the stem. Water well, then reapply the mulch on top of the compost for added winter protection. In spring, you won't have to worry about fertilizing for a few months. The compost will heat up as the temperatures rise, begin decomposing, and release nutrients into the soil, taking care of the job for you.

- In warm-winter areas, apply fertilizer one last time. Watering is less frequent, a good deep soaking about every 10 days.

- Bare-root roses may be available in warm-winter climates. Keep them moist and cool until you plant. When you have a hole prepared, carefully remove the bare-root rose from its medium. Clip its roots if they are broken, sliced, or damaged, just cutting off the wounded portion and no more. Use compost as mulch to give them a bit of extra warmth in cooler soils.

DECEMBER

- If you want to gift a mini rose to a friend, repot it into a container that is a bit larger than the display pot, prepare the roots before planting into fresh soil, incorporate timed-release fertilizer, water well and allow it to drain completely, and deadhead. This takes all the immediate worries away from the recipient so they can enjoy it without any stress. If they are new to caring for roses, tuck a care sheet into your card.

- Check the mulch depth around garden roses. Pile it up to 8 inches for winter. You can also use leaves, branch prunings, and conifer branches as extra insulation.

- Check potted overwintering roses often for water. Damp soil holds heat longer than dry soil. If they are stored in a garage or dark area, bring them out occasionally for a bit of sun during the day, setting them in warm spot (if temperatures are above freezing) at midday for a few hours. If they are in a greenhouse, keep them cool so they remain dormant, check for moisture and water deeply, but infrequently, to avoid too-damp and too-cool soils, which lead to root rot.

SHRUBS
for the Southwest

When we acquired our little bit of land in southern Utah, other than native scrub, juniper, and pinyon trees, there was not much of anything going on in the neglected landscape. We planted trees first. The next step was to establish the foundation, give form to the landscape, and to fulfill background, midground, and foreground functions in the design. The answer to all our needs: shrubs.

SHRUB LANDSCAPE DESIGN

For screening or framing a view, select large shrubs, 10 to 20 feet x 5 to 15 feet (height x width). Large shrubs work singly as a focal point in a landscape or planted in a large pot on a patio. A green screening wall is created when large shrubs are planted *en masse* in the landscape. Some large shrubs can be trained when young to a small tree form, a perfect solution for gardening in small spaces. Interplant various types of large shrubs to form a textural hedge with differing foliage and blooms. Large shrubs make a statement in the garden, provide backdrop to the landscape, and give a garden its structure.

For accenting other plants or enclosing a space, select medium-sized shrubs, 5 to 10 feet x 3 to 10 feet (height x width). Mid-sized shrubs fill a space with color and texture, drawing the eye through the garden, bringing continuity and flow to the bed. They are suitable for pots as a focal point plant. Medium-sized shrubs are perfect for small-scale gardens where they become the background or are the tallest plants in a bed, with small shrubs becoming midground fillers, and groundhugging plants filling the foreground. Plant medium-sized shrubs to form drifts, borders, and hedgerows.

For filling and defining a space, choose small-sized shrubs, 1 to 5 feet x 1 to 5 feet. Small shrubs do triple duty in the garden serving as fillers, borders or ground covers. Small shrubs pull the landscape composition together, enhance the features of other plantings, and anchor the color palette. Because of their small size at maturity, they can be tucked into bare areas that need a bit of color or they can serve as focal points for small garden vignettes. Plant groupings of two or three different species in the space, intertwining them for a diverse texture. Plant small shrubs *en masse*, forming broad sweeps to line a drive, cover a slope, or to form a garden border.

Unless you are using a singular shrub as a main focal point, use it in groups of threes, fives, sevens, etc. Planting in groups of odd numbers makes a landscape cohesive and mimics nature's design. Grouping similar shrubs together in the bed, arranged in a triangular or irregular pattern, brings attention to the individual features that might otherwise be unnoticed. Repeating the shrub in the landscape gives continuity and focus to the landscape. Select a shrub for a landscape bed and use the same plant two or four more times in different areas of the garden to draw the eye throughout the space.

Select combinations from each of the mature-size categories below to create beautiful, all-season garden spaces. Mix evergreen with deciduous types, plan combinations to give season-long color through foliage or flower, create movement with open airy types, or seclusion and quiet with dense habits. The combinations are endless.

BACKGROUND: LARGE SHRUBS REACHING 10 TO 20 FEET X 5 TO 15 FEET (HEIGHT X WIDTH)

NAME	FOLIAGE	FALL COLOR	FLOWER, SEASON	NOTABLE CHARACTERISTICS
Mock Orange	Evergreen	N	White, fragrant, spring, summer	Glossy leaves, dense habit
Photina	Evergreen	N	White clusters, spring	New foliage is red to orange-red
Butterfly Bush	Deciduous	N	Fragrant, pink, lavender, hybrids in more colors, summer	Semi-deciduous arching branches
Vauquelinia	Evergreen	N	White clusters, spring	Blooms turn amber in fall, seed capsules in winter
Chaste Tree	Deciduous	N	Fragrant, lavender-blue, summer	Aromatic leaves, spikes remain through winter

MIDGROUND: MEDIUM SHRUBS REACHING 5 TO 10 FEET X 3 TO 10 FEET (HEIGHT X WIDTH)

NAME	FOLIAGE	FALL COLOR	FLOWER, SEASON	NOTABLE CHARACTERISTICS
Boxwood	Evergreen	N	Insignificant	Soft and billowing form if unsheared
Cotoneaster	Deciduous	y	White, pink	Small berries in fall through winter
Lilac	Deciduous	N	Lavender, pink in spring (new cultivars are white)	Deliciously scented
Nandina	Evergreen	y	Pinkish white, spring	Berries in fall, lovely bamboo form

FOREGROUND: SMALL SHRUBS REACHING 1 TO 5 FEET X 1 TO 5 FEET (HEIGHT X WIDTH)

NAME	FOLIAGE	FALL COLOR	FLOWER, SEASON	NOTABLE CHARACTERISTICS
Barberry	Semi-deciduous	y	Yellow, spring	Beautiful natural form if deciduous, unsheared
Featherduster	Evergreen or deciduous	N	Red, pink, spring, summer	Open, airy habit, feathery foliage
Shrubby Senna	Evergreen	N	Fragrant yellow, spring to fall	Open, airy habit
Spirea	Deciduous	N	Pink, red, purple, summer	Hybrids have bronze new foliage
Sumac	Deciduous	y	Yellow, spring	Red fruits at maturity

As with any plant you use in your garden, match the garden space to the mature size of the shrub. Shrubs that are allowed to grow naturally will be healthier plants and siting with this consideration limits pruning to crossing, damaged or errant branches. Less pruning means less stress on the plant and less work for you. Some drought-tolerant shrubs are slow growers, so fill the space until they grow into it. Add perennials, annuals, bulbs, and groundcovers or top the bed with some mulch, beneficial to the plants and aesthetically appealing.

PLANTING AND MOVING SHRUBS

Shrubs are amenable to being moved. Of course, the larger they become, the more difficult it is to dig up those huge rootballs, but most are tough plants and can take the transplant. If a shrub is not happy in its surroundings after it has been in the ground for a year or you are just not happy with the design results, then plan to move it in very early spring before it is actively growing or in the fall when temps are cool. Dampen the root zone and surrounding soil deeply. Prepare the new site and dig the hole before digging the shrub. Trim ripped or broken roots and cut back the top growth by half. Keep it well watered and mulched through the first season after moving.

Shrubs, with their seemingly endless list of attributes and aesthetic qualities, fulfill many roles in the garden. Versatile in their style, reliable in their ability to survive, amenable to being moved, and undemanding in their needs,

they are background, midground, or foreground plants in the landscape. Allow them to grow naturally, give them lots of water to form deep, far-reaching, strong roots and they will surprise you with rewards.

Moving shrubs in the fall after they have slowed in growth or dropped their leaves causes less trauma to the plant.

131

ABELIA
Abelia × grandiflora

Why It's Special—Abelia is low-maintenance, drought-tolerant, evergreen to semi-evergreen that forms a dense green screen when planted in drifts or as a border. A heavy bloomer, it's a good focal point shrub with its arching habit.

How to Plant & Grow—Plant in spring or fall, in summer if given ample water and afternoon semi-shade. In hot inland deserts, plant in part sun to part shade. Abelia need well-draining soil, so deeply work unamended native soil. Water deeply, three times a week, for two to three weeks. Add 3 to 4 inches of mulch.

Care & Problems—Fertilize in spring or fall with a timed-release fertilizer if growth slows or they're nutrient deficient. Don't prune except for errant branches. Shear to rejuvenate, if necessary, every few years. No pests or diseases but powdery mildew occurs in dense shade.

Water Needs—Water deeply twice a week if temperatures exceed 90 degrees Fahrenheit; otherwise, water weekly. Water twice monthly in winter if there's no rain.

Bloom Color—Pink, white

Peak Season—Summer to fall

Mature Size (H x W)—6 feet x 6 feet

Hardiness—Zones 7 to 11

ARIZONA ROSEWOOD
Vauquelinia californica

Why It's Special—Arizona rosewood is a full, rounded, bushy, deeply rooted shrub, reminiscent of the habit and vigor of oleander but without its disease problems. Its blooms only come in white, but they are numerous, long-lasting, and showy in contrast to the foliage. This large evergreen shrub makes an excellent screen planted *en masse*, a border planting along a drive (where it can take the reflective heat), or as a standalone focal point shrub.

How to Plant & Grow—Plant anytime into well-draining, deeply worked, unamended soil. Water deeply every three to four days for two to three weeks to establish. Add 3 to 4 inches of mulch.

Care & Problems—No fertilizing is needed. Only prune winter damage in spring when new flush of green growth appears; otherwise no pruning needed. No pests or diseases bother it.

Water Needs—In low deserts, water deeply every three weeks in summer; once every eight weeks in winter. Elsewhere, provide supplemental water only in extended drought or heat.

Bloom Color—White

Peak Season—Spring to summer

Mature Size (H x W)—15 feet x 15 feet

AZALEA
Rhododendron spp.

Why It's Special—Azaleas may take a bit more soil prep, a bit more pest monitoring, a bit more fertilizer, and moister soil (although they can be drought tolerant in favorable conditions), but they're worth the work to have a container on a deck, a small drift under the dappled shade of a favorite tree, or as bright accents in the part-shade perennial border.

How to Plant & Grow—Plant in spring as soon as ground can be worked in colder climates; otherwise, plant in fall into well-worked, well-draining soil. Amend alkaline soils, incorporating equal quantities of native soil and peat for backfill. Water-in, and top-dress with 3 to 4 inches of organic mulch.

Care & Problems—Feed each spring with fertilizer formulated for azaleas. Prune lightly to shape just after blooming, before late summer. Watch for lacebugs and control leaf gall at the first symptoms. Refresh mulch. It's a shallow rooting plant.

Water Needs—Keep soil moist but not soggy. Provide short, frequent waterings.

Bloom Color—Pink, red, coral, white, lavender, salmon

Peak Season—Spring

Mature Size (H x W)—3 to 10 feet x 3 to 8 feet

BARBERRY
Berberis spp.

Why It's Special—Barberry species include low growing for groundcovers, short and stout for borders or containers, mid-sized bushy shrubs for drifts under dappled shade, and large, multi-trunked, densely rounded ones for sunny focal points or *en masse* for hedgerows. Evergreen types have deep green, blue green, and reddish foliage; deciduous barberries have beautiful fall colors.

How to Plant & Grow—No amendments required, but deeply work a well-draining soil to plant in summer, spring, or fall. Check plant labels for exposure, which vary widely by species. Water deeply every two to four days for two to three weeks, then every seven to ten days its first summer. Top-dress with 3 to 4 inches of mulch.

Care & Problems—Fertilize in spring with an organic fertilizer the first year, then don't fertilize. Remove winter-damaged branches in spring. No pests or diseases.

Water Needs—Water deeply every two weeks during growing season. Winter water if there's no precipitation for extended periods.

Bloom Color—Pink, red, yellow

Peak Season—Spring to fall

Mature Size (H x W)—2 to 10 feet x 2 to 8 feet

'BLUE MIST' SPIREA
Caryopteris × clandonensis 'Blue Mist'

Why It's Special—Gray-white aromatic foliage on mounding plants and scented nearly blue blooms held high above the foliage make this drought-tolerant shrub a floral arrangement all by itself.

How to Plant & Grow—Plant in fall or as soon as ground can be worked in spring. Prepare well-draining soil by working it deeply, no amendments. Water deeply every three to four days for two to three weeks, then every seven to ten days its year to establish. Mulch 3 to 4 inches.

Care & Problems—Apply slow-release fertilizer in spring in year one; after that fertilization causes weak growth. Prune in spring to remove winter damage. There are no serious pests or diseases, but root rot occurs in soggy, cold soil.

Water Needs—Water deeply, weekly in hot summers, every two weeks otherwise. Water monthly in dry, warmer winters; no supplemental water needed in cooler climates.

Bloom Color—Dark blue to lavender

Peak Season—Spring, summer, fall

Mature Size (H x W)—2 to 3 feet x 3 to 4 feet

BOXWOOD
Buxus spp.

Why It's Special—Numerous species and cultivars offer a variety of forms. *Buxus microphylla* 'Compacta' grows small and tidy for containers. 'Suffruticosa' naturally mounds without pruning, and *B. sempervirens* can grow to 15 feet tall for a hedge (or you can shape it into a topiary giraffe if you desire).

How to Plant & Grow—Deeply incorporate compost or peat into a well-draining soil. Plant in spring or fall for best acclimation. Water deeply to seal in, then water regularly to maintain moist, but not soggy soil. Add 3 to 4 inches of organic mulch.

Care & Problems—Shear boxwood in spring to control size or anytime except in cold winters to keep compact. Fertilize in spring or fall with organic slow-release fertilizer. Nitrogen can burn its shallow roots. Spray off spider mites with water. Watch for fungal twig blight. Keep plants healthy and no problems arise. Refresh mulch.

Water Needs—Water one to three times weekly to maintain even moisture year-round.

Bloom Color—White

Peak Season—Spring

Mature Size (H x W)—1 to 20 feet x 1 to 6 feet

BURNING BUSH
Euonymus alatus

Why It's Special—Burning bush does look like it's on fire in fall, but it also makes a fine, bushy green screen, hedge (plant 'Compactus' for no pruning), or background shrub for flowering perennial beds. It is carefree and drought tolerant once established. Give it room to grow for a beautiful natural form.

How to Plant & Grow—No amendments are needed, but dig and work well-draining soil and plant in spring or fall. Burning bush loves full sun, but in low-desert areas give it part or afternoon shade. Water deeply to settle in, then water twice a week for three weeks to establish. Add 4 inches of mulch.

Care & Problems—Prune winter damage in spring. Allow it room to grow to limit pruning. Fertilize in spring with a water-soluble fertilizer. No pests or diseases. Maintain a thick layer of mulch.

Water Needs—Water deeply, weekly in summer and twice monthly in spring. Otherwise, water monthly if there's no rain or snow.

Bloom Color—Inconspicuous in spring

Peak Season—Fall foliage

Mature Size (H x W)—5 to 20 feet x 5 to 10 feet

BUTTERFLY BUSH
Buddleja spp.

Why It's Special—When butterfly bush blooms, its large clusters of butterfly- and hummingbird-magnet flowers become the stars of the garden. Some are scented, most are deciduous, a few are evergreen to semi-evergreen, but all are drought tolerant once established.

How to Plant & Grow—Plant in spring into well-worked, well-draining, native soil (though *Buddleja* tolerate any soil). Water deeply, twice a week for a month, then weekly through its first summer. Add 3 to 4 inches of mulch.

Care & Problems—To take full advantage of its arching growth habit, hard prune to 1 foot tall in spring before it begins to actively grow. This will also control spider mites. Don't fertilize; that causes spindly growth. Maintain a thick layer of mulch.

Water Needs—Water deeply every two weeks in summer; once a month in fall and spring. Don't water when it's dormant unless there is no rain or snow for extended periods.

Bloom Color—Blue, purple, pink orange, white

Peak Season—Summer to fall

Mature Size (H x W)—3 to 12 feet x 5 to 12 feet

CHASTE TREE
Vitex agnus-castus

Why It's Special—*Vitex* grows into a medium shrub in colder winters, sprouting back from its roots each spring. A large, multi-branching shrub in warmer-winter climates, it can be trained into a small tree for small xeric gardens and containers. Site carefully. The foliage is scented when it's brushed against, making you want to plant it alongside a path, but when profuse blooms blanket the plant, bees come buzzin'!

How to Plant & Grow—It's best to plant in spring or summer. No amendments needed, but work the well-draining soil. Water deeply every three to four days for two to three weeks, then water every seven to ten days through the first summer and fall.

Care & Problems—Prune winter-damaged branches back to new green growth in spring. No fertilizer. No pests or diseases. Maintain a thick layer of mulch.

Water Needs—Deeply water once a week in summer; monthly otherwise. No water needed in winter except in extended drought.

Bloom Color—Purple-blue, pink, white

Peak Season—Summer

Mature Size (H x W)—10 to 20 feet x 10 to 20 feet

COTONEASTER
Cotoneaster spp.

Why It's Special—Cotoneaster can cover the ground, tuck into rock gardens, drift among trees, surround perennial beds, or screen views. Many species and cultivars offer various foliage colors from green to gray-green, abundant blooms, and colorful berries.

How to Plant & Grow—Plant in spring or fall into well-worked, well-draining native soil. Locate in part sun to part shade in low-desert climates. Water deeply two to three times a week for three to four weeks. Add 3 to 4 inches of mulch.

Care & Problems—Feed with timed-release fertilizer in spring. Selectively prune damaged branches only. Fireblight causes burned foliage and stems. Cut back to healthy tissue, toss blighted branches in the trash, disinfect pruners in bleach (1:10 ratio bleach to water) after each cut, and clean and disinfect before pruning other plants.

Water Needs—Deeply water twice weekly when temperatures are above 90 degrees Fahrenheit; otherwise, water weekly, twice monthly spring, fall. Water monthly in winter if there's no rain.

Bloom Color—White, pink

Peak Season—Spring blooms

Mature Size (H x W)—1 to 8 feet x 3 to 10 feet

CRAPEMYRTLE
Lagerstroemia indica

Why It's Special—Crapemyrtle is often used as a small tree, but it makes an excellent, full, rounded shrub. When it blooms, it is a show stopper, so use it as a focal point in perennial beds, planted *en masse* as an outdoor room enclosure, singly in pots, and in drifts in shrub beds.

How to Plant & Grow—Plant in spring after last frost in cold-winter areas, otherwise spring to fall. Plant into deeply worked, well-draining native soil. Water deeply every week through its first summer if there's no rain. Add 3 to 4 inches of mulch.

Care & Problems—Prune in early spring before bud break to shape or train to tree form. Prune out winter damage to new green growth in spring. Fertilize with a timed-release fertilizer in spring. Keep mulched. Powdery mildew is common in extended wet weather. No pests.

Water Needs—Deeply water twice monthly during growing seasons. Water monthly in winter if there's no rain.

Bloom Color—Red, pink, white, purple, magenta

Peak Season—Summer, spring, fall

Mature Size (H x W)—2 to 25 feet x 2 to 20 feet

FEATHERDUSTER
Calliandra spp.

Why It's Special—A drought-tolerant, low-maintenance flowering shrub that thrives in heat and full sun is worth adding to the garden as a poolside planting (it's not a bee magnet), in the xeric shrub bed, in drifts along hot driveways or dry streambeds, or grouped in succulent gardens. Featherduster makes a strong textural statement for such a small plant.

How to Plant & Grow—Deeply work the native soil in spring to plant. No need to amend a well-draining soil. Water deeply and add 3 to 4 inches of mulch. Water twice weekly in low-desert areas, weekly otherwise, to establish.

Care & Problems—Prune winter-damaged branches only in spring. To rejuvenate leggy growth, cut to 2 feet in spring. No pests or diseases affect it and no fertilizer is needed.

Water Needs—Water deeply every two weeks in summer; monthly fall, spring. Water only if there's no rain in winter.

Bloom Color—Red, pink

Peak Season—Summer, spring, fall

Mature Size (H x W)—3 to 5 feet x 3 to 6 feet

Hardiness—Zones 9 to 11

FLOWERING QUINCE
Chaenomeles speciosa

Why It's Special—Flowering quince is an early bloomer in spring, followed by burgundy-tinged foliage. The bitter pear-shaped fruits are best eaten as jams and jellies. Use dense, thorny species as a security fence, garden border, or garden room enclosure. Less thorny cultivars are good to interplant in perennial gardens or in drifts lining a pathway.

How to Plant & Grow—Plant in spring or fall. Plant into well-worked, well-draining native soil. It doesn't like intense summer heat, so site it where it gets late afternoon part shade. Water deeply twice a week for three to four weeks to establish. Add 3 to 4 inches of mulch.

Care & Problems—If you need to shape, prune after blooming in spring. Fertilize in spring with a timed-release fertilizer if it's been less vigorous. No pests or diseases to be concerned about. Maintain mulch.

Water Needs—Water deeply once a week in summer, twice monthly in fall and spring. Winter water only if there's no rain or snow.

Bloom Color—Pink, red, salmon, white

Peak Season—Spring

Mature Size (H x W)— 4 to 10 feet x 4 to 10 feet

HEAVENLY BAMBOO
Nandina domestica

Why It's Special—Nandina offers pure-white spring blooms growing atop tall, bamboo-like stems covered in lacy foliage. Blooms persist through summer, replaced by bright red berries, which combine with red fall foliage. There are dwarfs for pots and borders, mid-sized shrubs for mid ground or focal points, and the species makes a colorful screen.

How to Plant & Grow—Incorporate compost deeply into a well-draining soil. Plant in early spring or fall. Water deeply two to three times a week for three to four weeks to establish. Mulch 3 to 4 inches.

Care & Problems—Never shear. Control size by cutting tallest canes to the ground, never removing more than one-third of the total stems. No fertilizer is needed. Pests or diseases aren't problems. Maintain mulch.

Water Needs—Deeply water twice a week if temperatures exceed 90 degrees Fahrenheit; otherwise water weekly in growing seasons. Water monthly in winter if there's no rain or snow.

Bloom Color—White

Peak Season—Spring, summer

Mature Size (H x W)—2 to 6 feet x 2 to 4 feet

Hardiness—Zones 6 to 9

HIBISCUS
Hibiscus spp.

Why It's Special—Native to southeastern Oklahoma, hibiscus grows throughout the Southwest. Blooming in the heat of summer until first frost, species and cultivars make great container plants, planted *en masse* for borders or floral hedges, in sweeps lining paths, or as focal points.

How to Plant & Grow—Plant containerized or bare-root hibiscus in spring into deeply worked, compost- or peat amended, well-draining soil. For hot-summer locales, provide afternoon part shade. Deeply water once a week when temperatures exceed 85 degrees Fahrenheit; otherwise, once every 10 days for two seasons until established. Add 3 to 4 inches of mulch.

Care & Problems—Apply timed-release fertilizer in spring its first two years, then don't fertilize. Remove one-fourth of older branches to permit light to the center of a plant. No pests or diseases bother hibiscus. Refresh mulch.

Water Needs—Deeply water every 10 days when temperatures exceed 70 degrees Fahrenheit; otherwise, once a month if there's no rain or snow.

Bloom Color—Pink, purple, white, red

Peak Season—Summer

Mature Size (H x W)—3 to 12 feet x 3 to 10 feet

INDIAN HAWTHORN
Rhaphiolepis indica

Why It's Special—Indian hawthorn is hard to miss, even traveling at speed when passing a highway meridian strip full of its rosy pink blooms. Many cultivars make it perfect for the color bed as a border, in containers, or *en masse* as a hedge. When not blooming, it makes a dense green screen with its leathery, oval leaves.

How to Plant & Grow—Deeply work a well-draining native soil to plant in spring. Site for afternoon part shade in hot-desert climates. Water deeply twice weekly through its first summer to establish. Mulch 3 to 4 inches.

Care & Problems—It's slow growing so no pruning is needed. Apply timed-release fertilizer in spring. No pests, but it's subject to leaf spot in cool, wet climates. Refresh mulch.

Water Needs—Water deeply once every 10 days when temperatures exceed 70 degrees Fahrenheit, otherwise, twice monthly. Water monthly in winter if there's no rain.

Bloom Color—White, pink, rose-red

Peak Season—Spring

Mature Size (H x W)—3 to 8 feet x 3 to 6 feet

Hardiness—Zones 7 to 11; overwinter containers indoors in colder climates.

JAPANESE HOLLY
Ilex crenata

Why It's Special—Japanese holly is grown for its green foliage, which is not as spiny as other *Ilex*. Types include dwarfs, and variegated, evergreen, and deciduous forms. Use them a natural hedgerows, as accents, and in containers.

How to Plant & Grow—Plant in spring, early summer, or fall into well-draining, well-worked soil. Give part shade in the afternoon in low-desert regions. Water deeply, twice a week for three to four weeks, weekly until winter, and twice a month through winter if there's no precipitation. Follow this regime until establishment—about two years.

Care & Problems—Prune in early spring as growth emerges to control size or to shape by shearing (formal hedging) or by selective pruning (natural form). Fertilize in spring to midsummer with timed-release fertilizer. Pests or disease aren't a problem. Refresh mulch.

Water Needs—Water deeply every 10 days when temperatures exceed 75 degrees Fahrenheit. Otherwise, water twice monthly, monthly in winter if there's no rain or snow.

Bloom Color—Black, red berries

Peak Season—Fall, winter

Mature Size (H x W)—4 to 6 feet x 3 to 5 feet

LILAC
Syringa spp.

Why It's Special—Continuous breeding is creating hybrid lilacs that flower in warmer climates (Descanso hybrids); there may be a lilac for almost every gardener in the Southwest. Now there are lilacs that just need a bite or two of frost, some stay small and compact yet produce those heavenly scented blooms. Others remain bushy and green with good form when not in flower.

How to Plant & Grow—Deeply work a well-draining soil. Plant in spring. Water deeply, weekly when temperatures exceed 85 degrees Fahrenheit; otherwise, twice monthly until established (3 years). Apply 3 to 4 inches of mulch.

Care & Problems—Choose mildew-resistant and heat-tolerant types for your zone. Apply slow-release fertilizer in spring. Heat-stress related issues are lilac borer and powdery mildew. Prune winter-damaged branches in spring but don't shear. Keep well mulched.

Water Needs—Deeply water every two weeks when temperatures exceed 70 degrees Fahrenheit; monthly in winter if no rain or snow.

Bloom Color—Purple, lavender, blue, pink, white

Peak Season—Spring

Mature Size (H x W)—4 to 15 feet x 4 to 15 feet

MOCK ORANGE
Philadelphus spp. and hybrids

Why It's Special—Its intense fragrance gives this shrub its well-deserved name. These small, tight little shrubs carry a big shrub scent. Every gardener in the Southwest can grow mock orange; some are native and most that we can grow here are drought tolerant once established. Use in pots by seating areas, as shrub borders, and in drifts in shrub beds.

How to Plant & Grow—Plant in spring into well-worked, well-draining, native soil. Locate in afternoon part shade in hottest climates. Water deeply two to three times a week for three to four weeks, then weekly, if there's no rain, through three growing seasons to establish. Add 3 to 4 inches of mulch.

Care & Problems—Prune each spring, cutting old wood and overly dense branches to the ground. Rejuvenate by cutting to the ground in spring. No fertilizers, pests, or diseases. Refresh mulch.

Water Needs—Deeply water twice a month when temperatures exceed 80 degrees Fahrenheit; once a month if there's no rain or snow.

Bloom Color—White

Peak Season—Spring, summer

Mature Size (H x W)—3 to 10 feet x 3 to 8 feet

OREGON GRAPE-HOLLY
Mahonia spp.

Why It's Special—Oregon grape-holly begins the season with fragrant flower clusters backed by blue-green foliage that's copper-colored when emerging. Some low-growing mahonia species are for groundcovers; smaller cultivars for shrub borders and midground; taller types form thickets for screening. Mahonia prefer part to full shade, another bonus in the quest to find plants for understory plantings.

How to Plant & Grow—Incorporate compost into a well-draining soil in spring. Deeply water once a week when temperatures exceed 85 degrees Fahrenheit for three to four years to establish. Add 3 to 4 inches of mulch.

Care & Problems—Apply timed-release fertilizer in spring for two years to establish, none after that. No pruning is required. It suffers no pests but leaf spots can occur in moist or low airflow conditions. Keep well mulched.

Water Needs—Deeply water every two weeks when temperatures exceed 70 degrees Fahrenheit; weekly in hotter summers, monthly otherwise.

Bloom Color—Yellow

Peak Season—Spring, winter

Mature Size (H x W)—1 to 6 feet x 3 to 5 feet

PHOTINIA
Photinia × frazeri

Why It's Special—Photinia shows its true beauty with its new red-tinged growth. Some cultivars are purple, turning green and glossy, covering this bushy plant. Use photinia as a natural hedge, focal point, or plant in drifts along a drive. Evergreen photinia may die to the ground in Zone 5 but it usually comes back from its base in spring.

How to Plant & Grow—Plant in spring or fall, giving ample spacing to grow and for air movement. Plant into well-worked, well-draining soil. No amendments are necessary. Water deeply two times a week for three to four weeks to establish. Add 3 to 4 inches of mulch.

Care & Problems—Fertilize in spring with a timed-release fertilizer. Pinch tips to encourage new red growth. Prune errant branches or winter damage. It has no pests; control leaf spot by watering soil, not foliage, and avoid overfertilizing. Maintain thick mulch.

Water Needs—Water deeply, weekly in summer; twice a month other times. Water monthly in winter if there's no rain or snow.

Bloom Color—White

Peak Season—Spring

Mature Size (H x W)—10 to 15 feet x 8 to 10 feet

PITTOSPORUM
Pittosporum spp.

Why It's Special—There are pittosporum cultivars that are low growing, tiny leaved, and deep rooting for slopes; species that are willowy, open branched, and desert tough; and large, bushy shrubs that grow dense and round year-round. There are so many variations you wouldn't imagine they belong to one genus. One trait they share is heavenly fragrant blooms.

How to Plant & Grow—No amendments are needed, but deeply work a well-draining soil before planting in spring, summer, or fall. Water deeply, two to three times a week for three to four weeks, then water weekly through its first summer. Mulch 3 to 4 inches.

Care & Problems—Prune to shape; to control growth, cut out deadwood in spring. Fertilize in spring with a timed-release fertilizer. Aphids and scale may be problems, but no diseases bother it. Keep well mulched.

Water Needs—Deeply water every 7 to 10 days in summer, spring. Water twice monthly other times if there's no rain.

Bloom Color—Yellow, red, white

Peak Season—Spring

Mature Size (H x W)—2 to 25 feet x 3 to 25 feet

Hardiness—Zones 6 to 10

PRIVET
Ligustrum spp.

Why It's Special—Privet evokes images of formal hedges and lots of pruning, but if you are not inclined to that style, then find a privet to fit your space. Smaller-growing cultivars fill pots for terraces, mid-sized shrubs can be planted in drifts under the dappled shade of trees, or large species can screen or form a natural hedge.

How to Plant & Grow—Plant in early fall or spring into deeply worked, compost-amended, well-draining soil. Water deeply every two to three days for three to four weeks, then twice a week through its first growing season. Mulch 3 to 4 inches.

Care & Problems—Prune weekly or bimonthly in the growing season to hedge (none in fall and winter). For natural growth, prune errant branches after bloom. Fertilize in late winter with a timed-release fertilizer. No pests or diseases. Keep well mulched.

Water Needs—Deeply water two times a week if temperatures exceed 90 degrees Fahrenheit; in cooler weather, water once a week.

Bloom Color—White

Peak Season—Spring, summer

Mature Size (H x W)—5 to 14 feet x 4 to 12 feet

RED TWIG DOGWOOD
Cornus sericea

Why It's Special—Dogwood is a four-season shrub. In spring, blooms cover the plant, then various shaped foliage unfurls in green, variegated, or tinged in pink, followed by orange-to-red fall foliage and berries. Its branches in gray, red, and purple form the scaffolding.

How to Plant & Grow—Plant in early spring for best establishment into deeply worked, well-draining soil. Amend very alkaline soils with compost. Plant in part to full shade, relative to summer heat. If planting in tree understories, place 20 feet from tree trunks. Water deeply once a week when temps exceed 85 degrees Fahrenheit for a few years to establish. Mulch 4 inches.

Care & Problems—Apply only timed-release fertilizer in spring. Prune dormant plants hard in late winter. It's subject to powdery mildew, leaf spot. Refresh mulch.

Water Needs—Water deeply every two weeks when temperatures exceed 70 degrees Fahrenheit, monthly otherwise. Don't water in winter unless there's no rain or snow.

Bloom Color—White, pink, purple

Peak Season—Spring, red–orange fall foliage

Mature Size (H x W)—7 to 9 feet x 4 to 12 feet

SHRUBBY SENNA
Senna spp.

Why It's Special—Shrubby senna, heat and drought tolerant, has an open, airy habit that shows off its feathery, finely cut foliage and prolific scented blooms. Use it along dry streambeds, as a shrub border in xeric gardens, or singly as a focal point with other drought-tolerant plants.

How to Plant & Grow—Deeply dig and work a well-draining native soil to plant in fall or spring. Water deeply every three to four days for two to three weeks, then water weekly its first year. Add 3 to 4 inches of mulch.

Care & Problems—Prune only winter-damaged branches in late winter while plants are dormant. If plants become rangy, hard prune to the ground in late winter every few years. No fertilizer, pests, or diseases. Keep mulched.

Water Needs—Water deeply every seven to 10 days in summer; supplement water in winter only if there are long dry spells.

Bloom Color—Yellow

Peak Season—Spring, summer, fall

Mature Size (H x W)—3 to 8 feet x 2 to 10 feet

Hardiness—Zones 8 to 10; shrubby senna is limited to frost-free climates.

SPIREA
Spirea spp.

Why It's Special—Spirea grow throughout all our climates, remain evergreen in warm winters, give some fall color, and drop their leaves in colder areas. All are drought tolerant once established. Choose the species, hardiness range, and cultivar to suit your need for colorful borders and midground and background plantings.

How to Plant & Grow—Plant in spring or fall into well-worked, well-draining native soil. Water deeply two to three times a week for three to four weeks, then twice a week through the first summer. Add 3 to 4 inches of mulch.

Care & Problems—Deadheading may extend its flush of blooms. Prune after blooming, cutting aged, overgrown canes to the ground; seasonal hard pruning is not recommended. Apply timed-release fertilizer in spring. No pests or diseases bother it. Maintain mulch.

Water Needs—Water deeply, weekly when temperatures exceed 80 degrees Fahrenheit, every ten days otherwise. Supplement water in winter if there's no rain or snow for a month.

Bloom Color—Pink, white, red

Peak Season—Spring, summer, fall

Mature Size (H x W)—1 to 10 feet x 2 to 12 feet

SUMAC
Rhus spp.

Why It's Special—Sumac is a native shrub, undemanding in its needs. Evergreen sumac makes a structural statement with twisted and gnarled branches covered in wavy-edged, glossy foliage, followed by blooms and berries. *Rhus aromatica* has fragrant foliage. Berries taste like lemons on *R. trilobata*. Cold-hardy *R. typhina* has brilliant red-orange fall foliage. Use 'Grolow' for groundcover, *R. virens* in the understory of open canopied trees, and *R. ovata* for natural hedges.

How to Plant & Grow—Deeply work a well-draining native soil (no amending) to plant in fall or spring. Water deeply every three to four days for two to three weeks, every seven to ten days for the first summer. Add 3 to 4 inches of mulch.

Care & Problems—Prune to remove old or dead wood in spring, cut down sucker growth. No fertilizers, pests, or diseases. Keep mulched.

Water Needs—Water deeply every two weeks in summer in low deserts; monthly elsewhere. Winter water only in extended drought.

Bloom Color—White, green, yellow

Peak Season—Spring, summer

Mature Size (H x W)—3 to 15 feet x 3 to 10 feet

VIBURNUM
Viburnum spp.

Why It's Special—Viburnums thrive in all areas. Evergreen types are more suitable to warmer winters while deciduous forms show scarlet fall foliage. Some have scented flowers, followed by berries. Use compact types in pots, mid-sized species in drifts or borders, and large growers as screens and hedges.

How to Plant & Grow—Deeply work compost into a well-draining soil to plant in fall or early spring. Water deeply two to three times a week for three to four weeks to establish. Add 3 to 4 inches of mulch.

Care & Problems—Prune after blooming to remove errant branches, but shrubby viburnum have a natural, bushy form, so other pruning isn't required. Fertilize in early spring with a timed-release fertilizer. No pests or diseases bother plants. Keep well mulched.

Water Needs—Deeply water twice weekly in summer in low deserts. Otherwise, water weekly in summer; twice a month in fall, spring. Water monthly in winter if there's no precipitation.

Bloom Color—White, cream, pink

Peak Season—Spring, summer

Mature Size (H x W)—3 to 18 feet x 3 to 12 feet

WEIGELA
Weigela spp.

Why It's Special—Wiegela is grown for its prolific blooms that blanket an entire plant from its base to its growing tips. When it's not blooming, the species fades into the background, but there are newer cultivars with variegated leaves or tighter forms for mid- or foreground plantings in color beds.

How to Plant & Grow—Plant bare-root plants in spring into well-worked, well-draining native soil. Water deeply two to three times a week for three to four weeks to establish. Add 3 to 4 inches of mulch.

Care & Problems—Prune after blooming, cutting faded bloom stems back to lateral branches and old canes to the ground. Or shear a shrub by one-third on alternate years, creating a tighter mound with lots of flowers. Fertilize with slow-release fertilizer in fall or early spring. It suffers no pests or disease. Keep well mulched.

Water Needs—Deeply water twice a week during growing seasons or once every 10 days in winter.

Bloom Color—Pink, red, white

Peak Season—Spring, summer

Mature Size (H x W)—3 to 10 feet x 3 to 12 feet

YEW
Taxus spp.

Why It's Special—Evergreen yew is renowned for hedgerows, lining an entrance drive, as windbreaks, and for natural groves, making its biggest statement when planted *en masse* or in drifts, clusters, and rows. Its deep-green foliage is the perfect backdrop for color beds. Yew offers further bonus in its love of part- to full-shade locations, always challenging sites to landscape.

How to Plant & Grow—Plant containerized or balled-and-burlapped yew in spring or fall. They need well-draining, rich, well-worked soil, so amend with compost or peat. Water deeply two to three times a week for three to four weeks. Mulch is critical; this is not a drought-tolerant plant.

Care & Problems—Do hard pruning and shearing in spring; reserve tip pruning throughout the season. Twig blight and root rot occurs in cold, wet soils. Yew naturally sheds older foliage. Apply timed-release fertilizer in fall. Keep well mulched.

Water Needs—Water deeply and regularly to maintain soil moisture, but less often in winter.

Bloom Color—Inconspicuous

Peak Season—Evergreen

Mature Size (H x W)—3 to 15 feet x 5 to 10 feet

SHRUBS MONTH-BY-MONTH

JANUARY

- Did you receive a rosemary shrub shaped like a Christmas tree during the holidays? It will need a bit of attention to regain its true identity. Remove the foil surrounding the pot. Examine the roots by gently pulling the plant from the container. They should be white to light tan and form a webbing. If the pot sat in its wrap for an extended period and the roots are brown, black, or mushy, the soil is soggy and has a foul odor, then it could have root rot. Rather than run for a fungicide, treat the problem passively. Dipping your shears into a bleach solution (1:10 ratio, bleach to water) between each cut, remove the bottom 2 inches of root mass and shave the sides of the rootball. Thoroughly wash and rinse the container. Using a lightweight, sterile (right out of the bag) potting soil, repot the plant, water deeply until water runs out the bottom of the pot. Don't water again until the soil is almost completely dry. Repeat the watering/drying regime until new roots form. Keep in a cool room with natural light or outdoors in full sun in frost-free areas. If, when you remove the plant from the pot, you see thick, white roots as big as a pencil wrapping around the bottom of the pot, then correct that problem now. Cut off the bottom 2 inches of rootmass, then make four or five vertical cuts around the rootball, add 2 inches of potting soil to the bottom of the pot, replace the plant, and water deeply, allowing the water to drain out the bottom. While it is still too cold to plant this Mediterranean shrub outdoors, repotting keeps it healthy until planting in the garden.

FEBRUARY

- In colder climates, rejuvenating pruning can be done on deciduous, dormant shrubs. Cut one-third to one-half of the oldest canes to the ground. You may sacrifice spring blooms in this hard pruning, but they will return the following year and the shrub will be refreshed.

- In warm-winter areas, shrubs can be planted in the garden. If any severe weather is forecast, such as high winds or freezing temperatures, then be prepared to offer extra protection to the new transplants. Add more mulch, cover the plants with sheets or frost blankets, and make sure the soil is moist.

- It's still too early to fertilize or to plant in cold-winter areas, but it's never too early to weed. Use a hand pick and cut them off at the soil line. Annual weeds will die, while perennial weeds will (hopefully) freeze to the roots from the exposed wounds.

MARCH

- March marks spring for warmer climates. Increase watering to every two weeks. In other areas, if you increase watering now, you risk the shrub putting out new green growth, making it susceptible to freeze and frost damage.

- Wait to cut out winter-damaged branches until you see signs of new green growth, then cut the damaged stems just to the point of new growth.

- If you are planning new shrub plantings, design the space with a shrub's maximum mature size in mind. This creates a healthier shrub, eliminates constant pruning to keep it within bounds, and shows the plant with its best features. Mulch between the shrubs to give the area a finished look until the plants fill in.

APRIL

- Shrubs that grow best in the Southwest are accustomed to alkaline, dry, lean, rocky soil. A few types may prefer acidic, moist, rich, loamy soil. If you amend the backfill with peat in order to provide more acidic conditions, the shrub gets off to a good start. However, eventually the soil reverts to alkaline, the roots extend beyond the amended soil into native soil. The easier practice is to plant the favored shrub in a large container where you can control the pH, watering, and fertilizer.

- If a shrub prefers a rich, garden soil, then spread 3 inches of compost over the area to be planted, thoroughly incorporating it into the native soil. If it is laid on top or used solely as backfill, an interfacing occurs, which is a definitive barrier between the compost and native soil. This can cause stunting, nutrient deficiencies, and lessen formation of healthy roots.

- All shrubs need a well-draining soil. If you fertilize shrubs in soggy, poorly draining soil, plants are unable to absorb the water or nutrients due to lack of oxygen; the root system collapses and the plant declines.

MAY

- There are organic and inorganic mulches. Choose the type based upon design style, availability, and the shrub. Shrubs native to the Southwest prefer inorganic mulches. Weed barrier with gravel, river rock, sand, decomposed granite, or cinder rock mimics their natural habitat. Organic mulches work well for deep-rooting, evergreen, coniferous, and deciduous shrubs. Use pine needles for acid-loving plants.

- If mulch is incorporated into the soil at planting, it can tie up the nitrogen in the soil, a requirement for decomposition. Rather than respond favorably, as they do to compost, the plants suffer nitrogen deficiencies. Use the mulch on top of the soil, allowing it to break down naturally.

- Increase watering now with warmer days. Check any drip irrigation systems by turning them on, then go from shrub to shrub, removing the mulch so you can see the emitter and the steady drip of water. If all is well, replace the mulch, covering the emitter and drip line.

JUNE

- In the lower deserts, it is much too hot to plant. If you are gifted a shrub or just have to have that buddleja on sale at the garden center, then plant in early morning hours into a moist soil, make sure to clip and slice the roots before planting. Make a broad, deep berm and basin, fill it to the top with water, allow to drain, then apply a 4-inch layer of mulch. Water daily in the morning or late evening. Water the soil, not the leaves.

- Use this design principle for shrubs: If the shrub is not being used as a focal point, then plant the shrub in groups or repeat in odd numbers. For a hedgerow, plant three, five, or seven shrubs. For vignettes, triangulate or plant three or five in a random cluster. For cohesive landscapes, repeat a shrub throughout the landscape three, five, or seven times.

- Check soil moisture. Deep watering is critical to shrub health in the heat of summer. A soil probe shows how deep the water is going. The deeper the water, the deeper the roots will grow, one of the features that helps plants survive drought.

JULY

- If you water by hand and the water runs off, then build a berm and basin to hold the water. If there are many shrubs, then snake a soaker hose around each one—close to its crown and at the outside of the drip line—to water the entire root area. If you have a drip system, add more emitters and increase the run time.

- Snails, slugs, earwigs, and sow bugs love mulch. For snails and slugs, move the mulch aside, toss down the organic bait, then replace the mulch so it is out of sight for kids and pets. For earwigs and sow bugs, wad up an old rag, and bury it under the mulch or in the underbrush. They will gravitate to the crevices in the rag. Throw it and the bugs in the trash.

- Some native shrubs drop their leaves in summer heat, others curl their leaves to hold in moisture, protecting leaves from sunscald. Check the habits on native shrubs, and feel the soil before watering. The natives may need this dormancy and their leaves may unfurl at day's end as the temperatures cool.

AUGUST

- Watering is the most important task for shrub health in August. Maintain a 3- to 4-inch mulch layer around shrubs. If you must handwater, run the hose at a trickle to fill the basin slowly. Avoid spraying the plant leaves. In the heat, evaporation increases and leaves can burn.

- Drought-tolerant shrubs may take up to three years to establish. Regular deep watering in summer, less-frequent watering in spring and fall, and supplemental water in winter may be necessary for these years. Then wean the shrub by spacing out watering over the next two years.

- Consider installing a drip system to conserve water for landscapes over 200 square feet. Spray system output is measured in gallons of water per minute (gpm). User-friendly retrofit kits convert spray systems to drip, which is measured in gallons of water per hour (gph). See the difference!

SEPTEMBER

- Plant cold-hardy shrubs in cooler zones in time to establish before winter. Days are still warm, but temperature differences can vary greatly between night and day. New transplants need frequent deep watering. Cooler soils and less daylight allow you to stretch the time between waterings.

- Don't fertilize until spring, although you can spread compost over the root zone to overwinter. The cool temperatures slow the decomposition process, but compost will do its magic come spring with warmer air and soils.

- Start spacing out the watering on established shrubs. In warmer parts of our region, water deeply twice per month; in cooler zones, water deeply every three weeks until October.

OCTOBER

- Fall is for planting. Evergreen shrubs can be planted in lower-desert climates. Water deeply two to three times a week for three to four weeks. Woody, deciduous shrubs will acclimate in colder regions. Water deeply after planting and every 10 days until the ground freezes.

- Stock up on mulch so you can add a 3- to 4-inch layer to new plantings and top off others for winter. An extra couple of inches on those shrubs that are new to the area or are on the edge of your hardiness zone make a big difference.

- Unless deciduous shrubs are in a lawn, there is no need to rake up leaves (unless diseased). Let them fall where they may. It's nature's mulch.

NOVEMBER

- In warm-winter areas, you can safely move shrubs that have not been happy with their site. But in cold winters, dig in early spring as soon as the ground can be worked. Dig the hole in the new location before moving the shrub. Deeply moisten the planting hole at the new site at least a foot beyond the hole and around the shrub, extending the moisture beyond the drip line.

- Using a round-point shovel, dig around the rootball at the edge of the drip line. Pry up as you dig, loosening the roots as you circle around until the rootball pops out. Clip damaged or frayed roots, then move the plant to its new site with as much of the soil intact as possible. Plant at the same level, make a berm and basin, and fill to the brim with water. Don't prune or fertilize until spring. Top-dress with 3 to 4 inches of mulch. Keep soil damp, but not soggy.

- In cold-winter zones, do one final deep watering, bleed the irrigation lines, drain the hoses, and stash away under the house or in the garage for winter.

DECEMBER

- If you see blooming azaleas for holiday sales, pick up a few to use for color in the home for winter, then plant them out in the garden or into containers in spring. For some of us coping with southwestern soils and aridity, this might be the best way to grow them successfully. Set the azaleas in a bright window, away from direct heat, vents, fireplaces, or wood stoves. Remove the foil overwrap and dump out standing water. Place in the sink and water, allow them to drain completely, rewrap if desired. Check the soil frequently for moisture; winter home heating dries them quickly. When they finish blooming, set in a cool room (not freezing) where they get indirect light. Remove the foil, water until it runs out the bottom of the pot, then wait until soil is dry down an inch before watering again. They need less water in a cool room.

SUCCULENTS
for the Southwest

I used to think, while living and gardening in southern California—which is the land of grow anything, anytime, anywhere—that succulents were for those who couldn't grow anything else. Landscapes planted with succulents were hot, dry, colorless places. I couldn't imagine why anyone would grow them when there were so many lush, flowering plants to choose from. Then I moved to the high desert.

My first succulents came from a gardening friend living in southern California. They arrived as sprigs after five days of mail travel, wrapped in separate little packs and layered in a cardboard shoebox. The card said, "Just stick these in a lightweight potting soil, water them, then leave them alone." I did as I was told. Now they grow in my landscape year-round or in pots that I overwinter indoors. I have since purchased new types to increase my succulent collection. It only took one shoebox full of succulents to make a believer out of me.

We learn as much from watching the plants as we do from other resources. Here are just a few lessons I have learned from watching and growing succulents. (I use the term "succulent" to include cactus, as they both store water in their leaves and spines.)

SUCCULENTS CAN TAKE EVERYTHING—MOSTLY

Succulents store water in their leaves and grow naturally in the desert, forming symbiotic relationships with other desert plants, sharing resources and given shade by taller or bushier types. Desert plant colonies form vast root systems that capture any moisture that might reside deeply in the soil. Their vast numbers equate to thousands

Echeveria glauca

of succulent leaves or thorny stems, holding huge quantities of water.

In cultivation, out of their natural habitat, it is a quite different environment. Upon planting, succulents need a steady supply of water to get them established. After that, most require a deep soaking throughout the growing season whenever the soil has dried. Winter-hardy succulents require a monthly watering if there is no precipitation.

Succulents grown in hot-summer climates prefer part shade or locations that receive shade in the afternoons. Morning sun is tolerated, but they need a cool respite in triple-digit heat. The dappled shade in the understories of trees, at the feet of taller plants that offer shade with their foliage, or under shady home eaves are all perfect succulent environments. Grouping the succulents together or planting them with other plants mimics their natural habitat.

Some succulents cannot take freezes or winter cold. These are summer plants; their soft tissues turn to mush in the slightest temperature drop, but they make excellent houseplants for overwintering. Many succulents are winter hardy, maintaining their evergreen foliage throughout winter in protected areas. Others freeze to the ground and new growth resumes in spring.

MULCHING SUCCULENTS

In succulents' native habitat, non-organic mulch comes as sand, gravel, and rock. Porous mulches such as these have a lot of airspaces, which allow the soil to dry out, but the mulch still offers all the benefits of mulch by cooling the soil and protecting it from erosion. To mimic their native environment in our gardens, add 2 to 3 inches of gravel, river rock, sand, decomposed granite, or cinder rock for mulch.

SUCCULENTS LOVE (SOME) CONTAINERS

While it's true that succulents grow well in containers, they have a preference for the type used. Clay pots breathe and wick moisture away from potting mix so the plants are never in standing water—sure death for succulents.

Hypertufa (pronounced hi-per-toofa) is a favored container, made of sand, peat, and cement; I add perlite to lighten the mix even more. Succulent cuttings can be rooted directly in hypertufa (a very porous material), topped with gravel mulch, and then live their entire lives in the pot.

SUCCULENTS IN THE LANDSCAPE

Succulents can fill a landscape all on their own. Use large types as background or focal plants, serving as hedgerows or security barriers, and as specimen plantings in large containers. Mid-sized types form drifts, colonies, borders, and accents. Smaller types, planted en masse, make great groundcovers and can cover broad sweeps. Interplant succulents with other drought-tolerant plantings. Use them in dappled shade, in dry, lean soil locations, in small spaces or large expanses. Plant drifts in the shrub bed, group as accents in the perennial garden, create a streambed, build a rock garden, and form a border.

With succulents, you can design outside of the (shoe) box!

AEONIUM
Aeonium spp.

Why It's Special—Aeonium is grown for its rosettes in various shades of green, tricolored, variegated, gray-green, or dark purple fleshy leaves. Bringing texture and color to the landscape, use them to line a path or along a dry streambed, in pots as focal points and with other succulents.

How to Plant & Grow—Plant in spring into well-worked, well-draining soil. Use a very light or cactus soil mix in containers. Aeonium needs part sun to part shade in hot-summer climates. Water deeply after planting, top-dress with 2 inches of gravel, river, or cinder rock.

Care & Problems—Fertilize in spring with water-soluble fertilizer at half-rate. Prune lanky stalks to encourage rosettes to form at the base. Watch for aphids and mealybugs.

Water Needs—Water deeply and infrequently, allowing soil to dry completely before rewatering. Don't water in summer dormancy.

Bloom Color—Yellow, pink

Peak Season—Spring, fall, winter

Mature Size (H x W)—1 to 5 feet x 1 to 4 feet

Hardiness—Not hardy below 50 degrees Fahrenheit. Overwinter indoors or take cuttings each season for new plants.

AGAVE
Agave spp.

Why It's Special—Agave is famous for its up to 30-foot-tall flower spike that occurs once every century, when the plant dies. When that happens there are pups to take its place, so its flowering is cause for celebration. There are cold-hardy agaves, shorter artichoke-looking types for covering slopes, and large, stately, dramatic forms for focal points.

How to Plant & Grow—Plant in spring when it's consistently warm into well-worked, well-draining soil. Agave take full, hot sun or dappled shade; avoid dense shade. Water deeply. Ensure that the crown remains at the same level or a bit above where it was planted before. Top-dress with gravel mulch.

Care & Problems—Prune out old, browned bottom leaves (wear protective clothes). No fertilizing needed. Agave is subject to agave snout weevil if it's overwatered. Transplant offsets to propagate.

Water Needs—Water deeply to 2 feet deep monthly in summer; no watering otherwise.

Bloom Color—Yellow

Peak Season—5 to 50 years

Mature Size (H x W)—1 to 6 feet x 1 to 6 feet

Hardiness—Not hardy below 40 degrees Fahrenheit. Overwinter indoors.

BLUE CHALK STICKS
Senecio mandraliscae

Why It's Special—Blue chalk sticks are grown for their true blue, elongated, succulent foliage. Use them in dry streambeds planted in drifts to give the effect of flowing water, *en masse* to cover slopes, in pots for contrast with other succulents and xeric plants, singly in hanging baskets, and in narrow beds along walkways as filler.

How to Plant & Grow—Plant into well-worked, well-draining garden soil or in a light or cactus soil mix in containers. *Senecio* can take full sun but prefer part sun to part shade in hot-summer locales when temperatures exceed 100 degrees Fahrenheit. Water deeply; mulch with gravel or stone.

Care & Problems—No fertilizers or pruning is needed. No pests bother plants, but do not overwater.

Water Needs—Water deeply twice a month spring through fall in low deserts; monthly elsewhere. Don't water if there are winter rains.

Bloom Color—Blue foliage

Peak Season—Evergreen

Mature Size (H x W)—1 to 2 feet x 2 to 3 feet

Hardiness—Hardy to Zone 8; plant them in clay containers, bury these in the landscape, then dig back up to overwinter indoors.

GOLDEN BARREL CACTUS
Echinocactus grusonii

Why It's Special—Slow-growing, drought and heat tough, the swirling rows of spines coming together at the feltlike growing point on a rounded top make barrel cactus sought after for their architectural form. Use singly in a pot for drama, as a focal point in the succulent or xeric garden, and in clusters for accent. Once planted, you'll never have to get close to the spines again, unless it's for the perfect photo op.

How to Plant & Grow—Handle carefully! Plant in spring in a full- or part-sun site. Dig well-draining soil deeply, but don't amend. Water weekly the first year. Mulch with gravel, river rock, or stone.

Care & Problems—Don't prune or fertilize. Agave weevils attack overwatered plants. Water when the cactus' ribs shrink so you cannot insert your finger between them.

Water Needs—Water deeply twice a month if temperatures exceed 100 degrees Fahrenheit; otherwise, water monthly. Water only if there's no rain for six weeks in winter.

Bloom Color—Yellow

Peak Season—Summer

Mature Size (H x W)—2 feet x 3 feet

Hardiness—Hardy in Zones 9–11.

HARDY ICEPLANT
Delosperma spp.

Why It's Special—Hardy iceplant is a drought tolerant, carefree, and profusely blooming groundcover. Use *en masse* for slopes and as a turf substitute (although it doesn't care to be trod upon). Allow it to trail over the edges of containers and hanging baskets, plant in drifts along dry streambeds, and group in the rock garden or native landscape.

How to Plant & Grow—Sow seed in early spring or plant container grown or rooted cuttings from spring to fall. Plant into well-draining, deeply worked soil. Hardy ice plant grow and bloom well in either exposure. Water deeply once a week through its first summer to establish. Use gravel or stone mulch. Bees are drawn to its blooms, so site carefully.

Care & Problems—Neither pruning nor fertilizing is needed. Overwatering causes crown rot; make sure soil is dry before watering. No pests or diseases bother *Delosperma*.

Water Needs—Deeply water weekly in summer if temperatures exceed 90 degrees Fahrenheit; otherwise, water twice a month.

Bloom Color—Purple, red, yellow

Peak Season—Spring, summer

Mature Size (H x W)—2 to 4 inches x 24 inches

Hardiness—Cold hardy to Zone 4.

PRICKLY PEAR CACTUS
Opuntia spp.

Why It's Special—Native to much of the Southwest, when prickly pear cactus bloom in the desert, you can't help but notice their large, boisterous, almost roselike blooms sitting atop thick spiny pads. It's dramatic and awe-inspiring that such a drought-tolerant, heat- and sun-loving plant produces such glorious blooms. Some types set fruits suitable for jelly and wine. Use the type hardy to your zone, and the size that fits into your xeric, succulent, or rock garden setting.

How to Plant & Grow—Plant in spring into well-worked, well-draining soil. Water deeply, weekly for a month. Mulch with gravel, river or cinder rock, or stone.

Care & Problems—Prune diseased, damaged pads in summer, removing at a joint. Spray pads with jets of water if cochineal scale is sighted. No other pests or diseases are a factor. Don't fertilize.

Water Needs—Deeply water monthly in summer in low-desert sites if there's no rain; in other areas, no watering is needed after establishing.

Bloom Color—Yellow, pink

Peak Season—Summer

Mature Size (H x W)—2 to 6 feet x 2 to 8 feet

Hardiness—Some species are cold hardy to Zone 5.

RED HESPERALOE
Hesperaloe parviflora

Why It's Special—Red hesperaloe form clumps of linear green leaves quickly, then send out tall flower spikes that persist into fall on xeric, hardy, sun-, and heat-tolerant plants. Plant masses along a driveway or on sunny, hot slopes, in drifts throughout the perennial bed, in containers, and singly as a focal point. It makes a garden statement long after other plants subside from the heat.

How to Plant & Grow—Plant in fall or spring in low-deserts, spring elsewhere. Plant into well-worked, well-draining soil. Water deeply every four days for the first month. Top with organic or inorganic mulch.

Care & Problems—Deadhead faded blooms and remove spent leaves when they pull away freely. Divide crowded clumps in spring. There are no pests or disease to worry about.

Water Needs—Deeply water every two to three weeks in summer in low deserts, every three to four weeks elsewhere. No winter watering needed except during extended drought.

Bloom Color—Rose, coral, red, yellow

Peak Season—Summer to fall

Mature Size (H x W)—3 to 4 feet x 5 to 6 feet

Hardiness—Cold hardy to Zone 5.

STONECROP
Sedum spp. and hybrids

Why It's Special—There are large, fleshy-leaved stonecrops for mid ground xeric plantings; longer-leaved types for foreground mass plantings; and mini-sized stonecrops that tuck into small spaces in rock gardens and work as groundcovers. This cold-hardy succulent maintains its leaves in winter in protected sites or dies to the ground, then sends out new foliage in early spring yet thrives in triple-degree summer heat.

How to Plant & Grow—Plant spring through fall, rooted cuttings in summer or fall, into well-draining, well-worked soil. Water deeply once or twice a week for a month, allowing the soil to dry to the touch between waterings. Top-dress with stone, river, or cinder rock mulch.

Care & Problems—Cut back old stems down to new green growth in spring. Don't fertilize. Overwatering causes rot. No diseases of concern but aphids can be a problem.

Water Needs—Water deeply, weekly when temperatures exceed 90 degrees Fahrenheit; every two weeks when temperatures are 70 to 90 degrees Fahrenheit. Water monthly in winter if there's no rain or snow.

Bloom Color—Red, pink, yellow

Peak Season—Spring, summer, fall

Mature Size (H x W)—4 to 18 inches x 12 to 24 inches

Hardiness—Cold hardy to Zone 3.

YUCCA
Yucca spp.

Why It's Special—Yucca is a mainstay in xeric gardens. It's used as background planting for a hedgerow, in midground drifts along a dry streambed, singly as a focal point, and in large containers. There are smooth spineless types, yuccas native to the Southwest, and also to the East Coast. Some have stiff leaves, and others are soft and drooping. They have blue, gray, and green foliage, with large clusters of flowers on tall stems reaching far above the clumps. Select a yucca suitable to your zone and design style.

How to Plant & Grow—Plant in fall or spring in lower deserts, in spring elsewhere, into well-worked, well-draining native soil. Water deeply every four days for the first month. Mulch with rock, stone, or decomposed granite.

Care & Problems—Remove old flower stalks and dead basal foliage as they occur. No fertilizer is needed. Agave weevils and borers may be a problem.

Water Needs—Water deeply once a month spring through summer. Don't water in winter.

Bloom Color—White

Peak Season—Summer

Mature Size (H x W)—3 to 25 feet x 3 to 10 feet

Hardiness—Zone 7

SUCCULENTS MONTH-BY-MONTH

JANUARY

- In mild-winter areas, plant winter-hardy succulents in-ground or in containers. Containerized succulents can be set in full-sun locations in winter, making them perfect for sunny decks or patios. In summer, move them to part-sun to part-shade locations, their preference when temperatures rise.

- Plant winter-hardy succulents where they will get afternoon shade or under the dappled shade of trees or shrubs in summer. They may thrive in full sun now, but it's best to plant them in a permanent location and get them off to a good start before summer heat sets in.

- Water established succulents and cacti every month if there has been no rain. Let the soil dry out thoroughly and check it before watering; less is better than too much. Since succulents (and I include cacti in the succulents group) store water, keeping them wet in winter can lead to freeze damage.

FEBRUARY

- Depending upon when it is safe to move overwintering succulents outdoors in your area (after the last frost), don't start fertilizing until about a month after the move. Then start them on a water-soluble fertilizer at half-strength.

- If you find aphids on overwintering succulents, don't use pesticides to control them, as most succulents will burn from this treatment. Put the containers in the bathtub and turn the shower on to rinse off the leaves. If the pot is too large, handpicking will have to work. Don't fertilize them, which encourages new green succulent growth that aphids love. Keep the overwintering succulents as clean as you can. Once you move them outdoors, nature will take care of the pests.

- With warming weather, increase watering frequency to every few days for all actively growing succulents. Stick with monthly watering for those that are still winter dormant or slowed in growing.

MARCH

- Spring is on the rise in some zones. Start planting outdoors and bringing succulents outside that have been overwintered. If occasional frosts might occur, have a sheet handy to throw over the succulents to save them from turning to mush in an overnight freeze.

- Prune any frost damage from succulents with a clean cut down to new growth. Trim cactus if they are becoming too large for their space. They will regenerate quickly with warming weather.

- If succulents are actively growing, deeply water landscape plantings twice each month. Containers need water more often, but the soil is still cool, so check before watering. If you find dry soil and water once a day, then move them to a part-sun to part-shade location. If you are not past your area's last frost date, then keep watering once a month.

APRIL

- Watch for signs of dry rot on prickly pear cactus (*Opuntia*), caused (variously) by cold, larvae, weevils, and sunburn. Remove affected pads and discard them.

- Succulents grow slowly and naturally in dry, lean, rocky, sandy soils. Use these features to your advantage and plant them in similar conditions, saving the deeply amended rich soils for hungrier, fussier plants. Consider those narrow spaces under a garage overhang, between boulders, tucked into rock walls, between pavers on shady walkways, under dappled shade canopies, in dry spots on the fringe of irrigation systems, or on slopes.

- Succulents can be planted in the heat of summer. Mulch after planting; deeply water every 7 to 10 days until they start sending out new growth.

MAY

- If you are just starting your succulent collection, check out the 2-inch pots for sale at garden centers and home-improvement stores. Plant them in the garden or in a larger pot when you get them home and you can build your collection's numbers by taking cuttings. As soon as you can grow 3 inches of stem without cutting the plant back to the base, you will have another succulent plant in no time.

- Dry succulent cuttings a few days before planting to increase callusing and decrease chances of rot. Cuttings can be long, up to 8 to 12 inches as for aeonium, or short sprigs, 3 inches long, as with iceplant and sedum. Cut them to the length you want, then allow the cut ends to dry up to a week for thick stems, a few days is fine for smaller sprigs.

- Use a potting soil mix, amended with 50 percent perlite, a formulated cactus mix, or directly plant the cutting into the garden. Dampen the soil first, then stick the cuttings. Iceplant and sedum root from their stems, so you can lay them sideways and cover the stems halfway or stick them upright. Water the soil to seal around the stems. Wait until it is very dry before watering again. Set pots in a part-shade location to root.

JUNE

- If you have a large area to plant in iceplant, you'll save money by purchasing a flat. Look for a nice, full, overgrown one with succulents trailing over its edges. Take tip cuttings to direct stick. If you can only find newly rooted flats, then buy one, space the plants as needed, fertilize, and water regularly. As the sprigs put on growth, trim the ends and direct stick the cuttings into the soil, placing them between the established cuttings. Once you have the area as full as you want, mulch.

- Planting cactus is tricky business. Buy plants as small as you can find. Dig a planting hole in native soil, 3 to 5 feet wider than the rootball, but just as deep. Wear thick leather gloves, full protective layers on your arms and legs, and sunglasses or goggles to protect your eyes while you are working nearby. Set the cactus in the hole, adjusting it so it is balanced and supports its weight. Backfill, tamping the soil to firm the plant as you go. Water deeply to settle. Make sure it is not deeply planted or that it sinks.

- Water new plantings deeply, once a week for a month. Water established plants, deeply, once each month if no rain.

JULY

- Container gardens should be in part sun to part shade. If you are hot, the temptation is to cool plants down. Resist; don't water if the soil is damp. Succulents are accustomed to heat and store water in their leaves, stems, and spines. Overwatering can cause rots and mildews in succulents, drought-tolerant, and native plants.

- Limit activities in the succulent garden. There's no pruning or fertilizing required. They are using their resources to withstand the heat. Don't interfere.

- If you plant succulents or cactus now, and they are full-sun lovers, provide shade to acclimate them their first summer. Use shade cloth, umbrellas, or temporary lattice panels to cool them down for the next few hot months.

AUGUST

- While in summer's low-maintenance mode, make hypertufa pots to allow them to cure in time for fall cuttings and for potted succulents. Gather cardboard boxes, plastic bowls or pots for molds, grocery or trash bags, a dust mask and gloves, a wheelbarrow or large bin for mixing, a hoe and shovel, a screwdriver, and a wire brush.

  1. Combine dry ingredients: 2 parts Portland cement; 3 parts peat moss (break up clumps to measure and incorporate); 3 parts sand; and 1 part perlite (optional) to lighten the weight.

  2. Prepare the mold, lining it with plastic bag. Fold any excess plastic over the rim to hang down the outside of the mold. You will be pressing the material inside the mold.

  3. Add water gradually, mixing as you go for desired consistency. The mix is ready when materials form a ball when hand-squeezed with a little water seeping out. Beginning with the bottom of the mold, press the mix firmly to form a base, ½ to 1-inch thick. Start working the material up the sides, pressing and firming as you go. Loosely tie the bag closed so the hypertufa pot sets up overnight.

4. After 24 hours, remove the pot from the mold. Turn the pot upside down and poke drainage holes in the soft bottom with a screwdriver or awl. Re-wrap the pot in plastic, leaving the bag open.

5. Wait another 24 hours, remove the bag, and lightly finish the outer surface using a wire brush.

SEPTEMBER

- Finish curing hypertufa in a shady, frost-free location. Fill the pots with water and hose off daily to leach out lime. The final curing takes about three weeks, just in time to pot up cuttings of overwintering succulents.

- The weather is cooling down. Maintain your summer watering regime until mid-month, then water large succulents and cactus that are remaining outdoors through the winter every five to six weeks. Smaller cold-hardy succulents should still be watered once a month through winter.

- Take cuttings or dig up and pot non-winter-hardy succulents. Create succulent garden combinations with cuttings. Use taller types as background plants, sticking cuttings closely together, allowing only enough space for the crowns. Then stick shorter succulent cuttings at their base, with trailing or clumping types in front or at the edge. Water them in, then top with gravel, stones, or cinder rock to anchor all.

OCTOBER

- It is the perfect time to plant agaves in low-desert climates. The warm days and mild frost-free nights give plants good conditions for establishing long before summer's heat and limits chance of sunburn. Established agave may have pups growing at its base. You can pull those off (gently) and pot them up or replant in other areas of the garden.

- In cold climates, any non-cold-hardy succulents should be indoors or in a greenhouse. If you pulled potted succulents from the ground, hose off the soil and pull out of the pots to check the roots, which are likely growing out the bottom of the pot. For a 6- or 8-inch pot, cut off the bottom 2 inches of root mass, make vertical slices up the sides, add 2 inches of fresh soil to the bottom of the pot, slide the plant back in, and water deeply until water comes out the bottom. It's ready for overwintering.

- Set overwintering succulents in pots on windowsills in the house, on shelves, or on the floor. If you use saucers under container plants, water the pots deeply first, allowing the water to drain out the bottom before you place the saucers. Keep them out of the way of heat vents or heat sources. Indirect or full sun is fine. A cool room is fine too, as long as there is no danger of freezing.

NOVEMBER

- Reduce watering in warm-winter areas to every five to six weeks. If it rains, check the soil first before watering. Overwatering now can cause root rot and if a frost occurs unexpectedly, the succulents could suffer due to all the extra water.

- Water container-grown succulents when the soil is dry halfway down the pot. You can fertilize container succulents growing outdoors with a water-soluble fertilizer at half-rate. Don't fertilize overwintering container succulents.

- Christmas cactus are showing up at the garden centers and elsewhere. To thrive, they need bright indirect light, a cool location away from heat sources, and a room that maintains an even temperature with no severe changes between day and night.

DECEMBER

- Be prepared to cover non-cold-hardy succulents if prolonged freezes occur. Cover them with frost blankets, sheets, or burlap, and don't water if frosts are in the forecast.

- All planting should be done for the year. Too-cool weather and soil would inhibit growth. If the nursery is having a sale, then get the deal and bring that succulent home. Repot it if it's potbound and leave it indoors to acclimate a few days. Place it outdoors during the day, but if overly cold temperatures prevail, bring it back inside to protect it.

- No pruning or fertilizing this month, even succulents you are overwintering. There's minimal watering outdoors, only if there's no rain for a month.

TREES
for the Southwest

What trees give back to the environment and to us and future generations far outweigh our efforts for the same. They command all the respect and nurturing we can give them. Most of us inherit trees with our homes. Some are native to the area and have been living and thriving on their own for possibly hundreds of years. Others may have been planted by another tree-lover years ago. If older trees are struggling, diseased, or their structure has been compromised, then it may be time to remove them and plant new trees. In new home developments, often a few saplings are included into the pre-designed landscape. For gardeners, it is inconceivable to have a garden without trees, and as their caretakers, it is our job to to maintain them.

I love trees, so if I were only allowed one plant in the garden, it would be a tree. When my husband and I moved to Utah, we nurtured the native trees that were living here, having a deep respect for them since they have survived hundreds of years all on their own. We added long-lived trees that would be here long after we are gone, a legacy to our grandchildren and their grandchildren. We planted drought-tolerant trees because we live in the high desert, where it will always be water challenged. Some trees we chose for their blooms. An entire tree covered in flowers is an awesome sight. We wanted some to have brilliant fall foliage, followed by winter interest of seedpods, roughly textured bark, or a silhouette in the winter snow. We commonly experience triple-digit heat in summer, so we planted trees with broad crowns covered in foliage to give us shade, while their bare branches allow the winter sun in.

GIVE THEM ROOM TO GROW

The best landscape situation would be starting with a clean slate, a new expanse where the design begins with trees. Trees form the foundation, then the rest of the garden spaces develop. They are the largest and longest-living plants in a garden, so it's best to give them the space they need to grow into their mature selves, even if that time won't come for many years. Planting the right tree into the right space is critical. Unlike shrubs, perennials, and other plants, trees are more difficult to move and take more time (sometimes years) to recover from a move. They take five to seven years to establish, so it's best to consider their mature growth at the onset, giving them the space and time they need to grow into their beautiful selves.

Dig a hole twice as wide and just as deep as the rootball.

Backfill with soil, firming around the plant to secure it in place. Make sure it is planted no deeper than it was in the container.

Top with 3 to 4 inches of mulch.

Consider the tree's criteria for growing and treat each design situation individually to choose the right tree. If you have power lines in your landscape, then select a tree that is considered small at maturity, 15 to 25 feet tall. This eliminates the need to control its size by continual pruning to keep it shorter than the lines. If you desire shade and a tree with a large canopy, then consider a tree's roots, which we now know extend far beyond the tree's drip line, and how they may conflict with structures and hardscapes as they grow. If you have a small garden space, allowing only container gardening, then select small trees (or large shrubs that can be trained as trees while they are young) and give them as large a container as possible to accommodate their roots. If you want to have a tree in a lawn, select trees that are not susceptible to root rot, that tolerate wet or dry soil, and then choose a lawn that can take some shade. Planning for trees requires looking to the future. When we plant trees, we assume their care for years to come. Plan and plant responsibly.

PLANTING TREES IN TODAY'S GARDEN

Years ago, when gardeners planted trees, we purchased bags of amendments, dug the holes twice as deep and as wide as the rootball, planted the trees, filled the hole with the fluffy stuff, watered the tree in, and our job was done. It's a wonder that any trees survived. Either they would succumb to crown rot years later from the deep planting, or their shallow roots would be unable to support the tree, toppling over and uprooting after a good wind or rainstorm.

Then we learned that trees planted in native soil produced healthier trees over time and the practice shifted to planting trees into well-worked native soils.

Adding amendments to the soil was done in the hopes that the end product would mimic the soil that the tree preferred. Peat was commonly used as the backfill in order to give an acid-loving tree what it needed. The tree responded favorably to the backfill, but then its roots extended beyond the peat and into the native alkaline soil. Stunting, nutrient deficiencies, leaf burn, and a host of secondary issues arose. Realizing that it is impossible to change the chemistry of the soil, we learned that it's best to match the tree to the soil. The increase in native, drought-tolerant, or alkaline-tolerant trees available in the nursery gives us a long list of tree choices suitable for our Southwest soils and gardens.

Mulching was once considered a new landscape technique, not readily embraced by the landscape industry nor the homeowners at its inception. Previously viewed as an added step that increased the landscape bid total and meant more labor, mulch was just a cosmetic addition. Research studies brought the benefits of mulch to light. Now, planting a tree, then topping the soil with a thick layer of mulch is a required step to ensure plant health. The practice of raking fallen leaves and hauling them to the compost pile has been eliminated, as we view tree litter as nature's mulch.

PRUNING TREES THE EASY WAY

Back in the 1980s, Dr. Alex Shigo, a brilliant plant pathologist, conducted research into tree decay and discovered how trees compartmentalize wounds, in essence, healing themselves. His studies and publications revolutionized how we view the ways that trees grow. The quest to eliminate the detrimental practice of topping trees and to encourage sound pruning techniques arose from his revolutionary work.

For the first two years, no pruning is needed on young trees, except to remove broken or damaged branches. Then prune selectively by eliminating crossing or inward-growing branches, to maintain the natural structure of the tree, and to encourage strong branching. If you need to lift the crown for clearance, then do so gradually as the tree grows, removing lower limbs each year until they are the desired height. If you properly prune while the tree is still establishing, then little or no pruning will be

WHAT WE HAVE LEARNED ABOUT PLANTING TREES

- Rather than try to change the soil pH, select trees that will grow in alkaline or lean soils or are not particular about soil type.

- If you live in the arid Southwest, add drought tolerance as a tree selection criteria.

- Prepare an area by wetting the soil beyond the site to avoid drier surrounding soil wicking moisture away from the tree.

- Dig the hole just as deep as the rootball and twice as wide.

- Work native soil with your hands to create airspaces and use only native soil for backfill.

- Provide a well-draining soil. If you must amend with organics to increase drainage, then amend the entire area, thoroughly incorporating the amendment into the native soil. Plant on a berm for better drainage.

- Stake a tree only if it needs it, and on two sides, allowing 3 to 6 inches of space between the stakes and the tree. Tie loosely enough to allow the tree to bend with the wind, but securely enough to keep it upright. Stakes are temporary. Remove them after a couple of years or as soon as the tree can stand on its own.

- Build a deep and broad tree berm and basin, extending beyond the drip line of the tree. Plan to widen the basin as the tree matures.

- Water deeply and frequently through the growing season, less in winter, but continuing the regime for at least five years, then wean the tree gradually over a few seasons so it can grow on natural rainfall or with minimal supplemental watering.

- Add 3 to 4 inches of mulch. Refresh mulch each spring.

Make two cuts, upper and lower, on a long branch you wish to remove. This eliminates strain on the branch that might lead to stripping and tearing. Remove the branch and then cut back the stub, but avoid cutting into the branch collar.

required when the tree is mature. Less is more when pruning young trees. If you have a mature, large tree in the landscape, hire a certified arborist to assess the tree and to provide proper pruning if needed.

FEED ME

Back in the day, we fertilized everything, whether it needed it or not. Springtime was fertilizer time and the bags of fertilizer, high in nitrogen to promote growth, flew off the nursery shelves. After a few passes with the spreader, it looked as if it had snowed in the garden. Now we know that overfertilization causes excessive and weak growth. Fertilizers contain salts and in our already-alkaline soils, salinity leads to stressed plants. Fertilizing a tree when it is young can be helpful, but for the most part, if there is organic mulch, deep watering, and well-draining soils, then the tree will get all the nutrients it needs from the soil.

WATER, WATER, WATER

Tree roots need to go deep and broad to support the canopy. Well-developed roots absorb the water and nutrients the tree needs to thrive. Deep, slow watering encourages the roots to grow and spread, forming a vast network that increases huge populations of mycorrhizae that help in absorbing nutrients.

Drought-tolerant trees need ample supplies of water in their establishment years to encourage good root development, which will be able to capture moisture that resides deep within the soil profile. If you are handwatering, fill the basin with water completely to the top of the berm, allow it to drain, then fill again. Do this frequently just after planting and through the first few growing seasons. Drip irrigation systems deliver the water slowly and can be adjusted to run longer, or you can add more emitters to give extra water while the tree is young. Deep, slow, regular watering will be necessary until the tree is established, not a very long time in tree years, considering that a healthy tree will live and thrive on natural precipitation for years to come.

The fact is that the more we learn about how trees grow, the less work is required on our part. Given well-draining native soil, deep watering, selective pruning and mulch, a tree will grow and thrive for years after we are gone. The early years of a tree's life sets the tone of how that tree will grow to maturity. Tending to basic needs from the time we plant, consideration of how a tree grows in its natural environment, and using best horticultural practices ensures success. Better care now equals little to no care when the trees are mature.

Jacaranda mimosifolia

ACACIA
Acacia spp.

Why It's Special—Acacia is an excellent xeric tree, with tiny or narrow, linear evergreen foliage, dark brown to maroon bark and fragrant blooms. Pendulous shoestring acacia, *Acacia stenophylla*, has the form of a willow but without willow's water needs. Use sweet acacia, *A. smallii* and *A. farnesiana*, for shade in small spaces.

How to Plant & Grow—Plant in fall or spring into a well-drained, well-worked soil. Deeply water every three to four days for two to three weeks, then every seven to ten days its first year. Mulch 4 inches.

Care & Problems—Prune in late spring or summer to remove dead wood, and damaged or crossing branches. Types with dense crowns need selective branch thinning to allow wind to pass freely through; thin every two to three years in spring. No fertilizer is necessary and no pests or diseases bother *Acacia*.

Water Needs—Deeply water twice a month in summer, once a month other times.

Bloom Color—Yellow, white

Peak Season—Fall to spring; summer to winter

Mature Size (H x W)—15 to 40 feet x 10 to 30 feet

Hardiness—Zones 7 to 11

ARIZONA CYPRESS
Cupressus arizonica

Why It's Special—Arizona cypress is one of the few conifers that thrive in the Southwest's aridity and heat. It's a moderate-sized tree with a beautiful pyramidal growth, green to gray-green scalelike foliage, and is suitable for focal point, as a grove, or background for shrubs.

How to Plant & Grow—Deeply incorporate a thin layer of compost into well-draining soil. Plant containerized or balled-and-burlapped trees in fall or early spring. Water deeply every three to four days for two to three weeks, then every seven to ten days for the rest of the year. It's not suitable in moist, eastern Oklahoma.

Care & Problems—Prune in spring only to remove damaged branches, cutting all the way back to the main leader. Fertilize only if deficiencies exist based on a soil test. Pests include cypress bark beetles in low deserts in drought-stressed trees and spider mites and leaf blights in wetter climates. Keep well mulched.

Water Needs—Deeply water twice monthly in summer, monthly in winter.

Bloom Color—Inconspicuous

Peak Season—Evergreen conifer

Mature Size (H x W)—20 to 40 feet x 20 to 25 feet

Hardiness—Zones 6 to 9

ASH
Fraxinus spp.

Why It's Special—Ash trees are large shade trees that are drought tolerant once established. They thrive in heat, cold, sun and lean soils. There are many species, cultivars, and sizes for small gardens to large landscapes. It's an open-crowned tree that gives fall color. *Fraxinus cuspidata* even offers fragrant flowers.

How to Plant & Grow—Plant in fall or spring or bare-root trees in spring into well-worked, well-draining soil; no amendments are needed. Water deeply every three to four days for two to three weeks, then every seven to ten days for the first year.

Care & Problems—Prune in winter to remove dead, diseased, or crossing limbs. Plant disease-resistant, cold- or heat-hardy types for your area. Aphids may attack. Fertilize the second to fifth year with a slow-release fertilizer in spring.

Water Needs—Water deeply twice a month when temperatures exceed 100 degrees Fahrenheit; otherwise, water monthly. No winter watering except in extended drought.

Bloom Color—White, green inconspicuous

Peak Season—Spring, fall foliage

Mature Size (H x W)—15 to 50 feet x 10 to 45 feet

Hardiness—Zones 5 to 9

BIRCH
Betula spp.

Why It's Special—Birch trees are grown for their magnificent size, form, and peeling bark. Newer cultivars are resistant to borers and possess more heat tolerance, try *Betula nigra* 'Summer Cascade' and 'Dura-heat'. Smaller types like *B. pendula* 'Trost's Dwarf' are right for containers. Choose a species or cultivar right for your climate and space.

How to Plant & Grow—Deeply work a well-draining native soil in fall. Where summers are hot, plant in part-sun to part-shade locations. Water deeply, two to three times a week for a month; then, once a week for two growing seasons. Mulch 4 inches.

Care & Problems—Prune only crossing or damaged branches in fall. Choose cultivars and species resistant to bronze birch borer. Fertilize with nitrogen in spring for its first few years to accelerate growth, but none after that. Keep well mulched.

Water Needs—Deep regular watering every 7 to 10 days in summer; twice monthly in cooler weather. Don't water in winter dormancy except in extended drought.

Bloom Color—Yellow–brown catkins

Peak Season—Spring, fall foliage

Mature Size (H x W)—40 feet x 40 feet

Hardiness—Zones 2 to 8

BLUE PALO VERDE
Parkinsonia floridum

Why It's Special—Blue palo verde is grown for its month-long flower show when this open-branching tree is covered in neon yellow blooms. It is native to low elevations of Arizona, growing along washes, a testimonial to its drought and heat tolerance. 'Desert Museum' grows 30 feet tall and wide, covered in 1-inch blooms in spring, again in summer, with fewer seedpods.

How to Plant & Grow—Plant in spring into well-worked, well-draining native soil. Water deeply every week for its first summer, twice monthly in winter if there's no rain. Add 3 to 4 inches of gravel, stone, river rock, or decomposed granite mulch.

Care & Problems—Prune out crossing branches in spring, keeping an open crown. Wear gloves for protection from thorns. No fertilizer is needed. No pests or diseases bother plants. Keep well mulched. The seedpods can be messy; site accordingly.

Water Needs—Water deeply twice a month in summer, none in winter unless there's extended drought.

Bloom Color—Yellow

Peak Season—Spring

Mature Size (H x W)—15 feet x 25 feet

Hardiness—Zones 8 to 10; cold hardy to 15 degrees Fahrenheit.

CALIFORNIA FAN PALM
Washingtonia filifera

Why It's Special—California fan palm is a heat-tolerant plant native to desert regions. It is large, slowly growing and displays large fan-shaped fronds that naturally self-clean. It is very drought tolerant once established. As the wind passes through, the fronds shimmer, creating a comforting and cooling sound. Give it vertical space to grow.

How to Plant & Grow—Wait until the last frost date passes to plant into a well-draining, deeply worked soil. Deeply water every two to three days for a month, then weekly through the first summer. Add 3 to 4 inches of mulch.

Care & Problems—Prune dead leaves and faded stalks anytime. Do not prune thriving fronds. Apply timed-release fertilizer in spring when plants are young and less than 6 feet tall; then don't fertilize. No pests or diseases bother it. Keep mulched.

Water Needs—Deeply water every 10 to 14 days in summer, monthly in winter.

Bloom Color—Cream

Peak Season—Summer

Mature Size (H x W)—40 to 50 feet x 20 to 25 feet

Hardiness—Zones 8 to 11; to 20 degrees Fahrenheit without damage.

CEDAR
Cedrus spp.

Why It's Special—Evergreen cedar has silver-gray to green, yellow (*Cedrus deodara* 'Aurea'), and even white (*C. deodara* 'White Imp') foliage with strongly arching pendulous or tiered branches. All are drought tolerant. Cedars come in all sizes from 2 feet tall ('Feelin' Blue') to towering giants to 80 feet tall (*C. libani*). Grow in containers, as a focal point, as windbreaks, or plant a grove in large landscapes.

How to Plant & Grow—Deeply work native, well-draining soil. Plant in late spring through summer. Water once a week for two to three weeks and when temperatures exceed 90 degrees Fahrenheit for its first four summers. Add 4 inches of mulch.

Care & Problems—Fertilize its first four years with timed-release product in spring. Thin twiggy growth. Remove lower branches as they naturally defoliate from being shaded by upper growth. No pests or diseases bother cedars. Maintain mulch.

Water Needs—Deeply water every two weeks when temperatures exceed 80 degrees Fahrenheit; otherwise water monthly.

Bloom Color—Insignificant

Peak Season—Evergreen needles

Mature Size (H x W)—40 to 60 feet x 25 feet

Hardiness—Zones 5 to 9

CHINESE PISTACHE
Pistacia chinensis

Why It's Special—Chinese pistache shows brilliant orange, yellow, and red fall foliage, even in the desert. It's slow to fill out and establish, but it's carefree and drought tolerant five years after planting. Use it as a specimen tree, plant three or more as a grove, or line a drive.

How to Plant & Grow—Plant in fall or early spring from 5-gallon or larger containers into well-worked, well-draining soil. Water deeply every three to four days for three to four weeks, then water weekly during spring and summer for two years. Use drip irrigation, extending beyond the drip line, to completely wet the rootball. Add 4 inches of mulch.

Care & Problems—Prune to remove damaged branches and to train while young, then no pruning is needed. Fertilize with timed-release fertilizer in spring its first four years, then don't fertilize. It's pest and disease free. Do not overwater. Refresh mulch.

Water Needs—Deeply water every two weeks in summer in low elevations; water monthly otherwise.

Bloom Color—Insignificant

Peak Season—Fall foliage

Mature Size (H x W)—30 feet x 20 feet

Hardiness—Zones 5 to 9

DESERT CATALPA
Chitalpa tashkentensis

Why It's Special—Having the heat toughness of the *Chilopsis* and the flowering habit of the *Catalpa*, this hybrid is a perfectly sized tree for small gardens. It has no messy pods but it does drop spent blooms and leaves, so site accordingly. A fast grower, there are two cultivars: 'Pink Dawn' with pink blooms and 'Morning Cloud' with white flowers.

How to Plant & Grow—Incorporate a thin amount of amendment into a well-draining soil to plant in spring. Water deeply two to three times a week for three to four weeks, then weekly for its first year.

Care & Problems—Prune young trees for form after its first two years to allow the trunk to gain girth. In mild winters they are semi-evergreen, otherwise deciduous, so prune while they're dormant or growth is slowed. No fertilizer. No pests or disease. Keep well mulched.

Water Needs—Deeply water once a week in lower elevations in summer, twice monthly otherwise.

Bloom Color—White, pink, lavender

Peak Season—Spring, summer

Mature Size (H x W)—20 to 30 feet x 20 to 30 feet

Hardiness—Zones 6 to 11

DESERT WILLOW
Chilopsis linearis

Why It's Special—Desert willow is a small drought-tolerant tree that blooms in the heat of summer, attracting hummingbirds and bees to its orchidlike flowers. Pods hang onto to the branches into winter. They don't mind reflective heat, so plant along the driveway or entrance, or use as focal point in a patio.

How to Plant & Grow—Plant in spring before trees leaf out, into well-drained, deeply worked soil. Water deeply every three to four days for two to three weeks, then every five to seven days for the first year. Add 4 inches of mulch.

Care & Problems—Prune in spring to remove winter damage. For a single trunk, prune the two to three lowest limbs each spring until a tree is at your preferred height, removing no more than one-fourth of the growth each pruning. No need to fertilize. No pests or diseases bother it. Maintain mulch.

Water Needs—Deeply water every two weeks in summer, monthly in winter.

Bloom Color—Lavender, pink, rose, purple, white

Peak Season—Summer

Mature Size (H x W)—10 to 20 feet x 10 to 20 feet

Hardiness—Zones 8 to 9

DOUGLAS FIR
Pseudotsuga menziesii

Why It's Special—Douglas fir is a beautiful majestic conifer with classic pyramidal shape. It's drought tolerant once established. Often sold as a potted Christmas tree, Douglas fir has a delicious scent when its needles are crushed. Dwarf cultivar 'Fletcheri' only reaches 6 feet, making it good for containers and small gardens.

How to Plant & Grow—Deeply dig a well-draining native soil to plant in winter or early spring. Disturb the rootball as little as possible. Water deeply every three to four days for two to three weeks, then water every seven to ten days for the first year. Add 4 inches of mulch.

Care & Problems—Prune low branches to lift the crown if desired in early spring, otherwise no pruning is needed. No fertilizer. Western spruce budworm, scale, and aphids can appear in excessive heat or on water-stressed trees. There are no diseases for concern.

Water Needs—Deeply water every two weeks in summer if it's exceedingly hot and monthly in winter during drought conditions.

Bloom Color—Tan cones

Peak Season—Spring

Mature Size (H x W)—70 to 100 feet x 30 feet

Hardiness—Zones 5 to 7

FALSE CYPRESS
Xanthocyparis nootkatensis

Why It's Special—False cypress are evergreen conifers with foliage from green to blue or gray-green, yellow to bronze, supplying texture and color to the background of the garden. Forms are pyramidal, columnar, or weeping. Trees slowly grow to 60 feet or choose dwarf cultivars 'Glenmore' and 'Compacta', growing to just 6 feet tall. Grow as a focal point, grove, screen, or in containers.

How to Plant & Grow—Plant balled-and-burlapped or containers in spring into well-drained, deeply worked native soil. False cypress struggles in southern Nevada. Site away from strong winds. Water deeply, regularly for one year until established. Mulch 4 inches.

Care & Problems—Prune to shape in spring, but don't cut its lower limbs. Apply timed-release fertilizer the second spring. Root rot occurs in poorly draining soil; occasional spider mites. Otherwise, no pests or diseases affect it. Keep well mulched.

Water Needs—Deeply water once a week in summer, monthly in winter if there's no rain or snow.

Bloom Color—Inconspicuous

Peak Season—Evergreen

Mature Size (H x W)—30 to 80 feet x 15 to 30 feet

Hardiness—Zones 4 to 7

FIG TREE
Ficus spp.

Why It's Special—Fig trees are prized for their large, stiff, deeply green foliage covering a broad crown that forms a dense shade canopy. The ornamental types set small fruits (for the birds) but the edible *Ficus carica* can also be grown in our area. Use as a focal point, in a drift to line a drive or in a grove.

How to Plant & Grow—Deeply incorporate compost into a well-draining soil in spring after last frost. Deeply water every three to four days for two to three weeks, then every five to seven days for the first year. Mulch 4 inches.

Care & Problems—Prune in late spring or summer to shape or remove winter damage. Apply timed-release fertilizer in the second spring for two more years, then no more fertilizing. No pests or diseases affect it. Refresh mulch.

Water Needs—Deeply water every seven to ten days in summer, every month or two in winter if temperatures exceed 60 degrees Fahrenheit.

Bloom Color—Inconspicuous

Peak Season—Spring, summer

Mature Size (H x W)—10 to 50 feet x 12 to 35 feet

Hardiness—Zones 6 to 11

FLOWERING CRABAPPLE

Malus spp.

Why It's Special—Flowering crabapple is grown for its outstanding floral show. Fragrant blooms cover bare-branched trees in early spring (sometimes with young foliage). These trees give good shade through the summer, when small, red, edible fruits ripen. Use flowering crabapple as a focal point, in large containers, or grouped for a grove.

How to Plant & Grow—Plant bare root or containers in late winter or early spring into compost-amended, well-draining soil. Water deeply two to three times a week for a month, then every five to seven days through its first summer. Mulch 4 inches. It's difficult to grow in southern Nevada.

Care & Problems—Prune lightly in spring after bloom. Apply nitrogen fertilizer in early spring. Select from the many disease-resistant types available. Watch for typical apple pests, caterpillars, apple maggots, scale, aphids, spider mites. Keep mulched.

Water Needs—Deeply water once every 10 to 14 days if there's no rain. Water monthly in winter if there's no precipitation.

Bloom Color—Pink, red, white

Peak Season—Spring

Mature Size (H x W)—8 to 25 feet x 10 to 20 feet

Hardiness—Zones 5 to 8

FLOWERING PEAR

Pyrus calleryana

Why It's Special—Flowering pear brings early spring blooms followed by dense, green shiny foliage, creating appreciated shade. Brilliant fall foliage in red, gold, orange, and purple, depending upon the cultivar. Many forms are available from columnar ('Capitol') for narrow spaces and espalier, to rounded canopy ('Autumn Blaze') for broad shade, to pyramidal ('New Bradford') for focal point.

How to Plant & Grow—Plant in fall or early spring. Deeply incorporate compost into well-draining soil. Water deeply two to three times a week for a month, then every five to seven days through its first summer. Add 4 inches of mulch.

Care & Problems—Prune young trees for a strong canopy; remove crossing branches in spring after bloom. Apply timed-release fertilizer after blooming. Watch for fireblight, typical pear pests. Keep well mulched.

Water Needs—Water deeply once a week when temperatures exceed 90 degrees Fahrenheit, otherwise, every two weeks until summer's end. Water monthly in winter if no precipitation.

Bloom Color—White

Peak Season—Spring, fall foliage

Mature Size (H x W)—30 to 50 feet x 20 to 40 feet

Hardiness—Zones 5 to 8

FLOWERING PLUM

Prunus cerasifera

Why It's Special—In spring, flowering plum's vase-shaped canopy is covered in blooms, followed by green or deep purple foliage ('Atropurpurea') that drops in late fall. Its small stature makes it perfect for patio gardens, for grouping together in a grove, or as background plantings in small spaces.

How to Plant & Grow—Plant in spring after last frost or fall in low-desert sites into well-draining, deeply worked soil. Water deeply every three to four days for two to three weeks, then every five to seven days through summer and fall, every two to three weeks in winter if no precipitation its first year. Mulch 4 inches.

Care & Problems—Prune during winter dormancy to remove damaged or crossing branches. Fertilize if needed in fall or spring before leaves emerge. No pests or disease. Keep mulched.

Water Needs—In low elevations, deeply water weekly in summer; twice monthly at other times. In other locales, water twice monthly in summer. No winter watering except during drought.

Bloom Color—White–pink

Peak Season—Spring

Mature Size (H x W)—15 to 25 feet x 10 to 20 feet

Hardiness—Zones 4 to 8

FREMONT COTTONWOOD
Populus fremontii

Why It's Special—Fremont cottonwood doesn't grow as large as cottonwoods found growing along waterways, but it makes a sizable shade tree for urban gardens with brilliant yellow fall color. The more water it gets, the faster it creates a broad crown, covered in shimmering green leaves from spring to fall. Grow one for a shady backyard, more for a grove in large settings.

How to Plant & Grow—Incorporate compost into a well-draining soil for spring planting. Water deeply every three to four days for two to three weeks, then weekly for the first year. Add 4 inches of mulch.

Care & Problems—Prune in winter to remove dead, damaged wood or suckers. No fertilizer is needed. No pests or disease. These trees naturally live along streambeds, so keep them well mulched and deeply watered.

Water Needs—Water deeply once a week in summer in low elevations, every two weeks elsewhere. Water monthly in low elevations in winter, rely on rain elsewhere.

Bloom Color—Insignificant

Peak Season—Fall foliage

Mature Size (H x W)—40 to 70 feet x 20 to 40 feet

Hardiness—Zones 3 to 9

GINKGO
Ginkgo biloba

Why It's Special—Ginkgo trees are treasured for their beautiful broad canopy covered in green, fan-shaped leaves that turn golden yellow in fall, dropping from the tree seemingly all at once, forming a golden carpet beneath. Ginkgos are slow-growing, drought-tolerant, long-lived trees. Plant a ginkgo for future generations.

How to Plant & Grow—Install 5-gallon or larger containers in spring or fall into well-worked, well-draining soil. Plant 25 feet from structures. Even though ginkgo grows slowly, eventually its root system extends wide and deep to support the crown. Water deeply, two to three times a week for the first spring, summer. Water twice weekly in fall, monthly the first winter if there's no rain or snow.

Care & Problems—No pruning is needed. Fertilize during years two to five with a timed-release fertilizer in spring. No pest or diseases. Keep well mulched.

Water Needs—Deeply water once a week during growing seasons. No water in winter unless there's no rain or snow.

Bloom Color—Insignificant

Peak Season—Fall foliage

Mature Size (H x W)—40 to 60 feet x 20 to 40 feet

Hardiness—Zones 5 to 9

GOLDEN RAINTREE
Koelreuteria paniculata

Why It's Special—Golden raintree grows into a perfect shade canopy with its compound leaves, clusters of flowers that drip in neon yellow, followed by ornamental pink to mauve seedpods resembling tiny lanterns. It ends the season with golden-yellow fall foliage. A good size for small backyards, it takes center stage as a focal point in large areas; plant a grouping for a small grove. It's heat, wind, and drought tolerant.

How to Plant & Grow—Deeply dig a well-drained native soil. Plant anytime, but provide consistent watering if transplanted in summer. They thrive in full sun, but tolerate part-sun/part-shade sites. Water deeply, weekly through its first year. Add 4 inches of mulch.

Care & Problems—Prune only dead, damaged limbs and sucker growth. No fertilizer is needed. No pests or diseases bother it. Keep well mulched. Seedpods may germinate under a tree's canopy; pull or transplant.

Water Needs—Water deeply every 7 to 14 days when it's blooming, once a month otherwise.

Bloom Color—Yellow

Peak Season—Spring

Mature Size (H x W)—25 feet x 25 feet

Hardiness—Zones 6 to 9, marginal in Zone 5 with protection.

GUM TREE
Eucalyptus spp.

Why It's Special—Eucalyptus has mixed reviews, but I love them for their scented evergreen foliage; smooth, mottled, or peeling bark; twisted and gnarly, picturesque and rounded, or stately linear forms; and puffy white or brilliant red flowers. They are drought tolerant, fast growing, and long lived; and there is a perfectly sized eucalyptus to fit any spot, even a container.

How to Plant & Grow—Plant in spring into well-worked, well-draining native soil. Water deeply, daily for one week, then water every 7 to 10 days for the first year. Add 4 inches of mulch.

Care & Problems—Selectively prune in early spring to remove dead, damaged, or crossing limbs. Maintain an open crown for wind to pass through. No fertilizing. Beetles and psyllids occur on drought-stressed trees, but no diseases. Maintain mulch.

Water Needs—Water deeply every three to four weeks in summer; rely on natural rainfall in winter unless extended drought.

Bloom Color—Red, yellow, white

Peak Season—Spring, summer

Mature Size (H x W)—6 to 30 feet x 10 to 30 feet

Hardiness—Zones 8 to 10

HACKBERRY
Celtis occidentalis

Why It's Special—Hackberry is a long-lived, deep-rooting, drought-tolerant tree offering lush green foliage on strongly structured branchwork. It takes a few years to grow its root system, then forms a round shady crown. Hackberry is fire resistant, making it a safe tree to plant alongside homes for shade, yet it will not lift sidewalks due to its deep roots. It's resistant to oak root fungus, and it can be planted as a lawn tree.

How to Plant & Grow—Deeply dig a well-draining native soil. Plant in spring or fall. Water deeply once a week for four to six weeks, then twice monthly during the growing season for a couple of years. Add 4 inches of mulch.

Care & Problems—Wait until the bark becomes woody, then thin and selectively prune for structure. No fertilizer necessary. No pests or diseases bother hackberry. Keep well mulched.

Water Needs—In hot summer locations, deeply water twice a month. Elsewhere, once a month during growing seasons. No water in winter.

Bloom Color—Insignificant

Peak Season—Deciduous foliage

Mature Size (H x W)—25 feet x 25 feet

Hardiness—Zones 3 to 9

HAWTHORN
Crataegus spp.

Why It's Special—Hawthorn is noted for its brilliant scarlet, purple, and orange fall foliage. It blooms later in spring than other trees, which are followed by small red fruits, persisting until winter. Many species and cultivars offer all sizes, thorny and thornless, and disease resistance.

How to Plant & Grow—Plant in fall or winter in part-sun/part-shade locations in low elevations, or in spring in other areas. Hawthorn needs cold winters to flower. Plant into well-draining, deeply worked native soil. Water deeply every 10 to 14 days the first couple of years. Mulch 4 inches.

Care & Problems—Prune after its first year to a multi-trunk or single trunk by removing lower branches. Then only prune to remove crossing branches. Pruning is optional on thorny types. No fertilizer. No pest issues if trees are healthy; select disease-resistant types. Keep well mulched.

Water Needs—Water deeply every two weeks when temperatures exceed 85 degrees Fahrenheit, otherwise monthly. No winter watering.

Bloom Color—White

Peak Season—Spring; fall foliage

Mature Size (H x W)—15 to 30 feet x 15 to 25 feet

Hardiness—Zones 3 to 9

JACARANDA
Jacaranda mimosifolia

Why It's Special—Jacaranda quickly grows into an open-crowned, graceful tree that is covered in blooms that drop to the ground at once, making a gorgeous floral carpet beneath. It's resistant to oak root fungus. Bonus: it can be planted in wet or dry locations.

How to Plant & Grow—Plant after last frost into deeply worked, well-draining soil. Water deeply every three to four days for two to three weeks, then every five to seven days for the first year. Jacaranda can be planted in lawns; provide supplemental watering. Mulch 4 inches.

Care & Problems—Prune to train early as a multi- or single trunk in spring until it reaches desired height; then selectively prune crossing branches. After its first year, apply timed-release fertilizers in fall and spring for a few years; no fertilizer after that. No pests or diseases bother it. Maintain mulch.

Water Needs—Deeply water every 7 to 10 days in summer, every three to four weeks in winter.

Bloom Color—Lavender, blue, purple, pink, white

Peak Season—Spring

Mature Size (H x W)—25 to 50 feet x 15 to 30 feet

Hardiness—Zones 9 to 11

JUNIPER
Juniperus spp.

Why It's Special—Junipers are native to some Southwest states, explaining their drought, heat, wind, and cold tolerance. Many forms include twisted, weeping, upright, columnar, and conical; foliage colors vary from green to yellow, gray-green, and metallic blue; sizes range from compact at 2 feet tall to a stately, yet manageable, 30 feet. Use for shade, background, screens, groves, and containers.

How to Plant & Grow—Plant anytime except midsummer in low deserts, where they fare better in part sun/part shade. Plant into well-worked, well-draining soil. Water deeply each week through the first summer, every 10 to 14 days in spring, fall for a couple of years, then water monthly for a year. Add 4 inches of mulch.

Care & Problems—Prune only to remove damaged branches. If you choose to lift the canopy, prune lower branches gradually over a few years. No fertilizer, pests or diseases. Maintain mulch.

Water Needs—Water deeply if drought prevails in spring and summer. Rely on rain or snow otherwise.

Bloom Color—Insignificant

Peak Season—Evergreen

Mature Size (H x W)—15 to 40 feet x 8 to 15 feet

Hardiness—Zones 2 to 10

KENTUCKY COFFEE TREE
Gymnocladus dioicus

Why It's Special—Kentucky coffee tree does produce a bean, used by settlers as a coffee substitute, but it's now grown for its fragrant bloom clusters in spring, broad shade canopy, the 4- to 12-inch pods for winter interest, and its winter silhouette. Give it room to grow as a focal shade tree or, if you have a lot of space, line a drive or form a grove.

How to Plant & Grow—Deeply work native, well-draining soil before planting bare-root or balled-and-burlapped trees in the fall or spring. Containers can be planted anytime. Water deeply, weekly through its first season. Top-dress with 4 inches of mulch.

Care & Problems—Fertilize after first year, in spring, with timed-release fertilizer for two years, then no feeding needed. Prune crossing branches every couple of years. No pests. Maintain thick mulch to control weeds and to avoid cultivating around the roots.

Water Needs—Water deeply every two weeks when temperatures exceed 75 degrees Fahrenheit, monthly otherwise.

Bloom Color—White

Peak Season—Summer

Mature Size (H x W)—40 feet x 25 feet

Hardiness—Zones 5 to 9

MAPLE
Acer spp.

Why It's Special—For gardeners in warmer zones pining for maples, try your hand at bonsai. Others can grow maples, renowned for fall foliage in red, orange, and golden yellow. Smaller types fit the urban landscape; *Acer campestre* 'Carnival' grows slowly to 10 feet x 15 feet.

How to Plant & Grow—Plant in early spring into well-worked, well-draining soil. In warm-summer areas, site in part sun/part shade. Water deeply every three to four days for two to three weeks, then every seven to ten days for the first couple of growing seasons. Mulch 4 inches.

Care & Problems—Prune after it's a few years old, during winter dormancy, to remove crossing or damaged limbs. Fertilize young trees with timed-release fertilizer in spring; then none is needed. No pests or diseases. Keep well mulched. Avoid water stress.

Water Needs—Water deeply, weekly when temperatures exceed 90 degrees Fahrenheit, every two weeks otherwise. Water monthly in winter if there's no precipitation.

Bloom Color—Insignificant

Peak Season—Fall foliage

Mature Size (H x W)—15 to 80 feet x 10 to 60 feet

Hardiness—Zones 3 to 9

MESQUITE
Prosopis spp.

Why It's Special—Mesquite are heat- and drought-resistant trees for hot summer deserts. Many are native to the Southwest. They're deep rooting, with airy strong branches accustomed to standing strong in high winds. Texas honey mesquite (*Prosopis glandulosa*) grows 25 feet tall, with thorny branches, fragrant blooms. Velvet mesquite (*P. velutina*) has gray-green, soft, deciduous leaves on low-branched small trees, 25 feet tall and wide.

How to Plant & Grow—Plant into a well-draining native soil, but work it deeply before planting in early spring. Water deeply every three to four days for two to three weeks, then every seven to ten days for the first year. Mulch 4 inches.

Care & Problems—Prune in late summer to shape, thin, or raise the crown. No fertilizing is needed. Pests or diseases aren't problems. Maintain mulch.

Water Needs—Water deeply every three to four weeks in summer, monthly in winter if there's no rain.

Bloom Color—White, yellow

Peak Season—Spring, summer

Mature Size (H x W)—15 to 30 feet x 15 to 35 feet

Hardiness—Zones 7 to 10; Zone 6 with protection.

MOUNTAIN ASH
Sorbus spp.

Why It's Special—Mountain ash forms a classic vase-shaped crown and is amenable to growing in a lawn, fitting into small spaces with its short and narrow form. Dark green foliage emerges in spring, followed by clusters of sometimes-fragrant blooms and small, orange berries in fall. It ends the season with yellow to orange-red foliage if frost is delayed.

How to Plant & Grow—Plant balled-and-burlapped or containers anytime except during winter into well-worked, well-draining soil. Water deeply every three to five days for two to three weeks, then weekly through the first growing season. Add 4 inches of mulch.

Care & Problems—Selectively prune in December or January for structure. Use timed-release fertilizer its second spring. It is not heat tolerant for southern Nevada. Wrap young trunks in southwestern exposures for the first two winters to protect from splitting. No pests. Keep well mulched.

Water Needs—Water deeply every 7 to 10 days during the growing season. Winter water in extended drought.

Bloom Color—White, red

Peak Season—Spring, summer

Mature Size (H x W)—20 to 30 feet x 15 to 20 feet

Hardiness—Zones 3 to 8

OAK
Quercus spp.

Why It's Special—Oaks are stately long-lived trees, faster-growing than you think (up to 3 feet a year), and more drought tolerant than imagined. Oaks provide year-round or seasonal shade and brilliant fall foliage. There is an oak for every garden.

How to Plant & Grow—Deeply work a well-draining native soil. Plant evergreen oaks in spring, or summer; deciduous oaks in fall, Water deeply twice a month from April through August, monthly in cooler weather for four to five years. Mulch 4 inches.

Care & Problems—Oaks need little pruning except for structure. But don't prune for two years, then selectively prune weak, broken, or crossing branches in late winter. Established oaks don't need pruning. Apply timed-release fertilizer their second through fifth year, in spring. No pests or diseases attack if trees are in well-draining soil, watered deeply, and mulched to within 1 foot of the trunk to beyond the drip line.

Water Needs—Water deeply once a month year-round if there's no precipitation.

Bloom Color—Inconspicuous

Peak Season—Fall foliage

Mature Size (H x W)—10 to 100 feet x 50 to 80 feet

Hardiness—Zones 3 to 9

ORCHID TREE
Bauhinia spp.

Why It's Special—Once you see an orchid tree in bloom, you will be willing to nurse it through any conditions just to see its spectacular flowers in your patio garden. It's a small tree, so it's easy to give a bit of extra attention in a sheltered spot where it is protected from winter cold and to keep it well watered and mulched.

How to Plant & Grow—Deeply incorporate amendments into a well-draining soil. Plant in spring, summer, or fall. Water deeply every three to four days for two to three weeks, then water every five to seven days its first year. Add 4 inches of mulch.

Care & Problems—Prune to remove frost-damaged limbs and apply timed-release fertilizer in early spring. *Bauhinia* is subject to salt burn, heat stress, and summer chlorosis, but not to pests or disease. Leach salts and refresh mulch.

Water Needs—Water deeply, weekly in summer, every two to three weeks otherwise.

Bloom Color—Pink, mauve, white, purple

Peak Season—Spring, summer

Mature Size (H x W)—6 to 30 feet x 5 to 25 feet

Hardiness—Zones 9 to 10

PINE
Pinus spp.

Why It's Special—There is a pine tree for every zone and garden space. For low elevations, *Pinus elderica* and *P. halepensis* are heat and drought tough. Native to the Southwest, *P. cembroides* (pinyon pine) produces pine nuts on mature 20-foot-tall trees. Select a pine for your zone and space for focal point, groves, windbreaks, screens, and background plants.

How to Plant & Grow—Plant when weather is cool, midwinter in areas where ground can be dug, into well-worked, well-draining native soil. Water deeply every seven to ten days in summer, every three to four weeks in winter for two years, then reduce gradually over the next two years. Add 4 inches of mulch.

Care & Problems—Prune only to clean out dead wood in spring. No fertilizer, pests, or diseases. Keep well mulched. Allow needles that shed naturally to remain at the base of tree as mulch.

Water Needs—Deeply water monthly in summer, every other month if there's no rain or snow.

Bloom Color—Insignificant

Peak Season—Evergreen conifer

Mature Size (H x W)—20 to 100 feet x 10 to 70 feet

Hardiness—Zones 3 to 10

REDBUD
Cercis spp.

Why It's Special—Redbud blooms for three to four weeks in early spring, followed by heart-shaped foliage on multi-trunked trees. Fall color ranges from yellow to red, and smooth, gray winter branchwork forms its shadow on a wall or in the snow. Redbuds are focal points for small gardens, and stunning in drifts or groves.

How to Plant & Grow—Plant dormant trees in fall or early spring in low elevations in part-sun/part-shade sites. Otherwise, plant in spring into well-worked, well-draining native soil. Water deeply every three to five days for two to three weeks, then weekly through its first growing season. Mulch 4 inches.

Care & Problems—Prune dormant trees to remove dead, damaged, or crossing branches and suckers. Apply timed-release fertilizer each fall for the first four to six years. No pests or diseases. Keep well mulched.

Water Needs—Deeply water every 7 to 14 days when temperatures exceed 85 degrees Fahrenheit, every month or less otherwise.

Bloom Color—Pink

Peak Season—Spring

Mature Size (H x W)—12 to 30 feet x 15 to 25 feet

Hardiness—Zones 5 to 9

SMOKE TREE
Cotinus coggygria

Why It's Special—Smoke tree has distinctive blue-green foliage on a multi-trunked tree. Its flowers form seedheads that form a puffy cloud around the tree in summer, yielding to yellow to red fall foliage. 'Royal Purple' is commonly seen, valued for its deep red-purple foliage with contrasting dusky pink seedheads. It's small enough for containers, for understory plantings, singly as focal points, or *en masse* for a screen.

How to Plant & Grow—Plant well-acclimated containers anytime into well-worked, well-draining native soil. Smoke tree struggles in southern Nevada. Water deeply two to three times a week for three to four weeks, then weekly for its first growing season.

Care & Problems—Prune in summer, removing suckers and lower branch offshoots. Fertilize three to four years in spring with timed-release fertilizer. No pests or diseases. Keep well mulched.

Water Needs—Deeply water every two weeks when temperatures exceed 90 degrees Fahrenheit or during blooming. Other times water monthly; none in winter.

Bloom Color—Pink seedheads

Peak Season—Summer; fall foliage

Mature Size (H x W)—12 to 15 feet x 12 to 15 feet

Hardiness—Zones 5 to 8

SPRUCE
Picea spp.

Why It's Special—Spruce trees are valued for their silver to blue-green needles and classic, full tapered form. They're long-lived, large conifers. Grow spruce as a focal point, giving room for its majestic mature size. *Picea pungens* 'Glauca' has true blue needles, 'Pendula' is weeping, and 'Fat Albert' is stout, growing 15 feet x 12 feet. Interplant young trees with groundcovers.

How to Plant & Grow—Plant in early autumn or early spring into well-worked, well-draining native soil. Spruce suffers in extreme summer heat and high humidity. Water deeply every three to four days for two to three weeks, then water weekly its first year. Add 4 inches of mulch.

Care & Problems—Do not prune. Use a timed-release fertilizer in spring for its first five years. Mites, aphids, and bagworms might occur, but not diseases. Keep well mulched.

Water Needs—Deeply water when temperatures exceed 85 degrees Fahrenheit every 10 to 14 days, monthly when weather cools. In higher elevations it survives on natural rainfall.

Bloom Color—Insignificant

Peak Season—Evergreen conifer

Mature Size (H x W)—30 to 60 feet x 10 to 40 feet

Hardiness—Zones 3 to 9

'SWAN HILL' OLIVE®
Olea europaea 'Swan Hill'

Why It's Special—'Swan Hill' Olive® is a picturesque, heat- and drought-tough shade tree that produces no fruit or pollen. Its multi-trunked form is white and becomes gnarled with age, while the leaves are green with lighter undersides. Slow-growing, it's as wide as it is tall. Use it as a focal point shade tree for year-round beauty. If you cannot get one, another option is New Mexico olive, *Forestiera neomexicana*, which has a curving trunk, small leaves, fragrant flowers, and blue fruits.

How to Plant & Grow—Deeply incorporate compost into a well-draining soil to plant anytime of the year. Water deeply twice a week until new growth occurs. Add 4 inches of mulch.

Care & Problems—Thin to let the light into lower branches (never top!). Allow soil to dry between waterings; too much water causes problems. Top-dress each spring with nitrogen fertilizer. Refresh mulch to avoid cultivating under trees. Resistant to pests and verticillium wilt.

Water Needs—Water deeply, weekly throughout summer. Water occasionally in winter.

Bloom Color—White

Peak Season—Spring

Mature Size (H x W)—30 feet x 30 feet

Hardiness—Zones 8 to 11

SWEETGUM
Liquidambar styraciflua

Why It's Special—Sweetgum is warm-winter climate's claim to fall color. The cooler the winter, the better the show. Red, orange, yellow, and burgundy maplelike fall foliage drop to show off the furrowed bark and open branch structure in winter. Choose 'Rotundiloba' for its rounder foliage, yellow to reddish purple fall color, and lack of spiny fruits.

How to Plant & Grow—Plant in spring or fall (which allows you to select by fall color) into well-worked, well-draining soil. Water deeply two to three times a week for three to four weeks, then weekly through the growing season for the first year. Add 4 inches of mulch.

Care & Problems—Prune only to remove damaged branches. No fertilizer is needed. No diseases, but tent caterpillars, aphids, and spider mites may attack. Keep well mulched.

Water Needs—Water deeply once every 14 days when temperatures exceed 85 degrees Fahrenheit; otherwise water monthly until winter dormancy. Water if there's no rain for extended periods.

Bloom Color—Insignificant

Peak Season—Fall foliage

Mature Size (H x W)—45 to 75 feet x 40 to 60 feet

Hardiness—Zones 6 to 9

TREES MONTH-BY-MONTH

JANUARY

- In warm-winter zones, plant any potted holiday tree this month. Make sure it is a species that thrives in your area. Bring it outdoors to a cool location to acclimate for a few days before planting. Moisten the planting area, extending the watering a couple of feet beyond the planting hole.

- Dig the hole and remove the tree from its container, taking care not to disturb the rootball, retaining as much of the soil around the roots as possible. Set in the hole, adjust the depth so the tree sits exactly at the same level or a bit higher than it was before. Backfill, using well worked, native soil, firming the soil gently around the rootball. Build a broad berm and basin. Fill with water, allow to drain, then cover with 4 inches of organic mulch, leaving 2 inches free from mulch right next to the trunk. Keep well watered.

- Prune deciduous trees, removing only damaged, diseased, or crossing limbs growing into the center of the tree or toward the ground. Raise the crown gradually, cutting lower branches each season until you get the clearance you want. Do not prune frost- or cold-sensitive trees yet.

FEBRUARY

- It's bare-root planting season. While planting can only be done in areas where the ground is not frozen, if you don't buy this month, supplies dwindle, depleting completely by month's end. Buy as late in the month as you can, then store the bare-root transplant in a cool, sheltered, shaded location. Heel in the roots by covering with dampened peat moss, sawdust, or sand, then cover with moistened burlap. Keep the roots moist and cool so the tree stays dormant.

- Continue to prune deciduous trees. If you live in a frost-free area, you may lightly prune evergreens. Prune winter-damaged branches only when you see new green growth emerging, then prune back to that spot.

- If the ground is not frozen, water established trees monthly if there's no rain. Deeply water newly planted trees every three weeks.

MARCH

- To plant bare-root trees, dig the holes first into deeply watered soil that has been moistened 2 feet beyond the hole. This assures that drier soil outside the planting area does not wick water away from the roots. Soak the bare-root tree in a bucket of water at least six hours before planting to rehydrate.

- Newly planted trees may require temporary staking to protect them from winds while their roots are developing to anchor them to the soil. If they come with a stake, remove it immediately and reposition after planting. Stakes butted up against the tree do not allow light to reach that part of the trunk, causing cells to elongate, weakening the tree over time. Stakes should placed 4 to 6 inches away from the trunk. The tree should be tied so it is supported yet allowed to move gently with the wind. Move the stakes out from the trunk as the tree grows, loosening the supports, removing the stakes when the tree supports itself.

- There is no pruning to be done on conifers. They grow beautifully all on their own. Exposed pruning wounds are an invitation for pests and disease.

APRIL

- If you plant a tree in the lawn, remove turf in a broad swath extending beyond the drip line. The sprinkler system for the lawn will not give the tree enough deep water, so you will need to supplement water until it is established. Fill the excavated area with mulch.

- Fertilize juvenile trees this month if they have been in the ground for a year. Pull the mulch back from the trunk, exposing the soil from the trunk to the drip line. Scatter fertilizer on the surface of the soil, per package recommendations, water it in, then replace or refresh the mulch to 4 inches thick, leaving a 2-inch bare space around the trunk of the tree.

- As temperatures heat up, check the water depth of the soil after spring rains before you water. If it was a good soaking, then don't water. Overwatering in cool soils can lead to root rot.

MAY

- As trees grow taller, their root systems grow wider and deeper. Adjust any drip irrigation tubing so it curls around a tree, starting a few inches out from the trunk, then winds around about halfway to the drip line, continuing the loop to just outside the drip line. Add a length of tubing to accommodate the extended loops and a few emitters to ensure the entire root zone is receiving water.

- If you are planning to add a new tree to your garden, allow enough space to accommodate the tree's crown at maturity. Sketch the area to scale, including any structures, then draw a circle representing the tree at its mature width. Then you can see if the tree will be bumping into the roof, blocking a window, or growing into the garage. Site it in an area where it can grow to its mature, glorious size.

- Resume deep, regular watering for trees that have been in the ground less than five years. It takes that long for a tree to become established (much longer than for a shrub), but it's not that long in tree years!

JUNE

- It's heating up and it's the perfect weather to plant palms. They like the warm air and soil. Make sure they are planted at the same level they were in their pot, water deeply every two days for two weeks throughout the first summer. Add 3 to 4 inches of mulch.

- Planting groundcovers in the understory of young conifers is one way to keep the soil cool and the humidity level up. The groundcover roots grow in their own space, while the tree roots go deep. As the conifers mature, the branches will shade out the groundcovers, providing their own shade to cool the soil and roots.

- If you have an aphid infestation dropping honeydew, try releasing ladybugs. It may take a few releases over two or three seasons. Release in the evening, wetting the trunks and limbs so the ladies can gain a foothold, and release them in a few sites throughout the tree. Repeat monthly during the growing season.

JULY

- If you inherit a tree with surface roots, remove turfgrass growing in the area, then mulch thickly, eliminating the chance of damage by mowers or line trimmers. If sidewalks or concrete slabs are lifting due to tree roots, consult a licensed arborist to see if anything can be done to stop the lifting without damaging the tree.

- If you are growing saplings and newly planted trees, watering deeply for their first five years encourages deep rooting. Some tree types are prone to surface rooting, but others have surface roots because they were only given shallow watering while they were young.

- Deep rooting trees carry some drought tolerance when the roots are able to absorb water that may be residing deep within the soil profile. Trees that are deemed drought tolerant are only able to tap into that resource when they are well established. They may require ample, regular watering for many years, then weaning for a few more, but eventually they will survive drought on their own.

AUGUST

- If you fill a hole with water and it takes many hours to drain, then you may have a poorly draining soil, which is treatable over the long term with repeated incorporation of organics. If it has not drained in 12 hours, you may have caliche, a deep impermeable barrier that has no remedy. Caliche may only be present in pockets throughout your garden, so find another spot for the tree.

- Search out sources for mulch for fall planting and extra winter protection. Sometimes arborists will deliver a load of wood chips for free if they are working in your area, saving them a trip to the landfill. Tree mulch includes all parts of the tree, branches, leaves, cones, and bark. Desirable mulch is chipped to 3- to 6-inch pieces, fairly uniform in size, and no trash in the mix. Palms don't make good mulch. It doesn't chip well and tends to shred, so should be taken to the landfill.

- Don't fertilize this time of year. Either the plant will burn because it's still too hot, or the tree will generate new soft growth, susceptible to fall cold and winter freeze damage.

SEPTEMBER

- Fall is a good time to plant trees. The weather and soil temperatures are still warm enough to get them established before winter, yet cooler nights eliminate heat stress.

- Balled-and-burlapped trees have healthy roots surrounded by the soil they have been growing in. Plant them right away into deeply worked, dampened, prepared native soil, maintaining as much of the soil around the rootball as possible.

- Container plants may be rootbound. Check planting instructions on the label to make sure you are not damaging the roots. Some conifers and native trees don't like to have their roots disturbed, but most deciduous and evergreens need some work. Remove the bottom 1 to 2 inches of rootmass, then make vertical slices down the sides around the outside of the rootball. If you try to encourage wrapping roots to spread by gently teasing them apart, the roots will continue to circle, eventually girdling the tree.

OCTOBER

- You can plant trees that are not deciduous or frost tender in warmer zones. It is too cold to plant palms at this time.

- Newly planted trees and young trees should be deeply watered until just before the ground usually freezes or first snow fall. After that, they will need to survive winter on what nature provides. Keep them moist (not soggy) through the month and add an extra couple of inches of mulch. If the tree is on a zonal edge, then it may require laying branches over the mulch for added winter protection until it establishes.

- Established trees should be watered monthly if they have been in the ground for five years. If they are entering their sixth winter, extend watering to every six weeks if no rain or snow falls.

NOVEMBER

- When leaves fall from deciduous trees and conifers shed needles, leave them where they fall for nature's mulch. If they fall on the lawn, they shade grass blades, so you need to rake. If they blanket evergreen shrubs, then use the fan rake to gently knock them off.

- Living, balled-and-burlapped Christmas trees purchased in December can survive the home environment for 7 to 10 days, but then need to be planted outdoors. In colder climates, prepare the soil and dig the hole now before the ground freezes. Pack mulch into the hole and cover the backfill soil with a tarp. At the first of January, you can plant the tree, watering it well, then covering with a thick layer of mulch.

- If you planted cold-sensitive trees this year, be prepared to cover the young trees on freezing nights. Throw a sheet or burlap over the tree in the afternoon, remove it when temperatures exceed 32 degrees Fahrenheit the next day.

DECEMBER

- In low zones, if no winter rain occurs within a two-month period, deeply water established trees. Either run the drip system so water slowly percolates into the soil or coil a soaker hose around the root zone of the tree, encompassing the area close to the trunk (but at least a few inches away), circling the hose to include all of the rootmass out beyond the drip line.

- Living Christmas trees are often Italian stone pine, Afghan pine, Aleppo pine, Arizona cypress, noble fir, Scotch pine, or Monterey pine. Be sure to check which species grows in your zone and if you can accommodate the mature size and habit before purchasing it to plant after the holidays. Some may be sheared to the classic Christmas tree shape. Upon planting they will revert to their natural beautiful form. Some may have a pyramidal form in youth, but develop a broader crown with maturity. For sure, all will grow much broader and taller.

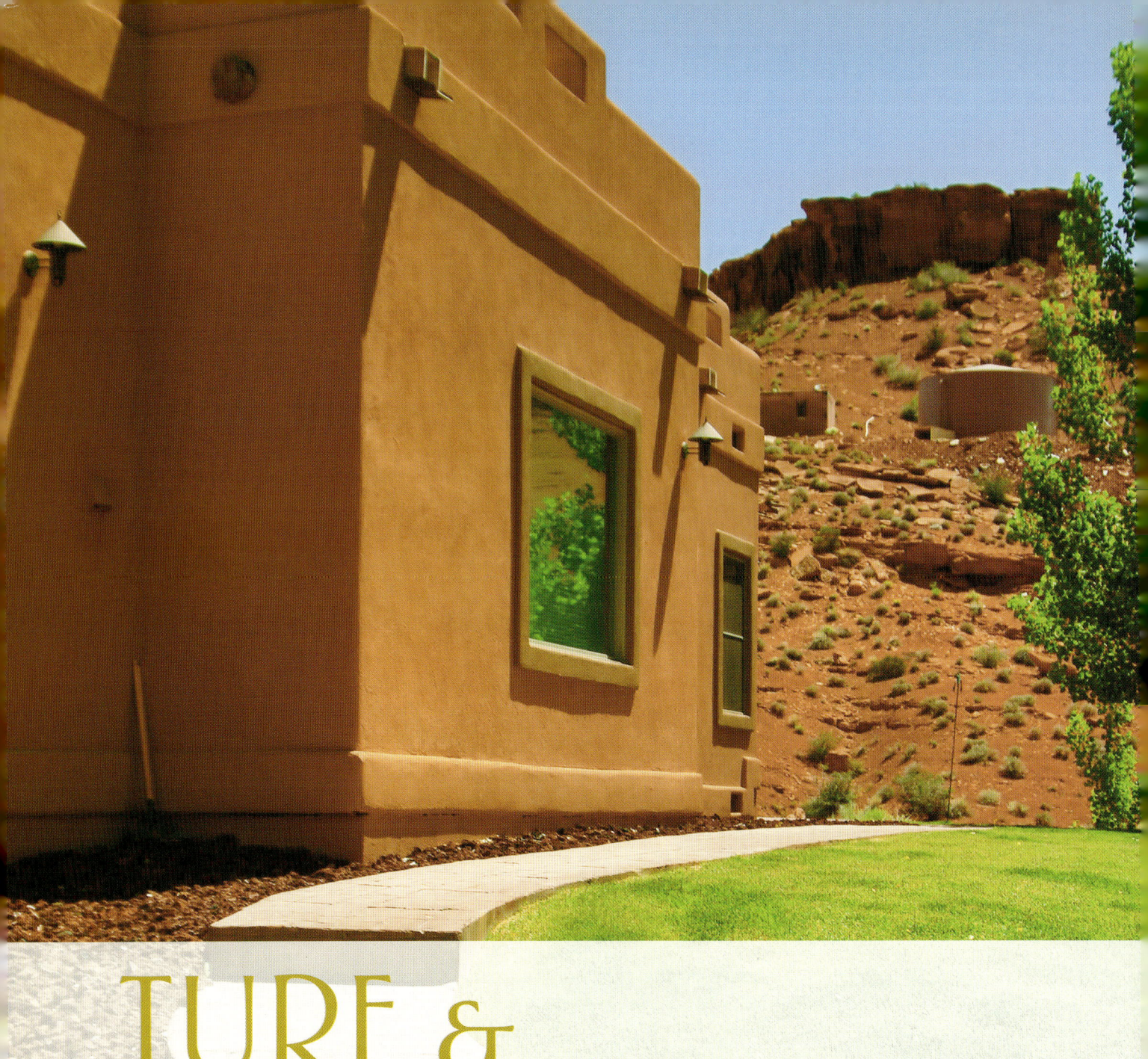

TURF & ORNAMENTAL GRASSES

for the Southwest

Turf grasses and ornamental grasses are often grouped together—after all, they are both "grass." They do have somewhat different functions, however. Lawns do more than simply provide a bit of green. They cool an area, anchor the soil, and are fire resistant. Thousands of leaf blades, each of which is an individual plant, emit oxygen, act as a filter for air pollutants, and diminish stormwater runoff. Growing lawns in the Southwest not only provides a cooling respite, it also offers valuable environmental benefits. Ornamental grasses provide texture, contrast, and movement in the garden. They can stand alone as a focal point or fill a container. Planted *en masse*, they cover and anchor a slope, surround a meadow, or line a driveway. They can be grouped to drift under trees, provide contrast in the perennial bed, create a visual barrier, or enhance a view. They come in all forms: upright, arching, clumping, tall, short, spreading, and tightly formed. There are tall, giant grasses that stretch even taller with their flower spikes, and diminutive types that remain tight in small tufts of green. Some have variegated, green, blue-green, gray-green, silver, or white foliage that change to golden amber, orange, or bronze foliage in fall. Most produce a flower on short little spikes held above the foliage or on towering plumes that add yet another dimension to their form, persisting for winter interest.

WE LOVE LAWNS

Many years ago, when I was younger and more energetic, I cultivated, harvested, and sold sod. I believe my love affair with turf began then. In the middle of a hot, inland San Diego summer, I sat on a mower, cooled by sprays of water from close-by sprinklers, with the aroma of fresh-cut grass enveloping me and the hum of the engine and the slapping of the blades lulling me into a state of relaxation and well being.

Many of us love our lawns. This sentiment may not be shared by all gardeners in the Southwest (who are often removing their lawns) as drought

An aerator pulls out 2- to 3-inch plugs of soil, creating spaces for air and water movement in a lawn that is stressed due to compacted soil or a thatch buildup.

and water challenges become the norm. A green expanse of lawn and cannon-like sprinklers going full blast with water running down the sidewalk is cause for the water patrol to come knocking. Large, so-green-it-hurts-your-eyes lawns should be a thing of the past, yet I still see them. My lawns are quite different, in quantity and quality, and are a compromise.

FACTORS TO GROWING A LAWN IN THE SOUTHWEST

GROW JUST ENOUGH LAWN TO DO THE JOB YOU WANT

Having a large expanse of lawn in the home landscape is a waste of space and resources. Site the lawn where it will be used and grow as much as you need to fulfill your purpose for it.

SELECT THE RIGHT TURF TYPE

Many cultivars and turf types are perfect for our climate and soil. Most will have a dormancy period, in which case you can overseed or even use a biodegradable turf dye if you can't tolerate a brown lawn for a few months. Some are more drought tough than others, some feel better underfoot, some need more care. Consider meadow plantings and lawn alternatives if you want the green, but might not be using it for play. Visit a local sod farm or research to see which turf types grow best in your area.

WATER THE LAWN EFFICIENTLY

Install a low-flow irrigation system that waters the area with minimal overspray or evaporation. Major manufacturers offer design assistance online, or hire a professional to design the system and you can install it yourself or hire it out. If you handwater, move the sprinkler often to cover all areas, while avoiding runoff. Adjust the irrigation system watering schedule to water in the morning, in short increments that allow the water to percolate into the soil, avoiding runoff.

LIMIT THE AMOUNT OF FERTILIZER USED AND CURB MOWING HABITS

Home lawns only require fertilizing twice a year, once in early spring and in late summer if the turf doesn't go dormant in winter. If the lawn is green and growing, then don't fertilize. The more you fertilize, the more it grows, hence the more water and mowing the lawn requires. Longer blades shade their roots, cooling the soil, cutting back on evaporation and requiring less water.

By following these guidelines, gardeners can enjoy the benefits of having a lawn and the design attributes it brings to the landscape, while conserving resources and minimizing labor. Sounds like a win-win situation to this seasoned sod grower.

ORNAMENTAL GRASSES COME BACK HOME

Ornamental grasses have been gaining in popularity quickly. I remember when pampas grass was the only "ornamental" grass people grew. Pampas grass is grown in colder parts of the country. It freezes back each year before its tall plumes, holding thousands of seeds, can disperse. I, however, spent a great deal of time eradicating it from the landscape, as it was labeled an invasive species in California. Planted as hedgerows here in Utah, I see its large, arching form with tall flower spikes blowing in the breeze, making quite a statement in the landscape. Any ornamental grass may be considered a weed in some gardens because, by definition, a weed is any unwanted plant and that is determined by the gardener, who is either pulling it out or planting it!

Many grasses grown in cultivation are derived from native species, bred to be more compact or controlled in size, tolerant of varied conditions and adaptable to landscape environments. Some come from deserts, where they thrive in the heat, full sun, rocky, sandy, and lean soils. Deep rooting, they are drought and wind tolerant, flowering profusely on tall stalks that send their seed in the breeze, perpetuating the species. Some grasses come from prairies, plains, and natural grasslands, from a time when their foliage fed grazing animals, regenerating their growth from rhizomes and stolons. And some come from swamps and streambed edges, waterways, and lakes, able to grow with their feet in consistently damp or slow-draining soils. The traits that helped grasses survive through the years make them tough-as-nails plants in our Southwest gardens.

Maintenance is simply a hard prune to just above the ground (don't cut into their crown) in fall or early spring, depending upon your winter climate. They never need fertilizing, have no pests or diseases, and most require only a supplemental watering after establishment. Grasses like mulches, but some are happiest with gravel, rock, or stone. They are amenable to being divided, don't miss a beat if transplanted, and are easy to grow from seed if available. If the ornamental grass sounds like the perfect plant to you, then maybe it is!

BEARGRASS
Nolina spp.

Why It's Special—Beargrass forms large clumps, similar to bunch grass, with long flower stalks covered in hundreds of small flowers. It's a heat- and drought-tolerant evergreen. Select the type to fit in rock gardens, for background borders, or along dry streambeds as a focal point.

How to Plant & Grow—Available as containers and seed. Plant February through October in lower elevations, otherwise, plant May through August into well-worked, well-draining native soil. Water deeply twice a week, allowing surface soil to dry between waterings, until new growth appears. Then water weekly through its first year. Apply gravel mulch.

Care & Problems—Remove spent flower stalks and dead leaves. Do not shear. No fertilizer. Do not overwater. Pests or diseases aren't a problem.

Water Needs—Deeply water every two to three weeks in summer in lower elevations, monthly in other locales. Water monthly in winter in low deserts, rely on natural rainfall in higher elevations.

Bloom Color—White

Peak Season—Summer

Mature Size (H x W)—2 to 6 feet x 4 to 10 feet

Hardiness—Zones 6 to 8; to Zone 5 if established by winter and well mulched.

BERMUDAGRASS
Cynodon dactylon

Why It's Special—Bermudagrass is the most drought- and heat-tolerant turfgrass that grows in the Southwest. It forms a dense, cushiony mat good for play, walking upon, or just relaxing.

How to Plant & Grow—Available as seed, sod, and stolons. Deeply work well-draining, pre-moistened soil in late spring or summer. Rake and level, then roll to settle. Cover seed or stolons with seed starter, sawdust, or sand; roll again. Keep moist, watering for short durations once or twice daily.

Care & Problems—Bermudagrass spreads by stolons and rhizomes so restrict its growth by concrete mow-strips or other barriers. Resume regular mowing and fertilize with a formulated turf fertilizer in spring. If drought is severe it will slide into dormancy, but resume growing once water is applied.

Water Needs—Water to 6 inches deep each week. When temperatures fall below 90 degrees Fahrenheit, water every other week. Water monthly in winter dormancy if there's no rain.

Peak Season—Warm season grass

Mowing Height—Mow to 1 to 2 inches, or taller

Hardiness—Zones 6 to 10; it goes dormant at the first frost.

BLOOD GRASS
Imperata cylindrica 'Rubra'

Why It's Special—Blood grass 'Rubra' offers outstanding red-tipped foliage, increasing in vibrancy and peaking at summer's end. It then turns copper for winter interest. Its size makes it perfect for containers, in the front of the part-shade border, and tucked into the edges of a pond or streambed.

How to Plant & Grow—Available as container plants. Plant into well-worked, well-draining, compost-enriched or sandy native soil in spring to early summer. Site in dappled shade or for afternoon shade. Water deeply, every three days, until new growth emerges. Add 2 to 3 inches of mulch.

Care & Problems—Blood grass doesn't like hot, dry locations. Prune to the ground each spring before new growth emerges. No fertilizer is needed and no pests or diseases are a concern.

Water Needs—Deeply water weekly during the growing season, twice weekly if temperatures exceed 90 degrees Fahrenheit. Water monthly while it's dormant if there's no rain.

Bloom Color—Red foliage

Peak Season—Summer

Mature Size (H x W)—15 to 20 inches x 15 to 24 inches

Hardiness—Zones 4 to 9

BLUESTEM
Andropogon spp.

Why It's Special—Bluestem naturally grows in prairies and some species are native to marshy damp sites, so it can grow in wet or dry soils. It ranges in size from columnar 8 feet in moist climates to 3 to 4 feet in drier locations, depending upon the species and cultivar. Its blades are pale green to silver blue, turning bronze-red, golden-red, and burgundy in fall.

How to Plant & Grow—Available as container grown. Plant in spring, summer, or fall into well-worked, well-draining native soil. Some species do grow in swampy conditions. If potbound, remove the bottom inch of roots and make vertical cuts around the remaining rootball before planting. Water deeply and frequently until new growth appears.

Care & Problems—Trim old growth down to new green growth in early spring. No fertilizer is needed. No pests or diseases bother bluestem.

Water Needs—Water deeply once a week when temperatures exceed 90 degrees Fahrenheit; every two weeks otherwise.

Bloom Color—White, purple

Peak Season—Summer, fall, fall color

Mature Size (H x W)—2 to 5 feet x 2 to 3 feet

Hardiness—Zones 2 to 7

BLUE AVENA
Helictotrichon sempervirens

Why It's Special—Blue avena's soft blue, stiff foliage holds its color through winter on a tidy clumping plant. It adds texture and color to containers, to drifts planted in perennial gardens, along meadow edges, singly in rock gardens, or along dry streambeds.

How to Plant & Grow—Available as container grown and divisions. When temperatures are below 75 degrees Fahrenheit, plant into well-worked, compost-amended, well-draining soil. In low deserts, site in part sun to part shade. Water deeply twice weekly until new growth emerges. Mulch 2 to 3 inches (organic mulch in full sun or gravel mulch in part shade).

Care & Problems—Cut leaves to just above the ground in early spring; remove drying flower stalks. Rust may occur in deep-shade sites. No fertilizing. No pests or disease. Keep mulched.

Water Needs—Water deeply once a week when temperatures exceed 85 degrees Fahrenheit, otherwise, every two weeks. Water monthly in cooler weather if there's no rain or snow.

Bloom Color—Blue panicles

Peak Season—Summer

Mature Size (H x W)—2 to 3 feet x 2 to 3 feet

Hardiness—Zones 4 to 9

BLUE FESCUE
Festuca glauca

Why It's Special—Blue fescue is a heat- and drought-tolerant, blue-foliaged, uniformly clumping plant offering multiple uses. Plant it in symmetrical formations to fill entire beds, in drifts on slopes, singly in containers, along dry streambeds, in rock gardens, or group for texture and color in perennial beds. Blue Crown™ stays a compact 4 to 8 inches tall and wide.

How to Plant & Grow—Available as container grown and flats. Deeply incorporate compost into a well-drained soil. Plant in early spring after last frost. Water deeply every three to four days for a month; then, every seven to ten days through its first summer. Add a thin layer of mulch.

Care & Problems—Cut back to a few inches tall in spring to refresh. If plants die out in the center, dig and divide. No fertilizer is needed. No pests or diseases. Refresh mulch.

Water Needs—Water deeply twice a month if temperatures exceed 80 degrees Fahrenheit; otherwise water monthly if there's no rain.

Bloom Color—Buff

Peak Season—Spring

Mature Size (H x W)—8 to 12 inches x 12 to 16 inches

Hardiness—Zones 4 to 11

BLUE GRAMA GRASS
Bouteloua gracilis

Why It's Special—Native blue grama grass is drought and heat tolerant. A cool-season grass, it awakens in early spring, turning amber in fall. It makes a showy ornamental when blooming, a softly swaying grass for meadows, and a traffic- or play-tolerant lawn.

How to Plant & Grow—Available as seed or plugs. Sow or plant in late spring or summer into deeply worked, pre-moistened, amended, well-draining soil. Cover lightly; keep moist by watering overhead daily until germination. Then water two to three times a week until it's well established. Keep weeded.

Care & Problems—Mow to 3 inches tall for lawns, but don't cut more than 1 inch at a time. For a meadow, mow in spring and late summer (sooner if you want to minimize self-sowing in small gardens). Fertilize in spring with a turf-type fertilizer to increase vigor.

Water Needs—Water deeply once a week when temperatures exceed 85 degrees Fahrenheit; otherwise, water twice monthly. Don't water in winter dormancy.

Bloom Color—Yellow-white

Peak Season—Summer

Mature Size (H x W)—18 to 24 inches x 12 to 18 inches

Hardiness—Zones 5 to 9

BLUE LYME GRASS
Leymus arenarius 'Glauca'

Why It's Special—Blue lyme grass is true silver-blue, with a clumping form and gently arching blades. It's salt, drought, and sun tolerant. Site in the rock garden, at the edge of an infrequently watered meadow, in drifts on slopes for groundcover, or under open-canopied trees.

How to Plant & Grow—Available as container grown. Plant anytime when temperatures are below 90 degrees Fahrenheit. Deeply work unamended, well-draining soil. Full-sun locations plus lean, rocky soils produce slower-spreading, more blue-tinted plants. Part shade increases the speed of rhizome growth.

Care & Problems—Cut off unattractive flower spikes as soon as they form. Cut back to the ground in autumn. No fertilizer. If grown in fertile, moist gardens, it spreads more, so either dig and divide in fall or spring or contain with barriers.

Water Needs—Water deeply weekly when temperatures exceed 85 degrees Fahrenheit; every two weeks when it's 60 to 85 degrees Fahrenheit. Water monthly during cooler weather.

Bloom Color—Inconspicuous

Peak Season—Spring through fall

Mature Size (H x W)—1 to 2 feet x 3 feet

Hardiness—Zones 4 to 9

BUFFALO GRASS
Buchloe dactyloides

Why It's Special—Drought-tolerant buffalo grass provides the look of a meadow grass, no mowing required. It spreads slowly by stolons, so it's not invasive. Seed is often mixed with blue grama for quicker fill. A tough, easy-care lawn, it turns golden-brown for winter dormancy.

How to Plant & Grow—Available as seed, plugs, and sod. Rototill amendments into a well-draining soil in late spring to early summer. Cover seedbed. Maintain moisture by overhead daily waterings until germination; then water weekly until well established.

Care & Problems—No mowing, unless you want a tailored look, then mow to 2 to 3 inches, not cutting more than an inch at each mowing. Mow to two inches in spring to encourage greening. Apply lawn fertilizer in April. No pests or diseases bother buffalo grass.

Water Needs—Water deeply, weekly when temperatures exceed 85 degrees Fahrenheit; every 2 weeks from 70 to 85 degrees Fahrenheit. Water monthly in winter if there's no rain or snow.

Peak Season—Winter dormant

Mature Size (H x W)—4 to 8 inches x 24 to 48 inches

Hardiness—Zones 2 to 10

FEATHER GRASS
Stipa tenuissima

Why It's Special—Feather grass (also named thread grass) has an upright form with gently arching, thin, threadlike blades. It emerges in spring with green growth, tips turning amber-gold as they mature, followed by fluffy seedheads on tall stalks. Then the entire plant transforms to golden wheat hues that persist through winter. Use at the edge of meadows, in drifts along a drive, interplanted with other xeric perennials as accents, tucked among boulders, or to line an open-air patio where they catch the breeze.

How to Plant & Grow—Available as seeds or container grown. Plant in summer into well-worked, well-draining native soil. Water deeply twice a week until new growth. Add 3 to 4 inches of mulch.

Care & Problems—Rejuvenate by shearing to the ground in spring. Cull fading plants; weed out unwanted seedlings once or twice a season. No fertilizer. Pests or diseases aren't a problem. Refresh mulch.

Water Needs—Water deeply, weekly in summer. Water monthly in winter if there's no rain.

Bloom Color—Yellow

Peak Season—Summer

Mature Size (H x W)—18 inches x 18 inches

Hardiness—Zones 7 to 10

FEATHER REED GRASS
Calamagrostis spp.

Why It's Special—Feather reed grass is prized for its tall, elegant flower plumes that double the overall height by season's end. Its blades are 2 feet long, slightly arching at maturity, forming an upright clump. Long-lived feather reed grass is best sited in the background of perennial beds, in narrow spots for linear accents, and in drifts lining a path.

How to Plant & Grow—Available as containers. Plant in spring, summer, or fall into sites receiving at least five hours of sun a day into well-worked, well-drained native soil. Water deeply two times a week until new growth appears. Add 3 inches of mulch.

Care & Problems—Cut down to just above the crown in spring. Remove seedheads to minimize reseeding. Rust occurs in heavy shade. No fertilizer. No pests or diseases.

Water Needs—Water deeply, weekly when temperatures exceed 80 degrees Fahrenheit; every two weeks if 60 to 80 degrees Fahrenheit. Otherwise, water monthly if no rain.

Bloom Color—Pinkish green

Peak Season—Summer

Mature Size (H x W)—2 to 6 feet x 2 to 4 feet

Hardiness—Zones 4 to 9

FOUNTAIN GRASS
Pennisetum alopecuroides

Why It's Special—*P. alopecuroides* is considered dwarf compared to its species relative, *P. setaceum*, which is invasive throughout the Southwest. Dwarf fountain grass stays a neat, tight, clumping grass with fountainlike foliage and flower spikes, valued for its place in smaller garden settings. Plant singly in containers, in rock gardens, as a focal point in perennial borders, in drifts in the understories of dappled shade trees, and *en masse* on seldom-watered slopes.

How to Plant & Grow—Available as containers. Deeply incorporate amendments into a well-draining soil in spring after the last frost. Site in part-shade sites in low deserts.

Care & Problems—Cut plants to the ground to rejuvenate in spring. Use chelated iron if plants are chlorotic in summer heat. Refresh mulch.

Water Needs—Water deeply every two weeks when temperatures exceed 85 degrees Fahrenheit, weekly at 65 to 85 degrees Fahrenheit. Water monthly in cooler weather.

Bloom Color—White, pink, mahogany

Peak Season—Summer

Mature Size (H x W)—1 to 5 feet x 1 to 5 feet

Hardiness—Zones 5 to 8

'JOSE SELECT' TALL WHEATGRASS
Elytrigia elongata 'Jose Select'

Why It's Special—'Jose Select' is a cultivar of the species, which is used as a grazing grass, giving this selection more ornamental value with its full, strong clump of dark green leaves and tall flower spikes held high above the foliage. In autumn, the plant turns amber-gold, giving the plants beautiful winter interest. Use singly as a focal point plant, for drama against a wall, or tucked next to a boulder.

How to Plant & Grow—Available as containers. Plant in spring, late summer, or fall into well-worked, well-draining native soil. Water two times a week until new growth appears. Add 3 inches of mulch.

Care & Problems—Cut previous year's growth down to the crown in spring. Strip off seedheads to minimize reseeding and keep plants tidy. No fertilizing. There aren't any pests or diseases.

Water Needs—Water deeply once a week when temperatures exceed 85 degrees Fahrenheit, every two weeks at 65 to 85 degrees Fahrenheit. In colder weather, if there's no rain, water monthly.

Bloom Color—Gold

Peak Season—Fall

Mature Size (H x W)—5 feet x 2 feet

Hardiness—Zones 3 to 8

LILY TURF
Liriope muscari

Why It's Special—Lily turf tolerates heat and humidity, growing in all exposures. Grown for its arching, clear green or variegated foliage, its flower spikes are a bonus. Use it to line an entryway, in drifts under dappled shade canopies, or grouped in perennial beds.

How to Plant & Grow—Available as container grown, seed, and divisions. Deeply incorporate compost into a well-drained soil in spring. Water deeply two to three times a week until new growth appears. Mulch 2 inches.

Care & Problems—Cut dormant foliage down to 6 inches in early spring before new growth emerges. Remove dead foliage anytime. Mass-planted lily turf may be mowed above the crown. Fertilize in spring with a timed-release fertilizer. Occasionally slugs, snails, mealybugs, scale, grasshoppers, or crown rot occur. Refresh mulch in spring.

Water Needs—Water deeply three times a week when temperatures exceed 90 degrees Fahrenheit, two times a week when they're 70 to 90 degrees Fahrenheit. Water weekly otherwise.

Bloom Color—Lavender, white, blue

Peak Season—Summer to fall

Mature Size (H x W)—6 to 24 inches x 12 to 18 inches

Hardiness—Zones 6 to 10

LOVE GRASS
Eragrostis curvula

Why It's Special—Love grass is a heat-loving summer/fall plant. It emerges in spring, quickly growing finely textured foliage that form dense tufts, followed by tall flower stalks bearing clusters of blooms in fall. The plant and flowers are bronze-red by late fall. Drought-tolerant love grass is at its best when all else is faded in the heat. Use its compact form in containers, in drifts lining paths, or *en masse* on slopes where its deep roots will stabilize the soil.

How to Plant & Grow—Available as container grown and seed. Deeply incorporate compost into a well-draining soil in spring. Water deeply twice a week until there's new growth. Add 2 to 3 inches of mulch.

Care & Problems—In February, prune to 6 inches above the ground. Prune back errant branches anytime to keep them neat. Apply a timed-release fertilizer when it's actively growing in spring.

Water Needs—Deeply water weekly in summer and fall; don't water in winter.

Bloom Color—Bronze-red

Peak Season—Fall

Mature Size (H x W)—3 feet x 3 feet

Hardiness—Zones 7 to 10

MAIDEN GRASS
Miscanthus sinensis

Why It's Special—Maiden grass is a robust, four-season clumping plant that emerges in spring with long, arching, finely textured green to silvery leaves. Flower plumes rise above the foliage adding contrast and texture in reddish bronze. The plant shimmers with winter frost and maintains its color through most of winter. Cultivars come in towering to dwarf, narrow to broad, solid or variegated foliage. Use maiden grass anywhere you want drama either singly for a focal point or in groups for a big statement.

How to Plant & Grow—Available as seed and container grown. Plant in spring into well-worked, well-draining, native soil. Water deeply twice a week until plants send out new growth and are established.

Care & Problems—Cut foliage back to 5 inches in spring to reinvigorate. No fertilizer is needed. Pests or diseases aren't a problem. It's short-lived, about four years; divide in spring and replant the offsets.

Water Needs—Deeply water weekly in summer; monthly in winter if there's no rain.

Bloom Color—Bronze

Peak Season—Fall

Mature Size (H x W)—2 to 10 feet x 4 to 8 feet

Hardiness—Zones 4 to 9

MONDO GRASS
Ophiopogon japonicus

Why It's Special—Mondo grass is a lush grassy mound in part- to fully shaded locations, making it a good choice for a patch of green under trees as living mulch. Deep green foliage in tidy tufts offer contrast and texture to shaded color beds; as a mass planting it slowly covers a shaded slope or a broad expanse with a rich carpet. There are variegated cultivars also.

How to Plant & Grow—Available as container grown and flats. Plant in spring to establish before winter. Plant into well worked, amended, well-draining soil. Water deeply, every two to three days until new growth. Maintain deep, regular watering until filled in. Add a thin layer of mulch.

Care & Problems—Shear or mow in spring after all danger of frost. Remove flower spikes its first year to promote root formation. Fertilize with a timed-release fertilizer in spring. No pests. Maintain light mulch.

Water Needs—Water deeply once a week in growing seasons, less in cool winter soil, but don't allow soil to dry.

Bloom Color—Blue

Peak Season—Summer

Mature Size (H x W)—6 to 12 inches x 4 to 18 inches

Hardiness—Zones 7 to 10

MUHLY GRASS
Muhlenbergia spp.

Why It's Special—Muhly grass is native to the southeastern US. In its native habitat, it gets more annual rain than we do in the Southwest, but still it is heat, drought, salt, and wind tolerant. Some species are more cold tolerant or heat tough.

How to Plant & Grow—Available as container grown and seed. Deeply work compost into a well-draining soil. Plant in spring or early summer. Water deeply every two to three days for a month, then weekly through the first summer. Mulch 3 inches.

Care & Problems—Shear to 4 to 5 inches tall in spring before new growth appears. Divide overgrown clumps in early spring, about every five years. Apply timed-release fertilizer in spring at half-rate. No pests or diseases. Keep mulched.

Water Needs—Water deeply every week when temperatures exceed 85 degrees Fahrenheit, every two weeks at 65 to 85 degrees Fahrenheit. Water monthly in cooler weather if there's no rain.

Bloom Color—Pink, purple, buff

Peak Season—Summer, fall

Mature Size (H x W)—2 to 4 feet x 2 to 4 feet

Hardiness—Zones 5 to 10

PLUME GRASS
Erianthus ravennae

Why It's Special—Plume grass has the presence of invasive pampas grass, but is more refined in its growth. It is a tall, clumping grass, sending out even taller flower plumes. Good fall color in orange to beige to purple develops. Grow it for a screen, a grassy green fence, a background plant, or *en masse* along a driveway entrance.

How to Plant & Grow—Available as container grown. Plant or divide in spring into well-worked, well-draining native soil that is not too fertile. Prepare roots on potbound plants by cutting off the bottom few inches and making vertical cuts on the rootball. Water deeply twice a week until new growth. Mulch 3 inches.

Care & Problems—Cut dormant foliage back in early spring when you see new growth. Cut off flower stalks in early winter. No fertilizer is needed. Pests or diseases aren't problems. Refresh mulch.

Water Needs—Deeply water once a month, if there's no rain.

Bloom Color—Silver

Peak Season—Summer, fall foliage

Mature Size (H x W)—8 to 12 feet x 4 to 5 feet

Hardiness—Zones 6 to 10

PRAIRIE DROPSEED
Sporobolus heterolepis

Why It's Special—Prairie dropseed is a four-season grass, slow to establish but worth the wait. Bright green, fine, soft foliage forms splayed clumps in spring; scented flowers appear in late summer, followed by burnished shades of gold and copper with frost, persisting for winter interest. Use in pots, rock gardens, perennials, color beds, and in drifts in dappled shade.

How to Plant & Grow—Available as containers and seed. Incorporate amendments into a well-draining soil in midspring. Prairie dropseed can't handle summer heat of southern Nevada. Water deeply two times a week until new growth appears. Mulch 3 inches.

Care & Problems—Cut foliage close to the ground in early spring before new growth. Trim fading seedheads. Apply timed-release fertilizer in spring or fall for first three years only. No pests or diseases.

Water Needs—Water deeply, weekly when temperatures exceed 85 degrees Fahrenheit, every two weeks from 65 to 85 degrees Fahrenheit. Water monthly in cooler weather.

Bloom Color—Green

Peak Season—Summer, fall foliage

Mature Size (H x W)—1 to 2 feet x 1 feet

Hardiness—Zones 3 to 7

RIBBON GRASS
Phalaris arundinacea

Why It's Special—Ribbon grass has beautiful variegated foliage that gracefully cascades with growth. It goes dormant in cooler climates, but grows actively in warmer-winter areas. Less-invasive cultivars include 'Dwarf Garters', staying a compact 8 inches x 12 inches, and 'Feesey', white stripes turning pink with age. Use in pots, and perennial and color beds.

How to Plant & Grow—Available as container grown. Plant so the crowns remain at the same soil level as the container. Set plants into a well-worked, well-draining soil. Water deeply weekly during the growing season. Mulch 3 inches whether direct-planted or in a container, filling containers with mulch to the top of the pot.

Care & Problems—Mow down in spring before new growth. *Phalaris* spreads by rhizomes and can be invasive. Grow species in pots in-ground or use barrier fabric to contain. Divide in spring. No fertilizer, pests, or diseases.

Water Needs—Water deeply twice a week in summer; once a week spring, fall. No water in winter.

Bloom Color—White, pink

Peak Season—Spring, summer

Mature Size (H x W)— 3 feet x indefinite

Hardiness—Zones 4 to 9

SEDGE
Carex spp.

Why It's Special—Sedge is grown for its mostly evergreen foliage, ranging in colors and textures from wider-bladed, variegated green/white striped to fine-bladed in reddish bronze, black, orange, and yellow. It's a good accent with other grasses, in shade as a groundcover, in sun as a path border, in containers at an entryway, in dry or wet streambeds, rain gardens, and meadows.

How to Plant & Grow—Available as containers. Incorporate amendments deeply into a well-draining soil in spring. In hot-summer climates, plant in part sun/shade. Water deeply twice a week until new growth. Mulch 2 to 3 inches.

Care & Problems—Remove winter-damaged foliage in spring; summer damage in fall. Trim close to the ground but not into the crown. Fertilize with a timed-release fertilizer in spring. Aphids may appear on stressed plants; watch for leaf fungus and rust spot. Keep mulched.

Water Needs—Deeply water weekly in summer, spring, but less in fall, winter. Keep soil moist.

Bloom Color—Insignificant

Peak Season—Evergreen to semi-evergreen

Mature Size (H x W)—1 to 2 feet x 1 to 2 feet

Hardiness—Zones 5 to 9

SWEET FLAG
Acorus gramineus

Why It's Special—Sweet flag make big statements as linear focal points in ponds, bogs, and streams. Combine with other moisture-loving plants in containers, shady perennial gardens as accents, or in sunny winter color borders for contrast. Its form is similar to sedge, with arching foliage, but variegated leaves are broader and have a delicious, cinnamon-like spicy aroma when crushed. It's semi-evergreen in warm winters.

How to Plant & Grow—Available as container grown. Plant in spring or summer into well-worked, compost-amended, moist soil. Divide in spring. Water deeply, as often as required to keep soil moist. Add 3 inches of mulch.

Care & Problems—Remove winter-damaged foliage in spring, cutting to the ground before new growth emerges. If garden-grown, apply timed-release fertilizer in spring when new growth is 4 to 6 inches tall. Maintain mulch in garden sites.

Water Needs—Deep water to maintain consistent moisture; it's a bog or water garden plant.

Bloom Color—Insignificant

Peak Season—Evergreen foliage

Mature Size (H x W)—10 to 15 inches x 12 to 15 inches

Hardiness—Zones 4 to 11

SWITCH GRASS
Panicum virgatum

Why It's Special—Switchgrass is not known for its refinement, but is desirable in landscape settings for its unreserved growth. It's a natural, full-bodied, clumping grass, early to bloom and giving good fall color that persists into winter. Its amber winter foliage is beautiful in contrast to a white carpet of snow.

How to Plant & Grow—Available as seed and container grown. Incorporate amendments into lean soils. Deeply work well-draining native soils before planting in late spring, summer, or early fall. If potbound, remove bottom 2 inches of rootmass, cutting the remaining rootball vertically. Water deeply once a week until new growth; then, every two weeks for the first growing season. Mulch 3 inches.

Care & Problems—Cut back dormant foliage in spring as new growth emerges. Fertilize cultivars when new growth in spring reaches 10 to 12 inches; no fertilizing for native species. No pests or diseases. Keep mulched.

Water Needs—Water deeply every four to six weeks if no rain.

Bloom Color—Purplish-red, beige

Peak Season—Summer, fall foliage

Mature Size (H x W)—4 to 8 feet x 2 to 4 feet

Hardiness—Zones 5 to 9

TALL FESCUE
Festuca arundinacea

Why It's Special—Tall fescue is a cool-season grass, tolerating summer heat, maintaining its color through mild winters, going dormant in colder zones. It takes some shade, so it can be interplanted with trees that give dappled shade. A rhizometous fescue-type eliminates seeding bare areas as it fills in but is not invasive. Many cultivars available.

How to Plant & Grow—Available as seed or sod. Sow or plant in fall in warm-winter areas, spring otherwise, into well-worked, amended, well-draining soil. Cover seed lightly. Maintain a moist seedbed until germination and rooting, watering for short periods two to three times daily.

Care & Problems—If not "manicured," mow as desired, but don't cut more than I inch off at a time. Fertilize with turf-formulated fertilizer in spring and fall in mild-winter areas where fescue does not go dormant.

Water Needs—Water deeply two to three times a week when temperatures exceed 85 degrees Fahrenheit; once a week otherwise. No water in winter dormancy.

Peak Season— Cool-season grass

Mowing Height—Mow 2 to 3 inches for a manicured lawn; 2 to 4 inches clumping grass.

Hardiness—Zones 2 to 10

TUFTED HAIR GRASS
Deschampsia cespitosa

Why It's Special—Tufted hair grass is a clumping, evergreen, delicate grass whose blooms put on the show, forming billowy clouds above the foliage on arching stems. Fall foliage brings bright orange to gold colors. Use *en masse* to cover a slope, line a driveway, at the edges of meadows or lawns, around a pool, or along a patio to soften hard edges. The more you plant, the bigger its impact.

How to Plant & Grow—Available as seed and container grown. Incorporate compost into a well-draining soil in early spring as soon as soil can be worked. Water deeply every three to four days for a month; then, weekly through its first summer. Mulch 2 inches.

Care & Problems—Prune to within a few inches of the ground in late winter. Apply a timed-release fertilizer in spring. No pests or diseases bother it. Refresh mulch.

Water Needs—Water deeply once a week in summer, more often if it's hotter and drier.

Bloom Color—Green, gold

Peak Season—Spring, summer

Mature Size (H x W)—I to 2 feet x I to 4 feet

Hardiness—Zones 4 to 9

ZOYSIA
Zoysia japonica

Why It's Special—Zoysia is a low-growing, drought-tolerant turf grass that forms a beautiful green carpet that can take some shade, without invasive tendencies. 'El Toro' is more shade tolerant and quicker to green up in spring. 'Emerald' is more frost tolerant. *Zoysia tenuifolia* is fine-textured and undulating, making a good meadow grass.

How to Plant & Grow—Available as seed, sod, and sprigs. Plant in early spring after last frost and soil is warm into well-worked, amended, well-draining soil. Do not plant in heavy shade or in areas where it is difficult to water. Cover sprigs. Keep consistently moist throughout its growing season. Sprigs take a few years to fill an area, so diligent watering, weeding and fertilizing is required.

Care & Problems—Mow with a reel mower to keep short and encourage spreading, but do not scalp. Its slow growth means less-frequent mowing. Fertilize when growth resumes in spring with a turf-formulated fertilizer.

Water Needs—Water regularly to retain its color and avoid wilting.

Peak Season—Warm-season grass

Mowing Height—I to 2 inches

Hardiness—Zones 4 to 11

TURFGRASS MONTH-BY-MONTH

JANUARY

- Lawns are dormant in colder zones, so no watering, fertilizing, or mowing is needed since the ground is frozen.

- In warmer-winter areas, water every 10 to 14 days, letting the water penetrate beyond the root zone. If water runs off the surface quickly or puddles, then water in short cycles, allowing the water to penetrate before watering again.

- When lawns need water, grass blades lose turgidity and change color. When you walk across a water-stressed lawn and look behind you, your footprints will show. A bright green lawn will change to a dull, muted shade. Water right away, deeply. Stay off the lawn until it dries and the blades have regained their stand.

FEBRUARY

- In warm-winter zones, plant ornamental grasses. Consider mature size and spread, if it is well behaved, has stolons or rhizomes, if it reseeds heavily, and its water, soil, and exposure requirements before planting. Grasses colonize and spread; they're not as easy to move to new locations in the garden. Plan before you plant.

- Mow overseeded lawns when grass blades begin to slightly bend, then only mow one-third of the tip growth at each mowing.

- Established ornamental grasses may show new green growth this month. As soon as you see active growth, cut back old foliage down to the point where you see green. The clippings make good mulch in open, dry areas to keep weeds down. Collect seedheads for sowing elsewhere, or compost.

MARCH

- Don't water or fertilize dormant lawns. Occasional rains may jumpstart the growing process, but snow and freezing weather is still likely in colder zones. You can clean up a bit with a light raking, but don't walk on a frozen lawn. Wait until the winter sun warms the grass and frost melts.

- Seed, stolons, or sod? All require similar soil preparation and watering until established. Seed is less expensive, goes down quickly, requires due diligence to pluck out weeds, possibly reseeding those bare areas, a long wait until you can walk on it—six to eight weeks. Stolons are not available for all types, more expensive than seed, require similar planting and water, and take a long time to establish, from months to years. Sod is the most costly, but there are no weeds, it is quicker-rooting, it requires less watering to establish, and you can be sitting on it within a month.

- Many ornamental grasses do not need a fertile soil. Rather than plant them in the flower bed where you have worked so hard to build the soil, use them on the fringes of the bed, in lean soils where you can't get anything else to grow, along a driveway or sidewalk (if they bask in the heat), in the understories of trees.

APRIL

- Bed preparation for lawns is time consuming so do it before you order sod or stolons, the shelf life is short—24 to 36 hours. Water the area at least 24 inches deep. Allow the soil to dry for a day or so before digging. It is not necessary to add topsoil or organics to the soil. If you do, then incorporate into the soil. Rototill deeply, making two passes at different directions. Remove all clods, rocks, and debris. Rake, rake, and rake some more to level the area. Undulating surface causes water to pool in low depressions, high spots lead to scalping when you mow. Fill the roller (you can rent them) with water to roll the area. Level any high/low spots. Keep the roller for use at the end of the planting process.

- For seed and stolons, you will need topsoil, potting soil, sand, or sawdust to top after planting.

- Sow seed thickly, accounting for birds and seed that doesn't germinate. Scatter stolons onto a pre-moistened soil. Top-dress to lightly cover. Drain the water out of the roller and roll over the surface again, pressing seed, stolons firmly into the soil. Keep moist.

- For sod, use a pre-plant fertilizer, 16-20-0 at 1 pound per 1,000 square feet. Scatter on a pre-moistened, prepared bed. There's no need to work it in. Beginning at a corner, lay the sod, butting edges together tightly as you go. Stagger the joints as you would laying bricks. Use full pieces to cover the entire area, then finish the edges with cut pieces to fit. Use the filled roller again, walking back and forth in both directions to press the roots to the soil. Keep moist until rooted in.

MAY

- Dormant lawns are awakening. Give them a good raking to remove thatch, and mow short with a bag on the mower to pick up debris. Water deeply, apply fertilizer, then surface water to wash fertilizer off grass blades and to water-in the fertilizer so it stays in the root zone.

- Mow emerging meadow grasses short, to 3 inches, to clean up last season's growth and encourage greening. Established ornamental grasses and meadows can be cut with a line-trimmer, cutting down to new tufts of green growth. Avoid cutting into the crown.

- If your lawns are interplanted with trees or shrubs, then remove the turf from around the base of the trunks, eliminating the danger of mower blade or line trimmer damage to the trees. Mulch the spots.

JUNE

- Established grasses need deep watering to reach their roots. Inline drip tubing has the emitter imbedded inside the tubing, spaced at differing intervals, eliminating attaching numerous spaghetti tubes or installing emitters manually. Inline tubing allows you to coil the line around the base of the grass so that water is delivered evenly into the entire root zone. Cover the tubing with mulch.

- Water lawns every three days in hot summer areas, once weekly elsewhere. If you water with a sprinkler, then turn it on low so it delivers larger water droplets, lessening the chances of over-spray and evaporation. Move the sprinkler a few times, allowing the watering pattern to overlap with each move so there are no dry areas.

- Bermudagrass needs to be mowed 1 to 1½ inches, depending upon the type, to encourage dense growth by stolons and rhizomes. The two create a tight web, causing a dense thatch buildup that blocks penetration of water and fertilizer. Rent a dethatcher, a small walk-behind machine that has slicing blades that lift the thatch. Use a mower with a bag to clean up debris. Fertilize and water deeply.

JULY

- If you notice yellow spots on your lawn and you do not have a dog, but do have an irrigation system, then you may not be getting head-to-head coverage. Evenly space jars or cans on the lawn, placing a jar on each of the dry spots, with others in the "green zones." Run the system for 10 minutes. If the jars on the dry spots have less water than the others, then you are not getting even distribution. Water longer or handwater the dry spots. A permanent solution would be to call an irrigation specialist to redesign for better system coverage, which may mean adding supply lines, additional heads or another valve and system to supply the needed water.

- More fertilizer equals faster growth, leading to more water and mowing. Be willing to have a less than a golf course-green lawn in the Southwest. If the lawn is green and growing, then don't fertilize. A fertilizer application in spring as lawns green up after winter dormancy, with another in late summer (only if needed) is plenty.

- Summer monsoons can bring mushrooms. If you have pets or children playing in the area, remove them. Otherwise, they don't hurt the lawn, disappearing as the lawn dries.

AUGUST

- Aerating compacted, slow-draining soil pulls plugs of soil and roots out at intervals, allowing more air and water movement. Aerate when the lawn is actively growing once a year or alternate years.

- If you are watering and maintaining a narrow strip of lawn running alongside a driveway, an unused expanse of lawn, a sloped area covered in green grass, or a side yard used for trash can storage, then consider sweeps of ornamental grasses, a drought-tolerant meadow, a deep-rooting, no-mow turf type, or a tall ornamental grass screen with a mulched pathway as alternatives.

- Long stalks and blooms on ornamental grasses sway in the wind and as they do, seed is dispersed. Decide if you want this to happen. Cut the stems before the tops dry and begin dispersing seed to minimize self-sowing. If you want the grass in other places, as the tops dry, carefully cut the stems, hang them upside-down in a paper bag to collect the seed for sowing in spring.

SEPTEMBER

- Overseed bermudagrass lawns with annual ryegrass. Scalp the bermudagrass, water deeply, then scatter seed. Keep moist. Annual ryegrass germinates within 7 to 10 days and grows through mild winters, creating a green lawn while the bermuda lies dormant. When the bermuda awakens in spring, the annual grass fades away.

- If you don't mind a brown bermuda lawn in winter, there is no need to overseed. Give it a close mowing and stop watering this month, allowing it to go dormant.

- Tall fescue retains its green throughout winter in warmer climates. A deep-rooting, clumping grass, consider it for other applications. Plant on a slope with drip irrigation, allow it to grow tall and its roots stabilize the slope. Use it for garden pathways. Make the path just wide enough for a lawnmower, which is also big enough for a couple of lawn chairs and a small table. Less is more!

OCTOBER

- If fescue lawns are waning in warm-winter areas when they should be lush and vigorous, apply fertilizer. Water in the morning, mow after lawn has dried, fertilize, then water just enough to wash off the blades and to water-in the fertilizer.

- Ornamental grasses are getting fall color. Warm-season grasses are going into dormancy, adding wheat colors to the mix. Stop watering lawns, but continue to water ornamental grasses once a month until first frost.

- Bring container grasses that you want to overwinter indoors. Water them deeply, allow to drain, then bring them into a cool, lighted space. Place away from heater sources. Water infrequently, when the soil dries (unless they are bog-types). Overwatering in cool soils can cause them to rot.

NOVEMBER

- Usually fallen leaves from deciduous trees and shrubs make good, natural mulch. If they fall on grasses, they shade the blades and as the leaves begin to decay, it can cause mold. Wait to rake the leaves until all have fallen. Use them for mulch or shredded into the compost pile.

- Plant spring flowering bulbs in meadows. Toss them out, dig the holes, sit them upright and bury. Until you are accustomed to their presence, place markers where the plantings begin and end. Plan on an early season meadow mowing in February, before the bulbs start growing.

- Mow overseeded lawns when the blades begin to bend, at about 2 inches, then only removed about ½ inch off the top. Mow at different directions each time to avoid compaction.

DECEMBER

- In warmer winters, cut back ornamental grasses at the end of the month to within 6 to 8 inches of the ground to revitalize.

- If the ground is not frozen and you can buy sod locally, then you can plant. Sketch the area on paper, squaring off irregular spaces. Measure the length by width for approximate square footage, then add 10 percent to account for waste. Give the square footage measurement to the sod farm; they will know how many pieces to cut to fill the order and usually add a couple extra pieces for good measure.

- If bermudagrass is encroaching into other areas, then while it is dormant, install a mow strip, edging, or barrier fabric. It's easier to remove and slice while not actively growing.

GLOSSARY

Acidic soil: On a soil pH scale of 0 to 14, acidic soil has a pH reading of 6.0 and lower. Mildly acidic is 6.0 to 7.0.

Aggregate: Soil particles that are massed together.

Alkaline soil: On a soil pH scale of 0 to 14, alkaline soil has a pH higher than 7.0.

Amendment: Organic or inorganic material incorporated into the soil to improve it.

Annual: A plant that germinates (sprouts), flowers, and dies within one year.

Balled and burlapped (B&B): Plants that have been grown in field rows, dug up with their soil intact, wrapped with burlap, and tied with twine.

Balanced fertilizer: A fertilizer with equal (or close to it) amounts of the three main plant nutrients—nitrogen, phosphorus, and potassium.

Bare root: Plants that are shipped dormant, without being planted in a container or having soil around their roots.

Beneficial insects: Insects that perform valuable services such as pollination and pest control. Examples: ladybugs, spiders, and bees.

Berm and basin: A berm is mounded soil that stops the flow of water, capturing it in a basin that holds the water until it can be absorbed into the soil.

Bulb: Swollen underground storage organs with small, living plants already growing inside. Examples: tulips, daffodils, and hyacinths.

Canopy: The overhead branching area of a tree, including foliage.

Chlorosi: When the space between the leaf veins turns yellow, signifying an iron deficiency.

Colonize: When plants spread or grow in a new area other than their native habitat.

Compost: The resulting material after decomposition of organic matter.

Conifer: A plant that produces cones. Most are needled evergreens, such as spruce, pine, and fir.

Container: Any pot or vessel that is used for growing plants.

Cool-season plant: A flowering plant that thrives in cooler weather.

Corm: A fat, flat, scaly underground stem that's planted underground similar to a bulb. Leaves and flowers emerge from nodes on the corm. Examples: crocus, gladiolus, and freesia.

Cultivar: A plant that has been bred or selected for having one or more distinct traits from the species, then given a name to set it apart, such as 'Pardon Me', a cultivar of daylily.

Crown: The branch work that makes up a tree canopy.

Dappled: Refers to open or light shade created by high tree branches or tree foliage in which patches of sunlight and shade intermingle.

Deadhead: To remove dead flowers in order to encourage further bloom, neaten the plant, and prevent the plant from self-sowing.

Deciduous: A plant that loses its leaves seasonally, typically in fall or early winter; some native plants in summer.

Decomposed granite: A soil type that has been formed from parent granite material. Also processed and used for permeable paths, roads.

Desiccate: When leaves completely dry up.

Diversion swale: A low-lying depression in the soil used to direct the flow of water to another location.

Divide: The process of digging up bulbs and clumping perennials, separating the roots, and replanting the pieces.

Drought tolerant: The ability of a plant to survive and tolerate periods of drought.

Dormancy: The period when plants stop growing in order to conserve energy in winter, summer in the case of some native plants and cool-season perennials, and spring-blooming bulbs.

Drifts: When plants are grouped together in curvilinear forms in the landscape.

Drip irrigation: The slow release of water delivered through tubing and emitters. Also called micro-irrigation.

Drip line: Refers to the outermost reaches of the branches of a tree.

Dwarf: Describes a plant whose size is less than that of the species' standard or usual size.

Emitter: A drip irrigation component that delivers water to plants, measured in gallons of water emitted per hour (gph).

En masse: When many plants of the same species are grouped and planted closely together in the landscape.

Evergreen: A plant that keeps its leaves year-round, instead of dropping them seasonally. These can be needled plants as well as broad-leaf ones.

Established plant: Refers to the stage when a plant reaches maturity and exhibits continued healthy growth. Varies with the type of plant. Perennials are established after two or three seasons, trees after five or more years.

Flats: Trays that hold smaller pots and cell packs.

Full sun: Areas of the garden that receive direct sunlight for at least six to eight hours a day.

Germination: The process by which a plant emerges from a seed or a spore.

Grafted: A plant that has two parts—a lower section with strong roots and a top part (the "scion") that has been attached for a desired growth habit, such as dwarf size, disease resistance, or improved flowering or fruiting.

Granular fertilizer: A type of fertilizer that comes in a dry, pellet-like form.

Green screen/wall: A screen or wall made of plants grouped closely together.

Hardiness Zone: A numeral system developed by the U.S. Department of Agriculture to designate an area's average annual low temperature. Plants are then given ratings according to the temperatures they'll survive.

Hardscape: Features in the landscape other than plants (softscape), such as benches, fences, sidewalks, etc.

Head: A spray irrigation component that delivers water to plants, measured in gallons per minute (gpm).

Hybrid: A plant produced by crossing two genetically different plants, usually to achieve a desired trait, new color, or some other perceived improvement.

Interplant: When two or more different types of plants are planted together in the same landscape bed so they share resources.

Invasive: Refers to a plant that multiplies by self-sowing seed or by self-dividing to the extent that it threatens growth of other plants.

Microclimate: Small sections of a property that deviate slightly from the prevailing, surrounding climate. A courtyard with stone walls, for example, will likely have warmer, less windy conditions than the rest of a yard.

Mulch: Any type of material that is spread over the soil surface, generally to suppress weeds and retain soil moisture.

Native plant: In terms of US native plants, these are species that were growing here before the arrival of European settlers.

Native soil: The soil that we have in our landscape before it has been amended. The soil in which native plants grow in their natural habitat.

Naturalize: When plants adapt, grow and spread as though it were native to the area.

Organic: Any carbon-based material capable of decomposition and decay. Here it refers to a fertilizer, mulch, soil amendment, or product derived from naturally occurring materials instead of synthesized in a lab or factory.

Ornamental: Refers to any plant favored for its ornamental characteristics, flower, leaf, structure, rather than for producing edible fruit, vegetable or foliage.

Part sun/part shade: Areas of the garden that get direct sunlight for part of the day (less than six hours) and that are in shade for part of the day (at least three hours of sunlight at some point). More than six hours of direct sunlight a day is full sun, and less than three hours is considered shade.

Perennial: A plant that lives for more than two years. Usually used to describe herbaceous plants.

pH: A figure designating the acidity or the alkalinity of soil as measured on a scale of 0 to 14, with 7.0 being neutral.

Pinch: The process of removing top or side growth on a plant to direct the growth.

Plug: A portion of a plant that has roots, allowing it to be planted to grow into a mature plant. Often used to plant a lawn.

Pollinators: Bees, butterflies, moths, or hummingbirds that transfer pollen for fertilization from the male pollen-bearing organ (stamen) to the female organ (pistil).

Retrofit: The process of keeping some elements, eliminating others, and rebuilding to fulfill new criteria. You might retrofit a landscape and irrigation system to be more water-thrifty.

Rhizome: An underground horizontal stem that grows side shoots. Examples: canna, ginger, and most irises.

Rootball: The network of roots and soil clinging to a plant when it is lifted out of the ground or pot.

Runner: A stem sprouting from a plant that roots itself as it goes. Also called a stolon.

Soaker hose: Attaches to a hose bib. A rubber hose that allows water to seep slowly out of the sides or flat tape with holes at intervals that allows water to slowly drip onto the soil.

Shade: A garden site that gets less than three hours of direct sunlight per day.

Slow-release fertilizer: A fertilizer that is prilled or treated so that it breaks down slowly over time. Often called timed-release fertilizer.

Sod: Pieces of turf, complete with soil, roots, and top growth, that are laid upon the ground to knit together to create a lawn area.

Species: A plant that's a variation or sub-group of a genus.

Soil test: An analysis of a soil sample, most often to determine its level of nutrients and pH (acidity) reading.

Succulent: A group of plants that have fleshy leaves that hold water, often includes cactus plants.

Sucker/ing: Twiggy growth emerging from roots around the base of trees and tall shrubs. Suckering diverts energy from desirable tree growth and should be removed.

Sweep: When plants are grouped together and positioned in broad stripes or sections, often in natural curvilinear fashion.

Terrace: A bench or shelf formed by a support wall, running parallel with a slope.

Timed-release fertilizer: A fertilizer that releases its nutrients slowly over time, meaning less-frequent applications are needed.

Thinning: In the context of pruning, it's the process of removing excess branches from woody plants to improve air flow, let more sunlight into the inner branches, and remove conflicts from branches that are rubbing one another.

Top-dress: To spread fertilizer on top of the soil (usually around fruit trees or vegetables).

Topiary: A specialized form of pruning and shearing to create geometric shapes, animals, and forms that are either freestanding or within a wire form.

Transplants: Plants that are grown in one location and then moved to and replanted in another.

Tree: A woody perennial plant that typically consists of a single trunk with multiple lateral branches.

Tree canopy: The upper layer of growth consisting of the tree's branches and leaves.

Tropical plant: A plant that is native to a tropical region of the world, and thus acclimated to a warm, humid climate.

Trowel: A shovel-like hand tool that is used for digging or moving small amounts of soil.

Tuber: Enlarged roots that send out shoots and roots from nodes along their surface. Examples: dahlia, cyclamen, and perennial (tuberous) begonias.

Turfgrass: Short grasses that are mowed and used in lawns as opposed to ornamental grasses, which are left to grow as landscape plants.

Turgidity: State of plump or swollen plant parts that have high levels of moisture.

Variegated: The appearance of differently colored areas on plant leaves, usually white, yellow, or a brighter green.

Vascular system: Refers to the circulatory system of a plant, the xylem and phloem.

Water-soluble fertilizer: Plant fertilizer in a liquid form, some types need to be mixed with water, and some types are ready to use from the bottle.

Wilt: To become limp from lack of water, heat, root failure, pests, or disease.

Wood chips: Small pieces of wood made by cutting or chipping and used as mulch in the garden.

Xeric, xeriphitic, xeriscape: Refers to needing only a small amount of water to survive.

Warm-season vegetable: A vegetable that thrives during the warmer months. Examples are tomatoes, okra, and peppers.

Watering wand: A hose attachment that features a longer handle for watering plants beyond reach.

Water sprout: A vertical shoot emerging from a scaffold branch. It is usually nonfruiting and undesirable.

Wheat straw: The dry stalks of wheat that are used for mulch. They retain soil moisture and suppress weeds.

Wood chips: Small pieces of wood made by cutting or chipping and used as mulch in the garden.

INDEX

Common Name Index

Botanical Name Index

PHOTO CREDITS

Bill Adams: 190 (right)

Liz Ball: 47 (right), 166 (middle), 171 (left)

Deneen Powell Atelier, Inc.: 18

Dreamstime: 186 (left)

Tom Eltzroth: 27 (right), 29 (right), 30 (left), 31 (left), 32 (left), 33 (right), 34 (left), 36 (right), 37 (both), 38 (right), 49 (middle, right), 52 (left), 61 (left, right), 63 (middle), 64 (middle, right), 66 (middle), 68 (right), 69 (both), 74, 79 (middle), 80 (middle), 81 (middle, right), 84 (left), 85 (left, middle), 86 (left), 87 (right), 95 (both), 98 (left), 99 (left), 100 (left, right), 101 (left), 106 (middle), 107 (left), 110 (both), 112 (left), 121 (both), 122 (both), 123 (both), 124 (middle), 132 (left), 134 (left), 135 (middle, right), 136 (middle), 137 (right), 138 (right), 139 (left, middle), 140 (left, right), 141 (middle), 142 (left), 149 (left), 151 (right), 152 (both), 156, 164 (middle, right), 165 (left, right), 167 (right), 168 (right), 169 (left), 170 (left), 171 (middle), 172 (left), 173 (middle, right), 181 (right), 183 (left), 185 (middle, right), 186 (middle, right), 187 (left, right), 188 (right), 189 (right), 190 (left)

Katie Elzer-Peters: 14 (all), 17 (both), 45 (both), 58 (both), 94 (both), 117, 158 (all), 179

Getty: 164 (right)

Lorenzo Gunn: 66 (right)

Mary Irish: 99 (middle)

JC Raulston Arboretum at NC State University: 38 (left), 149 (right), 165 (middle), 182 (left)

Bill Kersey: 8, 9, 44 (all), 157, 160

Dave MacKenzie: 188 (middle)

Charles Mann: 10, 80 (right), 101 (middle), 106 (right), 108 (left), 162 (left), 168 (left), 171 (middle), 184 (middle)

Diana Maranhao: 124 (right), 169 (middle), 181 (left)

Troy Marden: 59, 68 (left), 102 (middle), 106 (left)

Judy Mielke: 88 (right), 132 (right), 162 (right), 163 (left), 166 (right), 172 (right), 184 (left, right)

Jerry Pavia: 25 (right), 26 (right), 32 (right), 34 (right), 46 (left), 67 (left), 78 (left), 80 (right), 82 (left), 87 (left), 97 (all), 99 (right), 102 (right), 104 (left, right), 109 (right), 111 (left), 112 (right), 118, 119, 124 (right), 133 (right), 134 (middle), 138 (left), 139 (right), 141 (left, right), 142 (right), 149 (middle), 150 (left), 151 (left), 163 (right), 166 (left), 169 (right), 170 (right), 173 (left), 182 (right), 185 (right), 187 (middle), 188 (left), 189 (left, middle), 190 (middle)

Proven Winners: 25 (left)

Tom Russell: 174 (left)

Shutterstock: 12, 13, 16, 19, 21, 22, 25 (middle), 26 (left), 27 (left), 28 (both), 29 (left), 30 (right), 31 (right), 33 (left), 35 (both), 36 (left), 38 (middle), 43, 44, 46 (middle, right), 47 (left, middle), 48 (all), 49 (left), 50 (both), 51 (both), 52 (right), 56, 60 (all), 61 (middle), 62 (all), 63 (left, right), 64 (left), 65 (all), 66 (left), 67 (middle, right), 70 (both), 75, 76, 77, 78 (middle, right), 79 (right), 81 (left), 82 (middle, right), 83 (all), 84 (middle, right), 85 (right), 86 (right), 88 (left), 93, 96 (all), 98 (middle, right), 100 (middle), 101 (right), 102 (left), 103 (all), 104 (middle), 105 (all), 107 (middle, right), 108 (right), 109 (left), 111 (right), 116, 128, 131, 133 (left), 134 (right), 135 (left), 136 (left, right), 137 (left, middle), 138 (middle), 140 (middle), 146, 147, 150 (right), 161, 167 (left, middle), 168 (middle), 172 (middle), 174 (right), 178, 183 (right)

Neil Soderstrom: 23, 170 (middle)

Andre Viette: 79 (left)

RESOURCES

REFERENCES

Brenzel, Kathleen Norris, ed. The New Sunset Western Garden Book. Birmingham: Oxmoor House, 2012.

Brickell, Christopher and Judith D. Zuk. The American Horticultural Society A-Z Encyclopedia of Garden Plants. New York: DK Publishing, 1997.

Cretti, John. Month-by-Month Gardening in the Rocky Mountains. Minneapolis: Cool Springs Press, 2004.

Dobbs, Steve. Oklahoma Gardener's Guide. Minneapolis: Cool Springs Press, 2004.

Grant, Greg. Texas Fruit & Vegetable Gardening. Minneapolis: Cool Springs Press, 2012.

Greenlee, John. The Encyclopedia of Ornamental Grasses. New York: Rodale Press, 2000.

Groom Dale. Texas Gardener's Guide. Minneapolis: Cool Springs Press, 2002.

Irish, Mary. Arizona Gardener's Guide. Minneapolis: Cool Springs Press, 2003.

Irish, Mary. Trees & Shrubs for the Southwest.Portland: Timber Press, 2008.

Irish, Mary. Month-by-Month Gardening in the Desert Southwest. Minneapolis: Cool Springs Press, 2002.

Maranhao, Diana. Rocky Mountain Fruit & Vegetable Gardening. Minneapolis: Cool Springs Press, 2014.

Mills, Linn, and Dick Post. Nevada Gardener's Guide. Minneapolis: Cool Springs Press, 2005.

Phillips, Judith. New Mexico Gardener's Guide. Minneapolis: Cool Springs Press, 2005.

Plaster, Edward J. Soil Science and Management.New York: DelMar, Inc.,1985.

Soule, Jacqueline A. Southwest Fruit & Vegetable Gardening. Minneapolis: Cool Springs Press, 2014.

Sterman, Nan, Mary Irish, Judith Phillips, and Joe Lamp'L. Water-Wise. Plants for the Southwest. Minneapolis: Cool Springs Press, 2010.

GARDENING RESOURCES

ARIZONA

Arizona Municipal Water Users Association: www.amwua.org
Desert Botanical Garden, Phoenix, AZ: www.dbg.org
University of Arizona Horticulture Publications:
    www.cals.arizona.edu/maricopa/garden/pubs.htm

NEW MEXICO

New Mexico Master Gardener Program:
    www.nmsu.edu/ces/mastergardeners/programs.html
New Mexico State University: www.nmsu.edu
Santa Fe Botanical Garden: www.santafebotanicalgarden.org

OKLAHOMA

Oklahoma Cooperative Extension Services: www.oces.okstate.edu
Oklahoma Horticultural Society: www.ok-hort.org
Myriad Botanical Gardens, Oklahoma City: www.myriadgardens.org

SOUTHERN NEVADA

Southern Nevada Water Authority (SNWA): www.snwa.com
Springs Preserve, Las Vegas, NV: www.springspreserve.org
University of Nevada Cooperative Extension (UNCE):
    www.unce.unr.edu/programs/horticulture

TEXAS

Fort Worth Botanic Garden: www.fwbg.org
Lady Bird Johnson Wildflower Center: www.wildflower.org
Texas Garden Clubs, Inc.: www.texasgardenclubs.org

UTAH

Conservation Garden Park, West Jordan, UT:
    www.conservationgardenpark.org
Salt Lake City Community College: www.slcc.edu
Utah State University Extension: extension.usu.edu

SOURCES FOR PLANTS & SEEDS

Burpee Seed: www.burpee.com
High Country Gardens: www.highcountrygardens.com
Johnny's Selected Seeds: www.johnnyseeds.com
Monrovia: www.monrovia.com
Proven Winners: www.provenwinners.com
Territorial Seed Co.: www.territorialseed.com
The Whole Seed Catalog: Baker Creek Heirloom Seed. Co. 2014;
    www.rareseeds.com

GARDENING NOTES

GARDENING NOTES

MEET DIANA MARANHAO

Diana "Dee" Maranhao has been an active member of the horticulture and landscape industry for more than 35 years. Most of her professional career was spent in higher education, serving as a horticulture program manager, nursery production specialist, and as an educator specializing in xeriscape-low water use landscaping, nursery production, and plant propagation. She developed and taught a program called "Xeriscape for the Classroom" and presented a monthly, full-day workshop to K–12 educators to give them the tools to teach water conservation gardening techniques in the classroom.

Upon retiring from her career in education, Diana has served as horticulture editor and project editor for numerous educational texts, magazines, garden guides, and horticulture books. She has been a regularly featured garden columnist for more than 10 years, authoring hundreds of gardening and horticulture articles for the public and the horticulture industry. This is Diana's third book; she is the author of *Rocky Mountain Fruit and Vegetable Gardening* (Cool Springs Press, 2014) and *Water-Smart Gardening* (Cool Springs Press, 2016).

Diana earned a degree in ornamental horticulture, certificates in copyediting and merchandising, and holds a lifetime teaching credential from California specializing in ornamental horticulture. She serves as scholarship chair for the Desert Green Foundation, Las Vegas, a nonprofit group that presents a yearly educational conference for professionals to encourage continued learning in the landscape industry.

She received the "2014 Professional of the Year" Award from *Southwest Trees & Turf Magazine* at the Desert Green XVIII Conference in Las Vegas, Nevada.

Diana and her husband, Steve, live and garden in southern Utah. Combining her professional background and education with the constant learning experience, their gardens serve to encourage, to teach, and to inspire others to garden, and to do so with water conservation and sustainability of natural resources in mind.